D1564217

SOCIAL STRESS AND FAMILY DEVELOPMENT

SOCIAL STRESS
AND FAMILY DEVELOPMENT

Edited by

David M. Klein
Joan Aldous

University of Notre Dame

The Guilford Press
New York   *London*

© 1988 The Guilford Press
A Division of Guilford Publications, Inc.
72 Spring Street, New York, NY 10012

Printed in the United States of America

Last digit is print number: 9 8 7 6 5 4 3 2 1

Library of Congress Cataloging in Publication Data

Social stress and family development / edited by David M. Klein and Joan
  Aldous.
       p. cm.
    Bibliography: p.
    Includes index.
    ISBN 0-89862-079-1
    1. Family—United States.   2. Family policy—United States.
3. Family policy.   I. Klein, David M., 1943–   . II. Aldous, Joan.
HQ536.S67   1988   87-28195
306.8′5′0973—dc19   CIP

To Reuben Hill (1912–1985), on whose intellectual activities so many family scholars depend, and to Marion Hill, whose contributions to the study of families delighted Reuben and enriched his thinking.

Contributors

Joan Aldous, The William R. Kenan Jr. Professor of Sociology, University of Notre Dame, Notre Dame, IN

Kurt W. Back, The James B. Duke Professor of Sociology, Duke University, Durham, NC

Susan L. Bailey, Research Analyst, Research Triangle Institute, Research Triangle, NC (formerly at the University of North Carolina at Chapel Hill, Chapel Hill, NC)

Thomas A. Cornille, Assistant Professor of Interdivisional Program in Marriage and the Family, Florida State University, Tallahassee, FL

Wilfried Dumon, Professor of Sociology, Katholieke Universiteit Leuven, Faculteit Sociale Wetenschappen, Leuven, Belgium

Glen H. Elder Jr., The Howard W. Odum Professor of Sociology, The University of North Carolina at Chapel Hill, Chapel Hill, NC

Lerke Gravenhorst, Research Analyst, DJI-Deutsches Jugendinstitut, Munich, West Germany

Donald A. Hansen, Research Sociologist, Language and Literacy, Graduate School of Education, University of California, Berkeley, CA

Carla B. Howery, Assistant Executive Officer, American Sociological Association, Washington, DC

Stephen R. Jorgensen, Professor of Home and Family Life, Texas Tech University, Lubbock, TX

David M. Klein, Chairperson and Associate Professor of Sociology, University of Notre Dame, Notre Dame, IN

Yoav Lavee, Research Associate, Department of Family Social Science, University of Minnesota, St. Paul, MN

Hamilton I. McCubbin, Dean, School of Family Resources and Consumer Sciences, University of Wisconsin–Madison, Madison, WI

Gerald W. McDonald, Associate Professor of Sociology, Florida State University, Tallahassee, FL (deceased)

Brent C. Miller, Professor of Family and Human Development, Utah State University, Logan, UT

John Modell, Professor of History and Social Science, Carnegie Mellon University, Pittsburgh, PA

Phyllis Moen, Associate Professor of Human Development and Family Studies, Cornell University, Ithaca, NY, and Sociology Program, The National Science Foundation, Washington, DC

David H. Olson, Professor of Family Social Science, University of Minnesota, St. Paul, MN

Irving Tallman, Professor of Sociology, Washington State University, Pullman, WA

Acknowledgments

This book is the result of the efforts of a number of people. In addition to the chapter authors, we thank Graham B. Spanier, Program Vice President, and Brent C. Miller, Research and Theory Section Chair, for making possible the presentation of earlier versions of some chapters at the 1982 Annual Meeting of the National Council on Family Relations. Reuben Hill himself was enthusiastic about the project and made suggestions for strengthening several of the chapters. The continuing support of the Hill family has also encouraged us to complete the book. We want especially to thank Lori A. Butchko for turning the manuscripts into the final edited chapters that follow. A flip of the coin established the order of the editors.

David M. Klein
Joan Aldous

Contents

SOCIAL STRESS AND FAMILY DEVELOPMENT

THE CONVERGENCE OF FAMILY DEVELOPMENT, FAMILY STRESS, AND FAMILY PROBLEM SOLVING

1

The Linkages between Family Development and Family Stress

JOAN ALDOUS
DAVID M. KLEIN
University of Notre Dame

Time cures sorrows and squabbles because we all change, and are
no longer the same person. Neither the offender nor the offended is
the same.—Blaise Pascal (*Pensées VI*)

This book brings together papers on two themes, those of development
and of stress in families. Both themes emphasize time and the changes
associated with it. Family development is expected change over the life
course of families, while in the case of family stress, the focus is on
unanticipated events that encourage change. Both themes were central
in the writing and research of Reuben Hill, and the papers show the
influence of his work.

Change is an issue of importance today when families are currently
in flux in regard to age at formation, number of children, family duration and composition. Later ages at marriage, childlessness, and fewer
children affect the timing and occurrence of events demarcating family
time. The prevalence of unwed pregnant women, divorce, and remarriage modifies expected family sequences and stages. There is also the
attendant stress associated with compositional changes to single parenthood and families with stepchildren. After describing how this book
came to be, we will analyze the linkages of family development and
family stress. The introduction concludes with a discussion of how the
papers are connected with each other and with the book's themes.

Social Stress and Family Development is the result of a session we
organized at the 1982 Annual Meeting of the National Council on Family Relations. The session was dedicated to Reuben Hill, who had retired
that year as Regents' Professor of Family Sociology at the University of
Minnesota. As former doctoral students of his who had also co-authored
papers with him (and in the case of Aldous had been a faculty colleague
at Minnesota), we wanted to celebrate his continuing contributions to
the field of family sociology.

There were four papers at this session by persons who had shared
various portions of his intellectual pilgrimage. Wilfried Dumon had
come from the Catholic University, Leuven, Belgium, as a North Atlan-

tic Treaty Organization Fellow in 1965 to work with Hill. Don Hansen, a doctoral student of Hill's in the late 1950s, along with one of his last doctoral advisees, Phyllis Moen, were also in the session. The late Gerald McDonald, who had held a postdoctoral appointment in the family policy training program funded by the National Institute of Mental Health in the 1970s, was another presenter.

The session papers concerning family change from the developmental perspective and how governments and families deal with stress-creating problems attracted a large and attentive audience. We were, therefore, encouraged to ask others of Hill's associates to contribute the additional papers on family development or family stress that made this volume possible. Several former colleagues are represented. Kurt Back, along with J. Mayone Stycos, had worked with Hill in their widely cited research in Puerto Rico on the marital dynamics of contraceptive use. John Modell, from the Department of History at the University of Minnesota during the last years of Hill's Minnesota career, had found his interest in the timing of family events in the past congenial with Hill's ideas on family development. During this same time, David Olson and Hamilton McCubbin were professors in the Department of Family Social Science at the University of Minnesota. Hill acted as a consultant and supporter of their work on family systems and models of family stress management. Irving Tallman, while on the faculty of Minnesota's Department of Sociology, along with Hill, Aldous, and Murray Straus, had been co-investigator for a National Institute of Mental Health research project concerning family problem-solving that represented their shared interests and participation in the Minnesota Family Study Center.

Persons who were students or doctoral advisees of Hill were also represented. Stephen Jorgenson and Brent Miller completed their doctorates in the 1970s under his supervision while Lerke Gravenhorst, Carla Howery, and Yoav Lavee were participants in his graduate seminars. Finally, Glen Elder, although never a colleague or a student, represented the many scholars whose intellectual debts to Hill came about through conversations at meetings or letters on issues of mutual concern. Elder's co-author, Susan L. Bailey, like many of the readers of this volume, would know Hill through his writings.

THE LINKAGES BETWEEN FAMILY DEVELOPMENT
AND FAMILY STRESS

Family development and family stress share a temporal perspective on families that appears in the following chapters. The concern is with the change processes families initiate and/or respond to as a result of events of varying duration. The developmental perspective on family lives, an approach pioneered by Hill and his co-worker, Evelyn Duvall (Duvall & Hill, 1948), ranges from the formation to the dissolution of family units. The perspective covers the multiple careers over the life span of persons in the existing marital, parent–child, and sibling subsystems. Families are followed as they move through stages of development and the tasks associated with each, as well as through the transitions between stages that punctuate the life cycle and represent major additions, losses, or modifications of roles. The most important family events that signal role changes are couple formation, the coming of children, their departure, and couple dissolution, along with significant educational, occupational, and residential changes experienced by members.

While the emphasis in family development is on when change occurs, as Olson, Lavee, and McCubbin point out in this volume, the family stress literature covers what causes the change. In Hill's (1949) classic ABCX formulation, the stressor (A) in association with the family's resources for meeting it (B), and the family's definition of the stressor (C) affect the response (X) in terms of distress and some way for handling it. However, family stress and family development are also directly linked. Changes in family life associated with different stages—the coming of children, their entering different levels of school or leaving home, and occupational retirement—all create stress in interaction patterns. Transitions made while new patterns are being established join stages in the family sequence. Stress due to the intercontingent careers of members as spouses, parents, children, and siblings, and also as workers and students is, therefore, associated with the expectable changes in families.

Family development contributes to thinking about family stress through its emphasis on time. Very often stress is seen in terms of events whose effects are over after they are lived through. The Holmes and Rahe (1967) scale, often used to measure stress, tends to represent this view. It underplays stress as a continuing process, a process that the family development approach points up by looking at consequences of stress-producing behaviors for later stages.

A consideration of family stress also enriches our thinking about family development. Stresses apart from the occurrences demarcating family stages are endemic in family life. These problems continue as "background noise" through stage transitions and the stages themselves. They constitute "limited linkages," or "carry-over" behaviors that limit possibilities for family behaviors in later stages (Aldous, 1978, p. 110). These carry-over processes can be part of the darker side of family life, distorting behavior patterns appropriate to a particular stage. Thus, for example, parent–child arguments about a child's use of drugs sour not only relations in a particular stage but cast their shadow over future stages. As a result, family members may not be able to change their interactions to take into account a high school youth's demands for more independence if she or he has a history of drug use.

Nevertheless, it should not be overlooked that stress can also have its positive aspects. Thus, although mothers' increasing attachment to the labor force brings attendant problems of child and household care, this attachment can be associated with greater conjugal solidarity in husbands during the busy preschool years and in wives during the school years (Simpson & England, 1982). These are periods when spouses' interests may diverge, as child responsibilities too often are largely allocated to women. When both spouses are employed outside the home, couples have concerns in common, putting pressure on men to be more involved in family matters, a positive change for wives and children.

Both family development and family stress share a social-psychological perspective on families. What goes on within families is central. In the family stress perspective, this social-psychological conceptualization appears in families' definitions of the stressor event, as well as in modifications in members' behavior patterns in response to it. Family development scholars also tend to concentrate on intrafamilial dynamics in their concern with the more enduring interaction structures of power, affection, communication, and division of labor, and changes in these situations during transition periods. In both approaches, the social context of family change, that is, the transactions whereby families are affected by external agencies (whether schools or workplaces) and in turn affect them, are less often specified.

In this volume, we have attempted to overcome this "nearsighted" perspective by including papers in which the larger societal context is taken into account. This macrofocus is consistent with sociologists' macroconcerns that have been coming to the fore in other scholarly areas in recent years (Kohli & Meyer, 1986). After noting the lack of material on the interface between families and institutions in the larger community, Hansen's chapter demonstrates the transactions between families and schools through children. The intercontingency of their student and family careers means that, unless school teachers planning their teaching strategies take into account family cultures at odds with conventional instructional techniques, these cultures constitute barriers to learning.

In contrast to these analyses of how families affect other institutions, chapters on the effect of economic catastrophe and war on family process are included in the volume. How the economic depression of the 1930s changed the transition to marriage through modifications in the institution of engagement is the subject of John Modell's chapter. Elder and Bailey look at whether military service in World War II influenced class differences in marriage timing and fertility.

More contemporary issues appear in chapters by Dumon and Gravenhorst. Dumon analyzes how a social-psychological perspective, as opposed to a more structural approach, affects policy-making views, while Gravenhorst highlights the structurally constrained opportunities over time for women in their families.

The chapter by McDonald and Cornille, with its discussion of the development of policies within families, represents well the contrast that Dumon discusses between a social-psychological and a more macro approach to policy. The authors attempt to bridge levels of analysis by borrowing concepts and principles from a societal policy framework and applying them directly to the family as a small group. Back, however, in his analysis of national family planning programs indicates why policymakers may prefer not to work directly with families in the programs they initiate. It is costly in time and effort, and there are ethical issues involved. Reuben Hill, whose Puerto Rican study showed how marital factors influenced fertility decisions, was a consultant to the Ford Foundation's population program. Back notes, however, that Hill emphasized economic development rather than family variables in population control plans. The review by Miller and Jorgensen suggests that progress has been made recently in moving between the extremes of individualistic and psychological orientations toward fertility on the one hand and societal and demographic orientations on the other. They point to research efforts incorporating relationship variables and family characteristics that carry forward the pioneering work of Hill and his colleagues decades earlier.

The chapters also indicate some of the methodological issues that have plagued family development and family stress studies, while also suggesting their solution. Both the Modell and the Elder and Bailey historical studies are necessarily dependent upon small, nonrepresentative samples, and in Modell's case, upon content analysis of popular literature to tease out relationships between variables. The Olson, Lavee, and McCubbin research is based upon a much larger contemporary sample, which they understandably regret is not longitudinal. These studies provide leads to be followed with data from the large-sample longitudinal data sets that have been amassed in the last several decades, such as the Panel Study of Income Dynamics.

The challenge, however, is to create relevant measures from these longitudinal studies designed for purposes other than the examination of family development and stress processes. Most do not provide information sufficient to identify stages of family development or transition periods. They also tend to be selective with respect to the types of stressor events covered and their timing in the family life cycle. Finally, existing large-scale longitudinal studies often focus attention on the experiences of a narrow range of age cohorts and are therefore unable to capture historical and cohort variations in an optimal way. Given these assorted limitations of even the best longitudinal studies, continued attention to alternative research designs for the collection of temporal data can be anticipated.

UNDERLYING ISSUES

We have divided the chapters into three sections. The first section brings together papers on stress and problem solving in the general context of family development. Stress due to historical and family events is dealt with in the second section. The third section relates issues arising in family lives to policy making. All the chapters, in one way or another, deal with the dynamics of family development, whether due to histori-cal, family, or individual changes. In addition, the policy chapters con-cern governmental and family attempts to mitigate family stress due to change. There are certain other underlying issues, however, joining the chapters and crosscutting the sections. They include the following issues: (1) family power and subjectivity; (2) families in historical or universal context; (3) the problems of family study; and (4) problem solving as a consequence of stress.

Power and Subjectivity

The power and subjectivity issue is particularly salient in the Gravenhorst, Hansen, and Dumon chapters. Gravenhorst gives a femin-ist critique of the family development approach while showing how the broadened perspective feminism provides is consistent with an earlier conceptualization of the approach. She sees a shift in emphasis in the family development perspective from its early years. Then, the concern was with how the needs of particular members were played out in the family interaction processes of specific stages. In the present concern with the acquisition and discarding of family roles, the earlier evalua-tive stance of whether families encourage individual development has been lost. The emphasis is also no longer on process, but on structure. The approach focuses on the "functional requisites for survival" and adaptation of family members to the "recurring life stresses" that the family faces as a system (Hill & Mattessich, 1979, p. 174). To look at families as systems, she contends, assumes an underlying consensus reflected in the role structures based on the decisions of husband/fathers. This masculine power to set the family interaction structures comes from a patriarchal tradition and greater physical and financial resources. Thus, family development, by focusing on structures and overlooking conflicting member needs reflected in family processes, does not come to grips with the issue of how stage change in families can serve or counter the development of individual members within them.

Dumon, too, in his comparison of family-policy views in the United States and Western Europe notes that power differences within families and among conflicting interest groups sometimes get overlooked in the United States. But with respect to policy, he argues that the United States has little concern for societal structures. Ameliorating family problems by working directly with families as they develop over time is an approach congenial to Americans. They have a predilection to see problems as having roots in individual weaknesses rather than in organizational structures. Reuben Hill's belief that a nonpartisan approach to family policy was possible also led him to concentrate on family interaction patterns and to downplay power politics concerning the allocation of resources. Dumon contents that it is hard to "do" family policy with this interactional framework because power differences among the interested parties affect how family policy is formulated. Gravenhorst writes of gender conflicts among members within families, but Dumon sees gender differences creating policy conflicts within European governments. Women pressing for governmental programs to enable them to combine more easily family and occupational roles come in conflict with family organizations committed to traditional household division of labor and power arrangements.

The subjectivity issue which Hansen, along with Gravenhorst, raises is also related to power. Both contend that family development, with its role theory underpinnings, is concerned with subjectivity. The subjective experiences and feelings of individual family members, even if they have little power, affects the way members behave and their interpretations of others' behaviors. To have knowledge of families, we must find out their members' perceptions of family life. Gravenhorst uses a case history to show how such a record of family processes over time, as reported by a working-class wife and mother, can add to our understanding. Hansen, though in agreement with Gravenhorst on this point, asks how we can get at another's subjectivity, particularly with respect to the family proscriptions that set limits on acceptable behavior. This issue of intersubjectivity is a methodological as well as philosophical concern.

We as family researchers need to get inside family members' thinking, but family routines are tacitly understood, and the overlap of family members' understandings can be hard to determine. Power differences between husbands and wives and between parents and children can limit what respondents say. Members may also have difficulty articulating their perspectives, and how they see those of others. Moreover, there are ethical issues involved in how far we as outsiders can go in our intrusions into family life. The further we go beyond the boun-

we've already this

daries of family privacy, the less permissible it is to maintain a scientific stance of noninvolvement in the stresses individuals reveal. These relationships usually stem from the belief that there will be, at the least, sympathetic understanding and, at the most, assistance in easing unpleasant situations.

A concern with subjectivity can be seen as going against the prescriptions for objectivity in scientific research to which Reuben Hill was so committed. Gravenhorst argues, however, that the latter approach often focuses too much on the family as a collectivity and overlooks the "motives, intersts and life trajectories" of its members. These experiences of both men and women are based on the feelings and interpretations of the reporters. Their accounts also possess their own logic. This logic can be studied objectively through the consequences that individual goals in one family stage have for the next, that is, the "limited linkages" they create.

Families in Universal or Historical Context

The issue of subjectivity also relates to whether one views families in historical context or seeks family propositions that hold regardless of time and space. This issue arises especially in the chapters of Moen and Howery, Tallman, and McDonald and Cornille. Moen and Howery discuss three different time metrics. Individual time is based on lives demarcated by age; family time is made up of family events; and historical time is time whose effects on families vary according to the ages of the individuals and their family stages during particular historical events. The authors argue that family development needs to be more concerned with transitions and the attendant flux in family patterns rather than with stages where there appears to be stability in sequences and in structures within stages. At the same time, families regardless of stage and age of members must be placed in historical context. The external stresses families adapt to, along with the changing demands of family members that are based on the intercontingent careers of persons in families, occupations, and schools, stem from what happens in society. Thus, the effect of feminism as an ideological approach to studying families (Gravenhorst) and as a political force (Dumon) is part of the present epoch. The studies in this volume that are concerned with changes in courtship, as a result of the hard times of the 1930s (Modell), and governmental post-World-War-II measures that smoothed-out class difference in the timing of marriage and childbearing (Elder and Bailey), explicitly take historical events into account.

Taken together, the contributions in this volume by Elder and Bailey, Moen and Howery, and Modell highlight what has perhaps become the most significant contemporary challenge to scholars committed to the study of developmental change and adaptation to stress in families. This challenge can be expressed in a single, if complex, assertion: The life courses of families and their members, as well as the stresses that alter those trajectories, are dependent upon the intersection of the accumulated developmental history of the family, current situational constraints, and societal transformations occurring outside the family. Put more simply, family development cannot be adequately understood without giving attention to cohort membership, sociohistorical contexts, and experiences affecting family members.

This orientation and the accumulating evidence in support of it do constitute a departure from earlier conceptions of family development and stress management as unaffected by context. The more recent view does not, however, fundamentally contradict the older view. Instead, the newer view supplements the older one by permitting more precise hypotheses based on developmental and stress theories, while taking into account historical and extrafamilial influences.

Yet, there are authors in the book who argue for seeking universal family propositions, propositions holding despite the immediacies of time and space. Tallman, in his analysis of the process of family problem solving, writes that the topic is beset by conceptual difficulties. He sees a need for greater precision in formulating definitions. This can be achieved, he believes by freeing concepts from empirical referents and thus from time and space particularities, since the goal of theory is propositions that hold universally. Tallman thus makes use of social exchange principles in his analysis of how family members respond to the stress they feel when routine activities no longer lead to goal attainment.

McDonald and Cornille also draw upon this conceptual approach in their discussion of how families themselves formulate policies concerning goals to be sought and means for reaching them. Their micro approach to family policy formation contrasts directly with Dumon's macro approach. Their concern with higher level propositions also is in opposition to the day-to-day power politics that Dumon examines, whereby policies get hammered out in both families and in legislative bodies. Hill himself was much caught up in the 1970s intellectual movement to develop family theory through a propositional approach. His own belief that social scientists should be objective tended to obscure an awareness of how sociologists might be affected by their own values in their interpretations of events. By being concerned with family policy as developed by families, the investigator renders less apparent struggles arising from members' conflicting interests, particularly when traditional power arrangements are taken for granted. The concentration on uncovering universal propositions for studying families allows some of the sharpness that characterizes the inherent conflicts of family life to be set aside.

The Problematics of Family Study

Along with the issues of whether to conceptualize families in terms of timeless universals or historical contexts, several of the authors discuss the problematics of engaging in family studies. Back, in his chapter on the family element in family planning, addresses the level-of-analysis issue. He looks at the relative failure of researchers and policymakers to build upon the insights concerning couple interaction and contraceptive use that Hill, Stycos, and Back (1959) offered in their Puerto Rican study in the 1950s. The difficulty of getting at the group qualities of couples or families leads population experts to design programs for individuals or to push for economic development in the broader society in order to lower fertility rates. Tallman, too, describes the difficulties in examining family as opposed to individual problem solving.

Miller and Jorgensen, however, in their review of the research on adolescent pregnancies, attempt to bridge the individual and family analysis levels by placing teenagers' sexual activities in a social and temporal context. Parents in the family of orientation, as transmitters of values and socializers of behavior, appear in the analysis, as in turn do the effects of teenage childbearing on adolescents' families of orientation. The authors attempt to deal with the group-versus-individual issue by tracing the interaction influences among family members across generations, while noting overall economic effects on family units. Olson, Lavee, and McCubbin, in their cross-sectional research on the number of problems families have at various stages and their adaptive strategies for handling them, also attempt to bring together the individual and family views. They discuss the school-age and adolescent stages, when family cohesion is lowest and family members feel less connected to one another. They find that identity with the family as a unit rather than member flexibility is associated with a lower sense of strain among family members.

Problem Solving as a Consequence of Stress

Stress as the cause of transitions between stages in which families are in flux because of new demands of external agencies and members is addressed in the problem-oriented chapters of Olson, Lavee, and McCubbin; Miller and Jorgensen; Tallman; and McDonald and Cornille. They see stress as triggering those family members activities that may produce group policies (McDonald & Cornille) or a greater sense of member efficacy as they succeed in removing barriers to group goals (Tallman). Thus, a positive outcome of stress can be activities that solve the stress-creating problems that arise from the disruption of routines following family events or changing individual life experiences. But in the work devoted to stress and family or members' responses to it, there is little directly on the emotions that stress engenders.

Tallman briefly mentions emotional commitment to solving problems and bonding to other members due to interdependency and the expectation of future payoffs. Olson and his associates use "cohesion" to cover the feeling element in family life. Hansen, however, specifically discusses how the disruption of established routines creates negative emotions. The sense of well-being that comes from expectations having been met is destroyed when members question the proscriptions that set boundaries around interaction variation. But, in general, the emotions members invest in family routines disrupted by change that Hansen discusses do not come through clearly in the chapters on family stress and the resulting change. Thus, the fact that husbands generally define the source of change and how it will or will not be addressed even if wives and children are in bitter disagreement is still largely unrecognized in these chapters. Just as the methodological issue of getting at the perceptions that generate behavior of members is often neglected in family research, so too a sociology of emotions does not yet inform it, even though it is the stressful emotions that give impetus to individuals' dealing with problems. Again, as with the issue of subjectivity, the conventional scientific stance of objectivity and rationality tends to rule out a consideration of family feelings (Oakley, 1981, p. 40). Families, however, are reunited and torn apart on the basis of emotions, and the indications of this in the chapters on problem solving keep us aware of their influence on family change and development.

CONCLUSIONS

Although we did not deliberately intend such a result, this book draws attention to general issues of theory formation, data collection and analysis, and policy application, all of which have significance throughout the social sciences and particularly in family studies. First, theory and research are moving more toward dynamic models in which concepts and measures of change occupy a central and explicit role. The analytical units assessed can vary from individual behaviors and group structures to societal events, and time may be conceptualized as episodic (e.g., particularly stressor events), developmental (e.g., careers of family groups), or historical (e.g., periods of rapid social change). Scholars appear to have become increasingly sensitive to these alternatives and to the need for integrated perspectives that do justice to several at once.

Second, there has grown a heightened awareness in recent years, inspired to a considerable extent by Reuben Hill's own work, of the need to move beyond miniature and middle-range theories of apparently distinct family phenomena. The goal is to create more encompassing frameworks that are adequate to tie together increasingly differentiated and complex bodies of research findings. The present book contributes to that goal by showing how family development theory and family stress theory, two orientations often addressed in isolation from one another, when brought together can result in an enriched perspective.

Third, this volume illustrates (without resolving) several of the debates that have both inspired and plagued family studies over the past half-century or more. One debate is between advocates of different disciplinary perspectives. The social psychologists represented in our volume see things differently from the macrocosm-oriented sociologists, demographers, and historians also represented here. For some contributors, thinking about the family as a unit is less problematic than it is for others. These latter prefer to focus on the behaviors, motives, and perceptions of individuals who interact with other significant individuals in and outside the family.

Still another ongoing debate illustrated by this book is taking place among advocates of different philosophies of science. While the more positivistically oriented push us toward universal propositions organized into causal models and deductive or axiomatic systems of reasoning, the more interpretively inclined highlight the fluidity of interaction and the importance of subjectivity constructed and negotiated orders of meaning and emotion. A third philosophical orientation, more critical than the others, is represented by feminism and its attack on the dominance and exploitation of women as a social class or category. This last perspective targets for criticism both the prevailing patterns of family life in societies today and the knowledge we have of these patterns. So long as male scholars dominate the intellectual scene, an incomplete and biased view of family development and stress management is likely to prevail. This may help, for example, to account for the fact that the emotional variations in family life have remained for so long underappreciated by all but a few family scholars.

Because this book recreates on a modest scale several of the ongoing controversies in the field as a whole, readers can expect to be confronted with dilemmas and alternative agendas. These should serve to sharpen their own positions on the issues treated. We invite such an internal dialogue rather than attempting any orthodox or programmatic solution of our own. Reuben Hill would have relished such an opportunity, particularly since the issues were of great importance to him. It is remarkable, and a genuine tribute to his enormously productive life and career, that this scholar has blazed so many trails and provisioned so many travelers. We urge others to make use of the material in this book to continue this intellectual heritage. Hill would have been the first to welcome the surpassing of his own achievements.

REFERENCES

Aldous, J. (1978). *Family carrers.* New York: Wiley.
Duvall, E. M., & Hill, R. (1948). *Report of the committee on the dynamics of family interaction.* Washington, DC: National Conference on Family Life.
Hill, R. (1949). *Families under stress: Adjustment to the crisis of war separation and reunion.* New York: Harper.
Hill, R., & Mattessich, P. (1979). Family development theory and life-span development. In P. Baltes & O. Brim, Jr. (Eds.), *Life-span development and behavior (Vol. 2).* New York: Academic Press.
Hill, R., Stycos, J. M., & Back, K. W. (1959). *The family and population control.* Chapel Hill, NC: University of North Carolina Press.
Holmes, T. H., & Rahe, R. H. (1967). The social readjustment rating scale. *Journal of Psychosomatic Research, 11,* 213–218.
Kohli, M., & Meyer, J. W. (1986). Social structure and the social construction of life stages. *Human Development, 29,* 145–149.
Oakley, A. (1981). Interviewing women: A contradiction in terms. In H. Robert (Ed.), *Doing feminist research.* London: Routledge & Kegan Paul.
Simpson, I. H., & England, P. (1982). Conjugal work roles and marital solidarity. In Joan Aldous (Ed.), *Two paychecks: Life in dual-earner families.* Beverly Hills, CA: Sage.

2

Types of Families and Family Response to Stress across the Family Life Cycle

DAVID H. OLSON
YOAV LAVEE
University of Minnesota, St. Paul

HAMILTON I. McCUBBIN
University of Wisconsin, Madison

Over the past 3 decades, much of the research and theory building on family response to normative transitions across the life cycle, as well as to nonnormative stressor events, has been inspired by Reuben Hill's pioneering works in the areas of family development (Duvall & Hill, 1948; Hill & Hansen, 1960; Hill & Rodgers, 1964) and family stress and crisis (Hill, 1949, 1958, 1970; Hill, Moss, & Wirths, 1953). These two areas of study, as Mederer and Hill (1983) noted, are similar in their foci: Both take the family as the unit of analysis with respect to its reaction to events, disorganization, renegotiation, and reorganization. Hill believed that apart from existing theories of individual or small group behavior, the family as a unit has certain characteristics that make it important to study its development, change, and response to demands over time. He also believed that families have some basic qualities that protect them from major disruptions and facilitate their adaptation to life's hardships.

Although the study of family response to normative and nonnormative demands was one of the areas of family research most productive of theory in the 1960s (Broderick, 1970) and the 1970s (McCubbin *et al.*, 1980), an understanding of the factors that make some families better able than others to cope with a normal range of stressors and strains has not progressed much since Reuben Hill's earlier landmark studies.

At least three basic reasons explain the delay in the systematic investigation of these questions. First, although much research effort has been concentrated on families' coping with major catastrophes, little has been devoted to "normal" or nonclinical families' responses to normative transitions and life events. Second, despite interest in family strengths and qualities that enable families to endure, research has not gone beyond descriptive variables. There has not been a search for multidimensional typologies of family dynamics that would identify the more resilient, or more adaptive, types of family systems. Third, researchers were slow to integrate the ideas and knowledge generated by the separate studies of family development, family response to stress, and family systems characteristics.

This chapter attempts to advance the study of family response to normative changes and life events by building upon the ties among three areas of research and theory: family development, family stress and adaptation, and family systems typology. Specifically, this study examines (1) the pileup of stressors and strains that families face across the life cycle, (2) changes in family system types across the family life cycle, and (3) response of families with different system types to the normal range of life events and changes.

FAMILY DEVELOPMENT AND CHANGING FAMILY PHENOMENA

Family development implies change over time. The developmental approach (Hill & Hansen, 1960; Hill & Rodgers, 1964) focuses on the changing characteristics of families over the period of their existence, from marriage through dissolution by divorce or death. Traditionally, family development has been described by stage progression, each stage being "a division within the lifetime of a family that is distinctive enough from those that precede and follow it to constitute a separate period" (Aldous, 1978, p. 80).

The question of what circumstances precipitate a shift from one stage of structural equilibrium to the next has barely been studied (Mederer & Hill, 1983). Most family development research has focused on description of family life *within* stages. Klein, Borne, Jache, and Sederberg (1978), for instance, have suggested that stages can be viewed as discrete entities and that differences in such phenomena as marital adjustment and family organization can be found between stages.

Family development includes two interrelated types of change: (1) change in role content of positions, due chiefly to changes in age norms for these positions, and (2) change in interactional patterns within the family. Changes in role content of positions have been used to describe family transition from one stage to another. These transitions, in turn, have been studied in terms of the demands for change they impose upon the family system. Change in one part of the system is believed to bring about changes in other parts of the system (Hill & Rodgers, 1964). Transitional change, therefore, brings about changes in family interactional patterns.

This process of change due to "external" sources (e.g., transitions, life events), which places demands on the family system to bring about internal change (e.g., of interactional patterns), has been described by both family development theorists and family stress and adaptation theorists. Despite sharing much of the same interests, however, these two areas of study have progressed along different paths.

There are probably three basic reasons for this. First, as Hill (1964, p. 189) noted, "family development studies at the descriptive level place their emphasis less on *what* [happens in the family] than on *when* it occurs, more on the timing and sequences . . . than on the content of behavior." Family stress theories, on the other hand, focus on *what* occurs in families when faced with a stressor event rather than on *when* it occurs.

Second, whereas family development scholars have focused on normative transitions as the critical life events that affect family interaction, family stress research has focused primarily on the impact of nonnormative, acute, and severe events. Third, whereas changing family interaction has been studied as a dependent variable and as an outcome in the developmental approach, it has been treated as an intervening variable in stress theories, as a factor that modifies family crisis or adaptation to stressor event(s).

Recent developments in family stress theory and in means of describing family interactional patterns now enable researchers to begin to connect the ties between these areas of study. The intent of this chapter is to describe changing family phenomena, with a view toward identifying family system characteristics that enhance family adaptation to normative and transitional changes as well as to nonnormative family life events.

Family Development and Family Stress

Although family stress research initially focused on the impact of acute and nonnormative events, there has been a recent shift toward describing the process of family response to accumulation of demands over time (Hansen & Johnson, 1979; Hill, 1973; Mechanic, 1974). McCubbin and Patterson (1983) listed five broad types of demands (stressors and strains) that may contribute to a pileup of demands in a crisis situation: (1) the initial stressor and its hardships, (2) normative transitions, (3) prior strains, (4) consequences of family efforts to cope, and (5) intrafamily and social ambiguity.

This concept of a pileup of demands, which includes both internal and external, expected and unanticipated, normative and nonnormative events and strains, has been incorporated into the Family Adjustment and Adaptation Response (FAAR) model (McCubbin & Patterson, 1982, 1983). The focus on a pileup of demands, rather than on a single event, may be useful for studying both demands described by the developmental framework and those referred to within the family stress framework.

Although both stressors and strains are sources of demand, a critical distinction is made between them. *Stressors* are discrete life events or transitions that have an impact upon the family unit and produce, or have the potential to produce, change in the family social system (Hill, 1949; Burr, 1973; McCubbin & Patterson, 1983). In family stress theory stressor events have been treated as independent variables with postulated effects upon the family.

Strain is defined as a condition of felt tension, or difficulty. It is usually associated with the need or desire to change something (Patterson & McCubbin, in press). Unlike stressor events, strains do not have a discrete onset; rather, they emerge insidiously in the family, whether from unresolved tension associated with prior stressors or from intrafamily relationships, without the occurrence of a specific stressor. Increased difficulty in performing roles (such as parenting), or increased interpersonal conflicts (such as between husband and wife, between parents and children, or with in-laws) are examples of changes in the family that may be indicative of an increase in intrafamily tension, or strain.

The causal relation between stressors (external sources of demand) and strain in the family (internal sources of demand) has been assumed by both developmental theorists and family stress theorists. Hill (1949) classified family demoralization (e.g., loss of a morale and family unity) as one of the crisis types and proposed that it is affected by stressor events. Rodgers (1962) suggested that failure to meet the demands of developmental transition (role expectation) brings about temporary disequilibrium and lack of integration in the family system. Intrafamily strain, therefore, may be treated both as a dependent variable affected by the occurrence of stressor events (as proposed by Hill's ABCX model) or as an independent variable affecting the level of family functioning and well-being.

Whereas Hill's (1949) ABCX model focused on the occurrence of *crisis* as an outcome variable, the FAAR model (McCubbin & Patterson, 1983) focuses on family *adaptation* following crisis and pileup of demands. Adaptation is achieved when the demands posed by stressors and strains are balanced by the family's capabilities. Since the family is in a constant process of adaptation to changing conditions (Angell, 1936; Hansen & Hill, 1964), however, family adaptation is difficult to define and measure.

One way to identify and measure a family's level of adaptation is by the outcome, or consequences, of adaptational efforts. Lazarus and Folkman (1984), for example, suggested that adaptation be examined by adaptational outcomes at three levels: the macro level (social outcomes), intermediate level (psychological outcomes), and micro level (physiological outcomes). Research on the detrimental consequences of prolonged crisis on physical, psychological, and interpersonal health leads us to believe that, following an accumulation of demands from stressor events and intrafamily strains, personal well-being and family well-functioning would be reasonable indications of family adaptation (Lavee & McCubbin, 1985).

Recently, Lavee (1985) has analyzed a multivariate path model of family stressors, strains, strengths, perception, and well-being and found that family well-being (as an indication of family adaptational outcome) is not directly affected by stressor events. Rather, he found that intrafamily strain mediates between these two variables: The accumulation of demands due to stressor events tends to increase intrafamily strain, which in turn has a negative impact upon the family's personal and relational well-being.

This causal linkage is depicted in Figure 2-1, which serves as a framework for studying family vulnerability to demands and family resiliency across the family life cycle. First, the pileup of stressor events (external demands) is believed to influence intrafamily strain. The degree of family vulnerability to stress, however, influences the amount of strain caused by the pileup of stressor events. This proposition is guided by Burr's (1973) definition of family vulnerability as "a family's ability to prevent a stressor event . . . from creating some crisis or disruptiveness in the system" and by his propositions regarding the effect of family vulnerability on the amount of disruptiveness in the family social system. It is reasonable to argue, therefore, that higher levels of intrafamily strain may be indicative of a greater family vulnerability.

Second, increase in internal demands (intrafamily strain) is believed to influence family well-being negatively. The degree of family resiliency, however, influences the amount of decrease in family well-being caused by strain: The more resilient the family, the greater will be its well-being following pileup of demands (strains and stressor events).

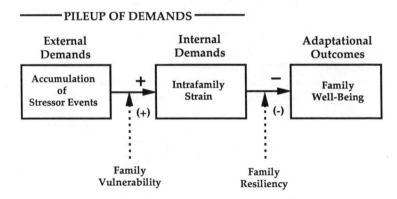

Figure 2-1.   Conceptual model for studying family response to stress across the family life cycle.

Family resiliency is defined as the ability of a family to recover readily from disruptiveness. This is similar to Hansen's (1965) concept of regenerative power, which Burr (1973) describes as the ability of the family to recover from a crisis. It is reasonable to argue, therefore, that following the accumulation of stressors and strains, a higher level of family well-being may be indicative of a greater family resiliency. In connecting the ties between family development and family stress and coping, the present study examines differences in the pileup of stressors and strains at various stages of family development, as well as families' level of well-being following these demands.

Family Development and Types of Family Systems

The description of family development over time has emphasized change in interactional patterns interspersed with periods of stability, or equilibrium. Klein, Jorgensen, and Miller (1978) pointed out that "the problem [then] becomes one of identifying shifts between one set of relatively stable relational networks and subsequent sets of such networks" (p. 114). In other words, a question of interest is what are the relational characteristics of families at various stages of their development.

The problem of identifying "sets of relational networks" may emerge, in part, from the fact that dozens of concepts are being used to describe family systems. Recently, family scholars became interested in (1) collapsing the wide range of descriptive variables of family interaction into a smaller number of umbrella concepts that would describe family dynamics more parsimoniously; (2) selecting the critical dimensions for understanding marital and family systems; (3) moving beyond single descriptive variables to a multidimensional approach that would capture the complexity of family systems; and (4) describing the total system rather than its parts.

In an attempt to delineate critical dimensions of family dynamics and to advance a model of family systems, Olson and his colleagues (Olson, Russell, & Sprenkle, 1979, 1983; Olson, Sprenkle, & Russell, 1979) reviewed over 50 concepts developed in family therapy, family sociology, social psychology, and family systems theory to describe marital and family dynamics. A conceptual clustering of these concepts yielded three major family dimensions: cohesion, adaptability, and communication.

The cohesion and adaptability (flexibility) dimensions were then placed orthogonally (property–space position) to develop the Circumplex Model of marital and family systems (Figure 2-2). The third dimension, communication, is not represented as a separate dimension in the model, because communication is considered as a facilitating factor in families' movement on the cohesion and flexibility dimensions.

The family's cohesion dimension is defined as the emotional bonding that family members have toward one another. It includes variables such as emotional bonding, boundaries, coalitions, time, space, friends, interests, and recreation. The family's flexibility dimension is defined as the ability of the marital or family system to change its power structure, role relationships, and relationship rules in response to situational and developmental needs. This dimension captures the range between family morphostasis (system maintenance through negative feedback) and family morphogenesis (system change through positive feedback), two central constructs in systems theory. Concepts used to define family flexibility rely heavily on family sociology, such as family power, negotiation, roles, and rules.

Family systems may range from extremely low cohesion (disengagement) to extremely high cohesion (enmeshment), and from extremely low flexibility (rigidity) to extremely high flexibility (chaotic system).

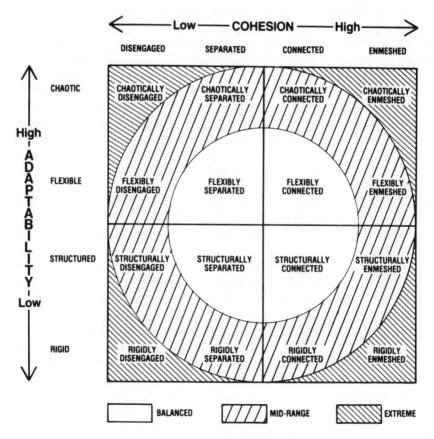

Figure 2-2.   Circumplex Model of marital and family system types.

Combining four levels of cohesion and four levels of flexibility in the Circumplex Model enables one to identify 16 types of marital and family systems. These 16 types can be grouped further into three more general categories: four balanced types, four extreme types, and eight midrange types (see Figure 2-2).

Much previous research has focused on problem families and has compared the functioning of balanced versus extreme family types. Whereas clinical families have been shown to be extreme in cohesion and flexibility (Olson, 1986), most "normal," nonclinical families tend be moderately cohesive units ("connected" or "separated") and moderately flexible units ("flexible" or "structured"). Indeed, when a large sample of predominantly nonclinical families was studied, the frequency of truly extreme families was quite small (Olson, Russell, & Sprenkle, 1983).

Since the typology of families by their cohesion and flexibility levels seems to be a useful approach for describing family systems (i.e., interactional patterns), the Circumplex Model may be used to classify nonclinical family systems into four types: (1) flexible-separated; (2) flexible-connected; (3) structured-separated; and (4) structured-connected.

If family interactional patterns are expected to change over the family life cycle, research may be able to capture this change in family system types. Unfortunately, previous studies on change of family systems over the life cycle are rare, and specific hypotheses as to the amount and directions of these changes are difficult to make at the current state of knowledge.

Family System Types and Their Responses to Stress

The question of what characteristics, traits, or qualities make some families less "crisis prone" (Hill, 1949) and/or more adaptive (McCubbin & Patterson, 1982) has attracted much research and theorizing efforts. As Burr's (1973) synthesis and other reviews (e.g., McCubbin *et al.*, 1980) indicate, numerous studies have attempted to identify critical dimensions of strong families. Of these, family integration (cohesion) and family adaptibility (flexibility), the two main dimensions of the Circumplex Model of family system types (Olson, 1986), have received most attention.

When focusing on the family's system type rather than on specific dimensions of the family's system, the question that arises is how families of various system types differ in experiencing intrafamily strains and level of well-being following a pileup of stressor events. Since the occurrence of stressor events is, for the most part, independent of the family's interactional pattern, it is not expected that family types will differ in the pileup of stressor events they experience. Stressor events, however, may affect some families more than others. Some families may be more vulnerable to the effect of stressor events and may experience more interpersonal conflicts, greater difficulties in role performance, and higher levels of internal strain following the accumulation of demands. Similarly, some families may be more resilient, that is, better able to recover from the impact of stressor events upon intrafamily relationships. In other words, it is predicted that following the accumulation of stressor events, families with different systems types will experience different levels of intrafamily strain as well as different levels of personal and interpersonal well-being.

To date, there is little data to derive specific hypotheses relating nonclinical family types to stressors, strains, and adaptational outcomes (i.e., well-being). Although more cohesive (in the moderate range) families may be expected to function better, Angell (1936) pointed to the importance of looking at family integration (cohesion) in conjunction with the family's level of flexibility:

> I did not see clearly from the start that integration alone would be no basis for predicting. . . . It seems now perfectly obvious that if one wished to define types in relation to a change of any kind, flexibility or adaptability with reference to that change was a very important consideration. (p. 290)

METHODOLOGICAL APPROACH: BRIDGING FAMILY DEVELOPMENT, FAMILY RESPONSE TO STRESS, AND FAMILY SYSTEM TYPES

This chapter integrates the theoretical works on the Circumplex Model of marital and family systems (Olson, 1986), the family adjustment and adaptation response model (McCubbin & Patterson, 1983), and the family development framework (Hill & Rodgers, 1964; Mederer & Hill, 1983), to more systematically investigate the relationships among them.

Empirically, this paper builds upon and extends the findings from a national survey of nonclinical families described in the book *Families: What Makes Them Work* (Olson, McCubbin, *et al.*, 1983). However, the operationalization of family development stages, family stress and adaptation, and family system types, and the analyses in the present study differ from those reported in the book.

Family Adaptability and Cohesion Scales (FACES III) was used to assess family system types and to describe extreme versus balanced types (Olson, Portner, & Lavee, 1985). FACES III was used in the present analyses to classify families by the four quadrants of the model. This "quadrant typological approach" seemed to be more appropriate for classification of "normal" (predominantly nonclinical) families where few legitimate extreme types exist. Additionally, whereas previous analyses of the Circumplex Model examined the separate dimensions of family cohesion and family flexibility (adaptability), this chapter focuses on both the separate and the interactional effects of these two dimensions.

While the book described specific demands that families struggle with, these events and changes were grouped in the present analyses into two factors: stressors (life events) and strains (ongoing issues). Additionally, separate adaptational outcomes measured in the national survey (marital, family, and life satisfaction) were combined here to create an index of family well-being.

Finally, in order to increase the sample size in each stage of the family life cycle, the seven stages described in the book were collapsed in the present analyses into four: young couples, families with young children (preschool and school age), families with adolescents, and older couples (postparental stage). While describing families by four developmental stages may not be as useful as the traditional classification into seven stages, smaller sample size at each stage could have produced less stable results. Additionally, previous analyses (Olson, McCubbin, *et al.*, 1983) indicated that the characteristics of families with preschool and school-age children, of families with adolescents and young adults (where at least one child was an adolescent who lived at home), and of families at the empty nest and retirement stages were similar enough to enable collapsing these pairs of stages without losing significant information. In summary, the purpose of the study was to describe differences in family system types, pileup of stressor events, intrafamily strains, and family well-being across the family life span, and to describe families' responses to the pileup of stressor events as a function of their system type.

METHOD

Sample and Data Collection

Data for the present study were collected as part of a larger national survey of families (Olson, McCubbin, *et al.*, 1983). That study of "normal" families included families from 31 states across the United States at all stages of the family life cycle. A stratified random sampling approach represented each of the seven stages of the family life cycle: newly married couples without children; families with children in the preschool years; families with school-age children; families with adolescents; launching families (at least one child has left home, other children still at home); empty nest families; and families in retirement.

To acquire a stratified random sample, initial lists were compiled by a large fraternal insurance organization with a system of branches serving families around the country. From this list, families were first grouped by their life stage, and a final group of participants was randomly selected from each category. Families were contacted and asked to participate in the study. Fifty-six percent of the families who were asked to participate in the study responded positively to the recruitment teams.

The overall sample (completed questionnaires) consisted of 1,251 families, with more than 100 families in each family life stage and more than 200 families with adolescents. Data were collected from both spouses in each family and from adolescents in families that included adolescent(s) at home. Analyses in the present study, however, are based on responses of adults (husbands and wives) only.

The sample consisted of predominantly white, lower- to upper-middle-class, Protestant families from both rural and urban areas. Husbands' ages ranged from 20 to 85 years (mean, 46), and wives' ages ranged from 19 to 84 years (mean, 43). Children's ages ranged from less than 1 year in the preschool age to more than 40 years in retirement-stage families. A large variety of occupations was represented in the sample. Average family income fell in the $20,000-to-$30,000 range. Data on education showed that 30% of the husbands and 20% of the wives had at least a college education. A more detailed description of sample characteristics is reported in Olson, McCubbin, *et al.*, 1983.

Though data were gathered from more than 1,000 families from a wide geographical area, the sample could not be considered as completely representative of U.S. families. Several groups were clearly overrepresented, others were underrepresented. For example, nearly all families in the sample were Lutheran church members. Comparison of the sample characteristics with a national Gallup poll on perceived quality of life (i.e., satisfaction with marriage, family, housing, health, etc.) indicated, however, that this uniformity in religious preference may not have been a biasing factor. Minority groups were also underrepresented. The sample consisted of intact marriages only and thus did not include single-parent families. The effect of potential biases cannot be ascertained, and generalization of results, therefore, may be somewhat restricted by the nature of the sample. This is, however, one of the largest data sets of intact families that have been collected in the United States, and it provides a unique opportunity to study "normal" families.

Measures and Scales

Family stressors were measured by a ten-item scale (McCubbin, Olson, Lavee, & Patterson, 1985). The scale lists events that represent family transitions (such as birth of a child, marriage, launching), work transitions, and nonnormative events (illness, death of a family member) that may have occurred during the past year. An event was considered to have happened in the family if either spouse indicated its occurrence. A family stressors score was computed as the number of events that occurred within the specified time.

Family strains were also measured by a ten-item scale (McCubbin, Olson, Lavee, & Patterson, 1985). This scale lists changes during the past year in family interaction and role performance that represent increases in interpersonal strain, financial strain, and role strain (i.e., difficulty in performing tasks). A change was considered to have happened in the family if either spouse indicated its occurrence. A family strain score was computed as the number of strain items indicated.

Family well-being (adaptational outcome) was operationally defined as a composite index of three measures: (1) marital satisfaction (Olson, Fournier, & Druckman, 1982); (2) family satisfaction (Olson & Wilson, 1982); and (3) quality of life (Olson & Barnes, 1982). The three measures were factor analyzed and loaded on a single factor. The factor score coefficients were then used to compute well-being scores (well-being $= .184 \, Z_1 + .705 \, Z_2 + .143 \, Z_3$, where Z_1, Z_2, and Z_3 denote standardized scores of marital satisfaction, family satisfaction, and quality of life, respectively). Family well-being, therefore, is a standardized score with a mean of 0.0 for the whole sample.

Family types were classified into four system types by the Circumplex Quadrants typological approach. Two scales were used to classify families: (1) family cohesion (ten items) measures the emotional bonding family members have toward one another; and (2) family flexibility (adaptability) (ten items) measures the family's ability to change its structural relationships. Both scales were measured by FACES III (Olson, Portner, & Lavee, 1985).

Family life cycle data were collapsed to *four* family life stages in the present analyses to obtain a large enough sample in each stage: (1) young couples without children; (2) families with young children (oldest child is either a preschooler or of school age); (3) families with adolescents (oldest child is an adolescent, or oldest child has left home but there are other children living at home); and (4) older couples (couples at empty nest stage or in retirement).

ANALYSES AND RESULTS

The data were analyzed in three consecutive steps in order to examine the following: (1) the accumulation of stressors and strains and the family's well-being at the four family life stages; (2) possible differences in family system types at the four family life stages; and (3) differences in stressors, strains, and family well-being in the four family system types.

Stressors, Strains, and Well-Being across the Family Life Cycle

The first analysis examined the accumulation of stressors and strains, and the level of family well-being, across the family life cycle. The results of this analysis are presented graphically in Figure 2-3.

The bar graph in Figure 2-3 shows very little difference in the accumulation of stressor events among the four family stages. An analysis of variance indeed indicated no significant differences in the number of stressor events ($F_{(3)}$ = 2.38, p < .10). On the other hand, there was a significant difference among families' levels of strain at the four stages ($F_{(3)}$ = 32.63, p < .01). Specifically, the results in Figure 2-3 indicate that families with children, either preschool and school-age or adolescents, experience higher levels of intrafamily strain than do childless couples or families at the empty nest and retirement stage. Furthermore, the results indicate that families at the latter stage experience the lowest level of strain despite having the same accumulation of stressors as those at the other stages.

When families' well-being is examined, the results show a pattern opposite to that of strains. (Note that the scale of well-being is different

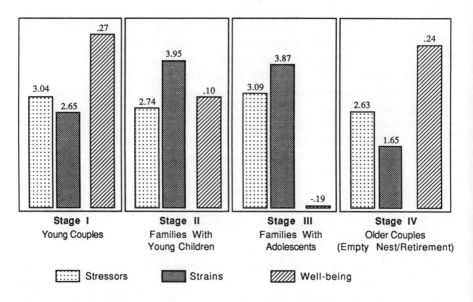

Figure 2-3.   Stressors, strains, and well-being across the family life cycle. Score for stressors and strains, and strains is the number of events/changes (range: 0 to 10). Well-being score is standardized (X = 0.0, range: −.19 to +.27).

from that of stressors and strains, and that it has been modified in Figure 2-3 to make the comparison among the four stages easier.) The results show significant differences in well-being among families at the various stages ($F_{(3)}$ = 4.50, p < .01). They also show that families at the first stage of family development (i.e., before children are born) and at the last stage of the family development (i.e., after all children have left home) are more satisfied with the marriage, the family, and their quality of life than are those with children at home. It is interesting to note also that families with adolescents have a level of well-being significantly lower than that of families with younger children, despite similar levels of stressors and strains.

Family System Types across the Family Life Cycle

Theoretically, "normal" or nonclinical families, should be equally distributed among the four family system types. In other words, it is expected that for a wide range of predominantly nonclinical families, approximately 25% would be classified as flexible-separated, flexible-connected, structured-separated, and structured-connected. Guided by this rationale, and using data from the whole sample (of normal families), norms were established for classification of families into the four types (see the above section entitled "Measures and Scales").

Table 2-1. Distribution of Families Classified by Circumplex Main Dimensions by Family Life Cycle Stage

	Cohesion		Flexibility		
	Connected	Separated	Flexible	Structured	Chi-square[a]
Theoretical distribution	50.0	50.0	50.0	50.0	—
Whole sample distribution	50.4	49.6	52.7	47.3	6.16
I. Young couples	70.7	29.3	62.0	38.0	17.89 **
II. Families with young children	62.7	37.3	36.9	63.1	42.16 **
III. Families with adolescents	40.4	59.6	55.2	44.8	18.56 **
IV. Older couples	46.9	53.1	62.5	37.5	8.91 *

[a] Chi-square for the whole sample's distribution is computed with theoretical distribution as expected values. Chi-square for distribution of families in the four stages is adjusted by the actual distribution of the whole sample (i.e., sample's distribution served as expected values).

 * p < .05.

 ** p < .01.

Given the even distribution of families among the four system types, the purpose of the next set of analyses was to examine the distribution among types at each of the four family developmental stages. Table 2-1 presents the frequency of families at each of the four development stages classified by the Circumplex Model's main dimensions, that is, connected versus separated and flexible versus structured families.

As the results in Table 2-1 show, the majority of young couples and families with young children (Stages I and II) are connected, whereas more than half of older couples and families with older children (Stages III and IV) are classified as separated. As to their flexibility, more than 60% of young and older couples (Stages I and IV) are flexible. Additionally, the majority of families with adolescents (Stage III) are classified as flexible. In contrast, more than 60% of families with young children (Stage II) are structured systems.

The combination of family classification by their cohesion and their flexibility yields a great variety of differences in family system types ɛ nong families at the four developmental stages. The distribution of family system types at the four stages is presented in Figure 2-4.

Stage I: Young couples (without children). Forty-six percent of these young couples are of a flexible-connected system type, and 25% of the families at this stage were classified as structured-connected. Only a small minority are either structured-separated (13%) or flexible-separated (16%). This distribution of family types could be expected for young married couples, whose system typically is cohesive and who have a great amount of flexibility in role sharing and family rules.

Stage II: Families with young (preschool and school age) children. Whereas families with young children mostly are connected, as young couples are (see Table 2-1), the most prevalent family system type of families with young children (37%) is structured-connected. One quarter of the families in this stage are flexible-connected (compared to 46% in Stage I), and about the same number of families are structured-separated (compared to 13% in Stage I). Only a small minority of families with younger children are flexible-separated (12%).

Stage III: Families with adolescents. Whereas the percentage of flexible-connected families remains the same as in families with young children (25%), there is a marked increase in the percentage of families who are flexible-separated (30% of families with adolescents, compared to 12% of families with younger children) and a large decrease in the percentage of families classified as structured-connected (16% of families in Stage III, compared to 37% in Stage II). There is also a small increase of families who are structured-separated (29% of families with adolescents). Loosely speaking, the greatest shift in family system types is from structured-connected to flexible-separated families.

Stage IV: Older couples (empty nest and retirement). Like young couples, older couples tend to be more flexible (62% of families) than

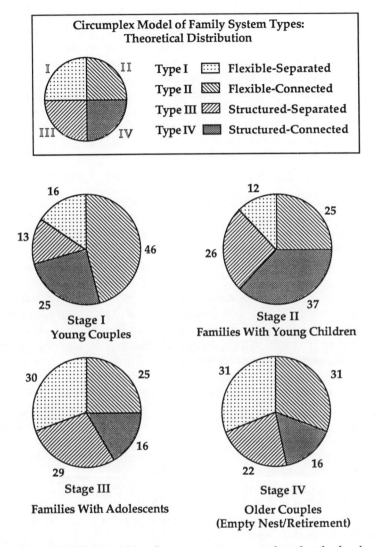

Figure 2-4. Distribution of family system types across four family developmental stages.

structured. Because older couples are not as connected as young couples, however, they differ in the distribution of family types. All in all, the distribution of system types among older couples resembles that of families in the previous developmental stage (families with adolescents) more than that of couples in the preparenthood stage. Most older couples, therefore, are either flexible-connected or flexible-separated (31% of families with each system type), and only a small percent of them (16%) are structured-connected.

In summary, the results indicate that all four system types can be found at the various stages of the family life cycle. Differences in cohesion and flexibility, however, yield a complex set of differences in the prevalence of family system types at different stages of family development. Most notably, more young couples tend to be flexible-connected, and more families with young children tend to be structured-connected. Families with adolescents tend to be either flexible or structured separated, and older couples tend to be of either a flexible-separated or a flexible-connected system type.

Stressors, Strains, and Well-Being in Family System Types

While the previous analyses focused on differences among families across four stages of the family life cycle, the next series of analyses examined differences in stressor events, strains and well-being among various types of family systems. Figure 2-5 displays this descriptive analysis graphically, and Table 2-2 presents analyses of variance for differences among types.

Figure 2-5 shows the accumulation of stressors and strains, and family well-being, at the four family types. As the bar graphs suggest, there were only slight differences in the experience of stressor events among the four family system types. In other words, the accumulation of these life events (but not necessarily the kinds of events) was evenly distributed among family system types. Analysis of variance for differences among the four family system types supports this observation (see Table 2-2).

There were, however, differences in intrafamily strain and well-being among families with various system types. Of the four types, flexible-connected families appear to have experienced the lowest intrafamily strains and the highest well-being. Flexible-separated families, on the other hand, suffered the most intrafamily strains and showed the lowest level of well-being. Additionally, as is evident in Figure 2-5, structured-connected and structured-separated families experienced similar levels of stressors and strains, but differed markedly in their well-being.

Table 2-2. One-Way Analyses of Variance for Differences in Stressors, Strains, and Well-Being among Family System Types

	Sum of squares	df	F	p
Stressors	9.54	3	.90	.442
Strains	266.27	3	17.49	< .001
Well-being	164.65	3	80.90	< .001

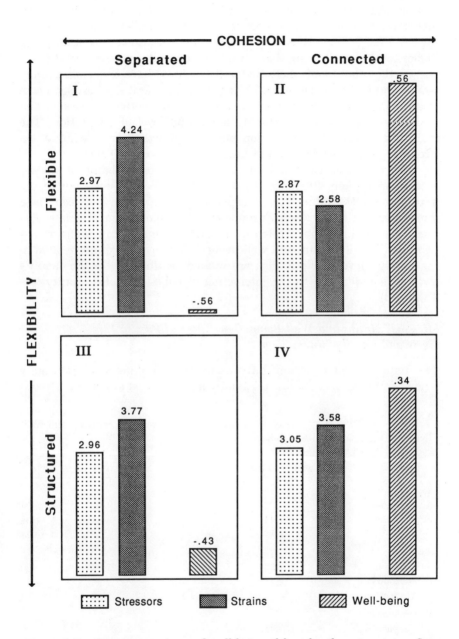

Figure 2-5. Stressors, strains, and well-being of four family system types. Score for stressors, and strains is number of events/changes (range: 0 to 10). Well-being score is standardized ($X = 0.0$, range: $-.56$ to $+.56$).

Close examination of the results presented in Figure 2-5 reveals that, overall, connected families do better (i.e., have lower strains and higher levels of well-being) than do separated families. The results also suggest that for connected families, flexible ones have less strains and higher level of well-being than structured ones. Among separated families, on the other hand, those that are structured have fewer intrafamily strains and higher levels of well-being than those that are flexible. These results suggest that there is an interaction effect between cohesion and flexibility in regard to intrafamily strain and level of adaptation. The main effects and the interaction effect of cohesion and flexibility on stressors, strains and family well-being are presented in Table 2-3.

The results in Table 2-3 indicate that the accumulation of stressor events can explain differences neither in the cohesion level, nor in the flexibility level. Neither can it explain the interaction between these dimensions. In other words, stressor events, which often originate outside the system, are not related to the system's main dimensions or system type. Family strains and well-being, however, though not related to the family's level of flexibility, are related significantly to the family's level of cohesion and to the interaction of cohesion and flexibility (see Table 2-3).

Stressors, Strains and Well-Being: The Effect of Family Life Cycle and Family System Type

The data presented so far have demonstrated differences in family strains and well-being across the family life cycle and among family sys-

Table 2-3. Two Way Analyses of Variance of Stressors, Strains, and Well-Being by Cohesion and Flexibility

	Sum of squares	df	F	p
Stressors				
A. Cohesion	.02	1	.01	.945
B. Flexibility	1.44	1	.41	.523
A × B	3.68	1	.12	.733
Strains				
A. Cohesion	137.92	1	27.92	.001
B. Flexibility	12.15	1	2.46	.117
A × B	96.54	1	19.55	.001
Well-being				
A. Cohesion	155.41	1	229.09	.001
B. Flexibility	.41	1	.61	.437
A × B	5.69	1	8.39	.004

Table 2-4. Two Way Analyses of Variance of Stressors, Strains, and Well-Being by Family Life Stage and Family System Type

	Sum of squares	df	F	p
Stressors				
A. Stage	24.71	3	2.38	.069
B. Family type	5.33	3	.52	.666
A × B	16.78	9	.55	.838
Strains				
A. Stage	417.91	3	32.63	.001
B. Family type	219.73	3	17.16	.001
A × B	39.46	9	1.03	.417
Well-being				
A. Stage	8.84	3	4.50	.004
B. Family type	144.90	3	73.77	.001
A × B	9.78	9	1.66	.095

tem types. They have also demonstrated differences in family system types across the family life cycle. A question that remains to be answered is whether differences in the experience of stressors, strains, and well-being are explained by these two factors separately, or whether there is an interaction effect as well. The results of two-way analyses of variances of stressors, strains, and well-being by family system types and developmental stages are presented in Table 2-4.

These analyses of variance show that (1) neither developmental stage, nor family type, nor the interaction between them account for significant differences in the occurrence and accumulation of stressor events; and (2) the variance in family strain and in family well-being is related to family developmental stage and to family system type, but not to the interaction between them.

As a way of summary, Table 2-5 presents mean scores of strain and well-being of family system types within the four developmental stages. Earlier (Figure 2-3), scores of family strains were shown to be highest in families with children at home (Stages II and III). The results in Table 2-5 indicate that *flexible-separated* families (Type I) in Stages II and III suffer the most intrafamily strains (4.89 and 4.68, respectively). The results presented in Figure 2-3 indicate that older couples (Stage IV) show least strains and that *flexible-connected* families (Type II) suffer less strains than other family types (Table 2-5).

As to families' well-being level, Figure 2-3 indicated that young couples (Stage I) and older couples (Stage IV) show higher levels of well-being than families with children, and Figure 2-5 indicated that flexible-connected families (Type II) tend to have highest level of well-

Table 2-5. Family Strain and Well-Being by Family Life Stage and Family System Type

Stage	Family type	Mean strain	Mean well-being
I. Young couples	I. Flexible-separated	3.00	−.24
	II. Flexible-connected	2.50	.60
	III. Structured-separated	3.92	.01
	IV. Structured-connected	2.52	.15
II. Families with young children	I. Flexible-separated	4.68	−.45
	II. Flexible-connected	3.66	.47
	III. Structured-separated	4.34	−.48
	IV. Structured-connected	3.92	.43
III. Families with adolescents	I. Flexible-separated	4.89	−.74
	II. Flexible-connected	2.87	.60
	III. Structured-separated	3.86	−.53
	IV. Structured-connected	3.58	.17
IV. Older couples	I. Flexible-separated	2.40	−.13
	II. Flexible-connected	1.25	.56
	III. Structured-separated	1.90	−.10
	IV. Structured-connected	1.37	.60

being, followed by structured-connected families (Type IV). Table 2-5 shows that families in Stage I (young couples) who are flexible-connected, and families in Stage IV (older couples) who are structured-connected, have levels of well-being higher than other subgroups (.60).

It is interesting to note that families with adolescents (Stage III) who are flexible-connected (Type II) also show high level of well-being (.60) despite the low level of well-being that families with adolescents generally show as a group (see Figure 2-3). As a matter of fact, families in this developmental stage (i.e., families with adolescents, Stage III) show both high levels of well-being, when they are flexible-connected (Type II), and the lowest level of well-being (−.79), when they are flexible-separated (Type I). In sum, the results presented in Tables 2-4 and 2-5 indicate that intrafamily strain and family well-being can best be explained by both the family's system type and its developmental stage.

DISCUSSION

Family scholars, researchers, and practitioners have been interested in identifying the factors that make some families more resilient than others in the face of life events and changes that may threaten family well-being and functioning. Implicit in these efforts were two assumptions: (1) that families differ in their critical interactional patterns, and (2) that families change over time.

The present study built upon these two assumptions in an attempt to advance the understanding of family systems and family response to change. Focusing on the pileup of demands rather than on specific sources of demand, the present study investigated differences in stressors, family strains, and family well-being across the family life cycle. Focusing on family system types as multidimensional indicators of interactional patterns rather than on specific interactional dimensions, the study examined differences in family interaction across the life cycle. Finally, guided by the need to identify strong families, the study investigated differences in intrafamily strains and well-being following the accumulation of stressor events among nonclinical families with different system types.

Implied in the examination of families' stressors, strains, and well-being was an assumption regarding a causal linkage among these factors, namely that increase in family strain is accounted for by external demands (pileup of stressor events), and that intrafamily strain negatively affects family well-being. Furthermore, it was argued that higher levels of intrafamily strain could be interpreted as indicative of greater family vulnerability to stress and that higher levels of well-being could be interpreted as indicative of greater family resiliency.

The present study has shown that families experience various degrees of demands due to life events and transitions. Neither family life stage nor family system type, however, could account for such variance in demands. These findings support the assumption that life events are external sources of demand. In other words, though families may experience different kinds of events (Olson, McCubbin, *et al.*, 1983), the accumulation of events is invariant across stage of family development or across family system types.

Families do differ, however, in their response to these external demands. Results of the present study suggest that both developmental stages and family system types account for these differences.

Stressors, Strains, and Adaptational Outcomes across the Family Life Cycle

Examination of the accumulation of family strain across the family life cycle indicated that families with young children (preschool and school age) and families with adolescents and young adults experience significantly higher levels of intrafamily strains than do families in the preparenthood stage (young couples) or postparental stages (empty nest and retirement). Families with children at home experience more interpersonal conflicts, role strains, financial strains, or social strains.

Furthermore, the results indicated differences in the major source of demand: Whereas families who have no children at home report more frequent occurrence of external demands (stressor events) than of internal demands (intrafamily strain), families with children report more internal demands than those stemming from life events and transitions.

These results are hardly surprising. First, they support numerous previous studies on the difficulties inherent in transition to parenthood and to the adolescent stage of the family life cycle. The present study did not focus on the transition per se, but it indicated that families at these stages suffer from more internal demands than families at other stages. Second, given the greater role complexity of families with children compared to families who are either childless or at postparental stages, it is not surprising to find greater frequency of conflicts between parents and children, among children, with in-laws, as well as greater financial hardships and difficulties in role performance (i.e., difficulty in managing children, increase in unresolved problems/issues, increase in number of chores/tasks that don't get done, etc.).

Based on the finding that the accumulation of life events and changes has a significant effect on increase in family strain (Lavee, 1985), it is reasonable to assume that while part of the increase in family strains at the parental stages originates inside the family, this increase also reflects a greater vulnerability of these families. In other words, the findings suggest that families with young children or adolescents are more adversely affected by accumulation of demanding events and changes than are families without children.

Whether demands have internal or external origins, both stressors and strains provide demands the family must cope with. This pileup of demands is relatively low at the preparental stage, increases as children are added to the family and grow into adolescence, and sharply decreases thereafter. How does this pileup of demands affect family well-being? How does family well-being change across the family life span?

The present study shows that levels of family well-being are inversely related to intrafamily strain across the family life cycle. Specifically, young couples and older couples report greater satisfaction with their marital relationship, family functioning, and their physical, psychological, and relational well-being than do families with young children or families with adolescents.

The results, however, indicated that families may differ in their vulnerability (i.e., strain level) and in their adaptational outcomes (i.e., well-being). For example, young couples suffer more stressors and strains than do older couples, but their level of well-being is similar (.27 and .24, respectively). Conversely, whereas families with young children suffer demand pileup similar to that of families with adolescents, their level of well-being is significantly higher (.10 and − .19, respectively).

Assuming that the level of intrafamily strain reflects family vulnerability to pileup of external demands (stressor events), and that the level of family well-being reflects family resiliency following pileup of demands, the differences noted between families with young children and families with adolescents may shed light on these families' vulnerability and resiliency. Specifically, the results suggest that families with young children are just as vulnerable as families with adolescents, in that they experience similar levels of strain following external demands (pileup of stressor events). Families with young children, however, show greater resiliency than families with adolescents in that they have a higher level of well-being despite a similar accumulation of stressors and strains.

Family System Types across the Family Life Cycle

In addition to the examination of changes in pileup of demands and well-being across the family life cycle, the present study examined differences in interactional patterns between families at various developmental stages. The Circumplex Model (Olson, Sprenkle, & Russell, 1979) was used to classify family systems because this typological approach has emerged from a conceptual clustering of numerous concepts of family interaction.

The results indicated differences in family types at different stages of the family life cycle. Some of the findings could be readily expected. For example, more than 70% of young couples were found to be "connected," with most of them being flexible-connected. It appears that young couples tend to have cohesive units, with stronger external than internal boundaries, and with flexible interactional rules and roles.

As families move from the first stage of development into parenthood and adolescence, family cohesiveness decreases. This trend was also expected, since a family's interaction with its environment increases (e.g., in school, with peers), thereby increasing the permeability of external boundaries and relaxing internal bonds. Of the four stages examined, families with adolescents are most "separated," as is normatively expected in our society.

Examining changes in family flexibility, the data show that families with young children are more structured (less flexible) than families at any other stage, and that families with adolescents tend to relax their rules somewhat. Because families with young children are more cohesive and less flexible than families with adolescents, they differ in the prevalence of system types. Structured-connected family systems, for example, are most common among families with young children but least common among families with adolescents. On the other hand, flexible-separated family systems are most common among families with adolescents but least common among families with preschool and school-age children.

Families in the postparental stage (empty nest or retired) show greater cohesion than families at the previous stage (families with adolescents). The findings suggest, however, that the cohesiveness of older couples does not return to the high level of earlier stages (young couples and families with young children). As to their flexibility, it appears that older couples are just as flexible as young couples. Because they differ in their cohesiveness, however, the majority of young couples are flexible-connected, whereas most older couples tend to be either flexible-connected or flexible-separated.

A note on developmental differences is in order here. It must be emphasized that, since the research approach has been cross-sectional, differences among stages of family development should be interpreted with caution. Specifically, while differences may indeed reflect changes in family interactional patterns over time, they may partly be accounted for by differences in cohort (Hill, 1964; Klein *et al.*, 1978).

Family Types and Family Resiliency

In connecting the ties between family development, family systems, and family response to stress, the final part of the analyses was geared toward better understanding the relationship between family system types and family adaptation to pileup of stressors and strains. A critical question has been what family characteristics best explain family resiliency. Although no differences in pileup of stressor events were found among the four types of family systems, there were significant differences in levels of strain and adaptational outcomes (well-being). These results suggest that some types of families are more vulnerable than others to the effects of external demands (i.e., they have a higher level of strain) and that some types are more resilient (i.e., they have more favorable adaptational outcomes).

In nonclinical families, family cohesion level accounts for level of family strain and well-being. In other words, "connected" (more cohesive) families have lower levels of strain and higher levels of well-being than do "separated" (less cohesive) families. Family flexibility, however, does not explain strain and well-being.

Of particular interest are findings that indicate an interaction effect between cohesion and flexibility. For example, connected families that are structured are more vulnerable (i.e., have greater levels of strain) than flexible ones. On the other hand, separated families are more vulnerable when they have a flexible system than when they are more structured. In other words, family flexibility, by itself, is not a critical factor in family vulnerability to stress and its resiliency in response to demands. But, as was suggested by Angell (1936), given differences in family cohesiveness, its flexibility needs to be considered in explaining family resiliency.

Conclusions

In the last decade, numerous studies have been conducted in an attempt to advance understanding of family response to stress. Theoretical formulations have been revised and new ones proposed to explain the process of adaptation and the critical factors of family resiliency. This chapter has attempted to examine some of these questions by addressing three relatively untouched perspectives.

First, whereas much previous research has focused on family coping with severe and acute stressor events, the present study examined family response to normative transitions and life events. Second, whereas much previous research has focused on specific dimensions of family resources as mediating factors between stressor events and family adaptation, the present study focused on a multidimensional typology of family dynamics in an attempt to identify what types of family systems are more resilient than others. Third, the present study has integrated ideas and knowledge advanced within three areas of study by connecting the ties between family development, family stress and adaptation, and a family systems typology.

REFERENCES

Aldous, J. (1978). *Family careers: Development change in families.* New York: Wiley.

Angell, R. C. (1936). *The family encounters the Depression.* New York: Scribner.

Broderick, C. (1970). Beyond the five conceptual frameworks: A decade of development in family theory. In C. Broderick (Ed.), *A decade of family research and action.* Minneapolis, MN: National Council on Family Relations.

Burr, W. R. (1973). *Theory construction and the sociology of the family.* New York: Wiley.

Duvall, E. M., & Hill, R. L. (1948). *Report of the committee on dynamics of family interaction.* Washington, DC: National Conference on Family Life.

Hansen, D. (1965). Personal and positional influence in formal groups: Compositions and theory for research on family vulnerability to stress. *Social Forces, 44,* 202–210.

Hansen, D., & Hill, R. (1964). Families under stress. In H. Christensen (Ed.), *Handbook of marriage and the family.* Chicago: Rand-McNally.

Hansen, D., & Johnson, V. (1979). Rethinking family stress theory: Definitional aspects. In W. Burr, R. Hill, F. Nie, & I. Reiss (Eds.), *Contemporary theories about the family* (Vol. I). New York: Free Press.

Hill, R. (1949). *Families under stress.* New York: Harper & Row.

Hill, R. (1958). Generic features of families under stress. *Social Casework, 49,* 139–150.

Hill, R. (1964). Methodological issues in family development research. *Family Process, 3*, 186–205.

Hill, R. (1970). *Family development in three generations.* Cambridge, MA: Schenkman.

Hill, R. (1973). *Family life cycle: Critical role transitions.* Paper presented at the Thirteenth International Family Research Seminar, Paris.

Hill, R., & Hansen, D. A. (1960). The identification of conceptual frameworks utilized in family study. *Journal of Marriage and Family Living, 22*, 299–311.

Hill, R., Moss, J., & Wirths, C. G. (1953). *Eddyville's Families.* Chapel Hill: University of North Carolina.

Hill, R., & Rodgers, R. (1964). The developmental approach. In H. Christensen (Ed.), *Handbook of marriage and the family* (pp. 171–172). Chicago: Rand-McNally.

Klein, D. M., Bourne, H., Jache, A., & Sederberg, N. (1978). *Family chronogram analysis: Toward the development of new methodological tools for assessing the life cycle of families.* Unpublished manuscript, University of Notre Dame.

Klein, D. M., Jorgensen, S. R., & Miller, B. C. (1978). Research methods and developmental reciprocity in families. In R. M. Lerner & G. B. Spanier (Eds.), *Child influences on marital and family interaction: A life span perspective.* New York: Academic Press.

Lavee, Y. (1985). *Family types and family adaptation to stress: Integrating the Circumplex model of family systems and the Family Adjustment and Adaptation Response model.* Unpublished doctoral dissertation, University of Minnesota.

Lavee, Y., & McCubbin, H. I. (1985, November). *Adaptation in stress theory: Theoretical and methodological considerations.* Paper presented in the Theory Construction and Research Methodology Workshop, Dallas, Texas.

Lazarus, R. S., & Folkman, S. (1984). *Stress, appraisal and coping.* New York: Springer.

McCubbin, H. I., Joy, C., Cauble, A., Comeau, J., Patterson, J., & Needle, R. (1980). Family stress, coping and social support: A decade review. *Journal of Marriage and the Family, 42*, 855–871.

McCubbin, H. I., Olson, D. H., Lavee, Y., & Patterson, J. M. (1985). *FIT: Family Invulnerability Test.* St. Paul, MN: University of Minnesota.

McCubbin, H. I., & Patterson, J. M. (1982). Family adaptation to crisis. In H. I. McCubbin, A. Cauble, & J. Patterson (Eds.), *Family stress, coping and social support.* Springfield, IL: Charles C. Thomas.

McCubbin, H. I., & Patterson, J. M. (1983). The family stress process: The Double ABCX model of adjustment and adaptation. In H. I. McCubbin, M. B. Sussman, & J. M. Patterson (Eds.), *Social stress and the family: Advances and developments in family stress theory and research.* New York, Haworth Press.

Mechanic, D. (1974). Social structure and personal adaptation: Some neglected dimensions. In C. Goelho, D. Hamburg, & J. Adams (Eds.), *Coping and adaptation.* New York: Basic Books.

Mederer, H., & Hill, R. (1983). Critical transitions over the family life span: Theory and research. In H. I. McCubbin, M. B. Sussman, & J. M. Patterson (Eds.), *Social stress and the family: Advances and developments in family stress theory and research.* New York: Haworth Press.

Olson, D. H. (1986). Circumplex model VII: Validation studies and FACES III. *Family Process, 25*, 337–351.

Olson, D. H., & Barnes, H. L. (1982). *Quality of Life.* St. Paul, MN: University of Minnesota.

Olson, D. H., Fournier, D. G., & Druckman, J. M. (1982). *ENRICH.* Minneapolis, MN: PREPARE/ENRICH, Inc.

Olson, D. H., McCubbin, H. I., Barnes, H., Larsen, A., Muxen, M., & Wilson, M. (1983). *Families: What makes them work.* Beverly Hills, CA: Sage Publications.

Olson, D. H., Portner, J., & Lavee, Y. (1985). *Family Adaptability and Cohesion Scales (FACES III)*. St. Paul, MN: University of Minnesota.

Olson, D. H., Russell, C. S., & Sprenkle, D. H. (1979). Circumplex model of marital and family systems II: Empirical studies and clinical intervention. In J. Vincent (Ed.), *Advances in family intervention, assessment and theory*. Greenwich, CT: JAI.

Olson, D. H., Russell, C. S., & Sprenkle, D. H. (1983). Circumplex model VI: Theoretical update. *Family Process, 22,* 69–83.

Olson, D. H., Sprenkle, D. H., & Russell, C. S. (1979). Circumplex model of marital and family systems I: Cohesion and adaptability dimensions, family types and clinical application. *Family Process, 18,* 3–28.

Olson, D. H., & Wilson, M. (1982). *Family Satisfaction*. St. Paul, MN: University of Minnesota, Family Social Science.

Patterson, J. M., & McCubbin, H. I. (in press). A family stress model for family medicine research: The family adjustment and adaptation response. In C. Ramsey (Ed.), *Family systems in medicine*. New York: Guilford Press.

Rodgers, R. H. (1962). *Improvements in the construction and analysis of family life cycle categories*. Kalamazoo, MI: Western Michigan University.

3

Schooling, Stress, and Family Development: Rethinking the Social Role Metaphor

DONALD A. HANSEN
University of California, Berkeley

[For the family developmentalist] the phenomenon of life-span ups
and downs of family organizational change is the puzzle to be
explained. We invite help in working toward this largely unfinished
goal of reworking and reformulating family development
theories.—Hill and Mattessich (1979, p. 200)

This chapter takes up Hill and Mattessich's invitation, suggesting reformulations in the social role metaphor that underlies our theories of family stress, change, and development. The reformulations emerge in the
consideration of a variety of family stresses introduced by the intercontingent careers of the child in the family and the school. As puzzles in
these stressors force closer attention to the intersubjectivity of familial
interaction, the limitations of traditional role theory are seen. These limitations do not indicate that we should abandon the role metaphor in
family research, however. Particularly when joined with "negotiation,"
social role concepts remain among our most useful tools. Yet, as we
recognize their limitations, their usefulness increases. The following sections, then, focus on some of these limitations, and suggest what seems
to be a promising path toward a social role metaphor that is more adequate to our continuing work on family development theory.

In brief, I will argue that everyday family interactions only occasionally are true "role performances," in the established meaning of that
term, that is, as behavioral responses to shared prescriptive expectations.
Few if any parents and children are so persistently rational and intentional as this conception of role would suggest; most family interactions
are more affective and habitual than role metaphors would allow. To be
sure, we sometimes play roles, but more often we follow "interaction
routines," which are based on the "assumed normalcy" of everyday life.
The tacit assumption that we agree on what is "normal" frees us from
having to continuously account for our behavior, as is implied in traditional role concepts.

I am indebted to Vicky Johnson, David Klein, and Joan Aldous for comments on an earlier version of this chapter, presented at the National Council on Family Relations meetings in Washington, DC, October, 1982.

Family stability and family change are then seen as moments in a continuing dialectic, involving the performance and negotiation of not only *prescriptive* roles, but also of *proscriptive* routines. The most profound moments of family change—including those we identify as transitions to a new phase of the "family career"—are marked by the negotiation of proscriptive rules. Importantly, these negotiations alter not only the proscriptive routines of family interaction, but also family members' individual and shared senses of "normalcy." Perhaps even more important to the study of family change and development, however, they also alter the boundaries of legitimacy and appropriateness within which negotiation itself is conducted. By comparison, the negotiation of role prescriptions, which has dominated our thinking about family development, is of far less consequence.

In the sections that follow I shall try to present these arguments cumulatively, but I must emphasize that I approach the venture in the spirit of theory exploration, rather than theory verification.[1] It may appear to some that my explorations take me far from the traditions of family theory. Yet most if not all of the basic ideas in this paper are already represented in family literature, though not so explicitly identified or systematically developed as I suggest they should be. Much of what I present is in fact explicitly developed (under different terminologies and with different emphases) in psychiatric and psychotherapeutic theories. And all of what I suggest is "clinically" demonstrated even more fully and richly in the fiction and autobiographical works of generations of creative writers such as Virginia Woolf, D. H. Lawrence, James Joyce, Harold Pinter, and Luigi Pirandello. All of it, I know, is part as well of my own family life, as it is, I believe, of virtually every family that has endured long enough to be considered a family by its members.

This exploration, I hope, will be only one of many in the search for a more workable method of inquiry into family processes. That method must allow fuller and more cogent understandings of family stress, family processes, and developmental transitions, and of the ways in which the outside world and the inner world of the family interrelate and influence one another. Within family development theory, the challenge is to distinguish those changes and elaborations that are needed from those that are not, while retaining the fundamental viability of the conceptual traditions nurtured by Reuben Hill over the past 4 decades.

Taking the perspective of a social interactionist, I rely particularly on the traditions that have developed from the works of George Herbert Mead and Max Weber. There are viable alternatives to this approach. I would hope, in particular, that others will propose reformulations of the basic concepts that underlie family development theories by drawing on

systems theories that are sensitive to the social workings of intersubjectivity, or phenomenological theories that are structurally aware. Alter-
nate reformulations are not necessarily incompatible with one another in
basic assumptions about intersubjectivity, interaction, and structural
processes, and each is likely to emphasize aspects of family development
and change that the others neglect.[2]

Whatever theoretical approach is taken, I believe that attention to
the intercontingent careers of family members may stimulate fundamental advances in our understanding of the intrafamily processes that lead
to family development, atrophy, and disintegration. The search for
closer understanding of career intercontingencies and stresses requires
that we move beyond the descriptive levels that have characterized family development theories to date, to search for the processes involved in
intrafamily stability and change over the life span.

ROLE AND SYSTEMS METAPHORS
IN FAMILY DEVELOPMENT THEORY

For the past 4 decades Reuben Hill and his colleagues have worked to
develop a conceptual perspective on the family that "sensitizes its users
to the changing interactional patterns of families over the life-span"
(Hill, 1981, p. 1).[3] At the core of this perspective is the concept of "family career":

> The term "family career" has been coined to encompass the timing and
> scheduling of [a host of functional, interactional, and structural] changes.
> The family career takes on a momentum of its own, but since it is also the
> convergent product of the intercontingent careers of the incumbents in the
> family's several positions, these role performances both stimulate and com-
> plicate the family's developmental achievements. (Hill & Mattessich, 1979,
> p. 175)

In their concern for the family career over the family life span, Hill
and his colleagues have raised new questions about family processes and
problems, sensitizing researchers and practitioners to similarities and
differences in the stresses of decision making and patterns of behavior at
various phases of the family career, as well as to the ways these phases
of family life are influenced by social, economic, and political processes.
(Among the notable examples of these contributions are Aldous, 1978;
Duvall, 1971; Hill, 1970; Hill & Mattessich, 1979.) In this effort, theorists have relied on an elaborate conception of family roles that are seen
to inhere in system-linked familial positions.

> In espousing the view of the family as a social system, the developmental
> approach emphasizes the interrelatedness of parts which exist in the family
> association. The concept of system carries with it the idea that change in

one part of the system brings about changes in other parts. This produces a state of interdependency which in the family involves positions and roles. . . .

Nevertheless, the family provides for liaison with other associations, building liaison roles into family positions and rules for transacting business with teachers, employers and the helping professions. . . .

Family development theorists see stages of development changing each time there is a marked break in the complex of positions and in the role content within these positions. New stages of development occur, therefore, with the addition of positions through births or adoptions and the loss of positions through death and through launching of members into jobs and marriage. New stages also occur each time there is a marked change in the age role content of any one of the several positions in the family requiring a rearrangement of role reciprocities. Thus, the family development approach enables one to anticipate stresses which normally accompany "growing up" by families and their members at the beginning of the cycle and "breaking up" toward the end of the life span. (Hill & Mattessich, 1979, pp. 166–168)

Although the family development perspective has informed hundreds of descriptive studies (see Hodgson & Lewis, 1979), relatively little attention has been given to its underlying assumptions and basic propositions, such as those concerning the processes of stability and change and the dialectics of "intercontingent influences." This deficiency has not gone unnoticed, and appears to be linked to a "descriptive bias" in family development approaches:

> In quick summary, although flourishing and cumulative in the research it has stimulated, the family development perspective remains at the descriptive level. Moreover, it appears to have been insensitive to historical contexts and events and to have been exclusively oriented to the developmental cycle of nuclear family units. (Hill & Mattessich, 1979, p. 170)

In part, the descriptive bias of the family developmental perspective may be seen as a consequence of the breadth and complexity of the areas it addresses, for the concept of family development raises substantive and theoretical issues that far outrun the energies available to address them. In this light, the descriptive bias of family development theory may be seen not as a failing, but as a judicious achievement.

There may be more to the descriptive bias than this, however, for that bias is also encouraged by the fundamental metaphors that have informed family development theories to date (cf. Weick, 1971). As they have been employed in family development approaches, the metaphorical terms of "family role" and "family system" have invited description and discouraged explanation.

Seen as metaphors, concepts and theories are recognized as never more than partial truths and partial untruths. Hall and Spencer-Hall (1981) argue that "There are numerous facets to reality or multiple realities, and thus many ways of presenting partial truths about the nature of reality." Seen as metaphors, concepts and theories are recognized as never more than vaguely accurate, always incomplete, at best merely suggestive and sensitizing to possibilities that otherwise might go unnoticed. Concepts and theories are never more than hypothetical and are to be assessed not in terms of their truth and completeness, but rather "in terms of their reasonableness, their plausibility and their illumination" (Blumer, 1969, p. 182).

Seen as metaphors, concepts and theories represent what Morgan (1980) calls "a form of creative expression which relies upon constructive falsehood as a means of liberating imagination" (p. 607). Even in the physical sciences, a good deal of problem solving employs metaphors, "with scientists attempting to examine, operationalize, and measure detailed implications of the metaphorical insight upon which their research is implicitly or explicitly based" (p. 612). With this understanding, let us consider the prevailing metaphors of family development theory, beginning with "family system."

Problems in the Social Systems Metaphor

It is important to note that, as used by Hill and Mattessich, "family as system" is only distantly related to general systems theory, or even to the "morphogenic systems" theories of Buckley (1967). Though Hill long ago challenged the field to consider the relevance of those theories to family development, little conceptual advancement has been made since he concluded that the formulators of the family development framework "have drawn somewhat uncritically from structure-functionalists' assertions about the family as a social system" (Hill, 1971).[4]

Perhaps the greatest promise of systems concepts for family development theory is in bridging the gap between the micro and the macro levels of analysis, involving historical and structural processes. The problems of interlinking these levels have long plagued interactional theories in general. In recent years, however, some impressive directions have been suggested by a small but increasing number of social theorists (see Collins, 1981; Maines, 1977; Strauss, 1979; Wentworth, 1980). Among other possibilities is a careful articulation of interactional theory with Buckley's social systems theory:[5]

> There is a close correspondence between the two, regarding domain assumptions (social systems and processual), the use of concepts ("feedback" is very similar to Mead's "role-taking"), the nature of structural constraint (transformational), and interaction (directed but not totally deterministic). It is clear, therefore, that symbolic interactionism can maintain its conceptual integrity and at the same time embrace a social structural position expressed in terms of information-systems theory. (Maines, 1977, p. 243)

It is hoped that over the coming few decades considerable attention will be turned to linking the interactional processes of the family to compatible constructs that are more appropriate to large-scale sweeps of social structure and historical time. For the furthering of this effort, family theorists may indeed look to social systems theory as a vehicle to understanding the historical, structural, and cultural foundations of family interaction over the life span.[6] To date, however, little use has been made of systems theory at this level of family development theory. Those few areas in which interactions and transitions are historically and structurally situated have been couched basically in role metaphors. These discussions, mostly of social-class differences in family careers, have generated some stimulating propositions, such as those concerning the differing "life-cycle squeeze" felt by middle-income and lower-income families (see, particularly, Aldous, 1978, pp. 275–280). But it is role theory rather than systems theory that has offered the sensitizing concepts.

In practice, systems concepts have been applied mostly in describing the interactions and transitions of the family group. However, promising the metaphor in linking family processes to larger-scale processes and structures, it has to date been mostly an encumbrance, perhaps as a result of the fact that attention has been focused only on intrafamily processes. Rather than sensitizing the reseacher and theorist to unnoticed possibilities, it simply demands another layer of description that adds little to the description already available through the role metaphor.

For example, most discussions of family change that employ a social systems approach say little more than this: "When role changes occur in the family we can say there has been morphogenesis in the family system." Despite the burden of excess conceptualizations, however, many of these discussions are incisive. Aldous, for example, suggests that we view the "critical role transition points" of individual family members as demarcations of periods in the life cycle of the family:

> Take getting married, as an example of a critical role transition point. The new spouses have moved from the son or daughter positions of the families of orientation—in which they grew up—to spousal positions in the new family of procreation—which they create by their marriage. Morphogensis occurs in the couple relation. . . .
>
> Previous arrangements of interaction are no longer sufficient, and every couple has to initiate morphogenic processes. Couple interaction is tentative, as spouses grope for new solutions and experience conflicting expectations. Communication and power patterns have to be worked out so mutual socialization into marital roles can occur. Work arrangements within the home and the demands of the occupational structure must be integrated to facilitate tasks of physical maintenance.
>
> The roles of individuals in work life and schooling also contain critical role transition points for the individual. . . . In the educational career,

entry into and graduation from school at various levels can be critical role transition points. The individual involved in these family-member, work-life, and educational careers has to synchronize their demands, just as the various career demands of other members have to be reconciled within the family as it develops over time. Accordingly, information on these multiple careers must be taken into account in establishing family stages as well as in understanding the lives of individuals. (Aldous, 1978, pp. 8081; see also Elder, 1975)

Aldous' discussion of critical role transitions in sensitizing, but not because of systems concepts. It is role perspectives that inform her analysis. Again, I am not suggesting that the metaphor of the family as a social system is useless to family theory, but rather that its utility has not yet been demonstrated. Further, if the systems metaphor does prove useful, it may be at levels other than those of intrafamily processes. To date, at least, it appears that systems concepts have provided family theory only with an unproductive overlay for descriptive analyses that are basically informed by social role metaphors.

Problems in the Metaphor of "Social Role"

In family development theory, then, the prevailing metaphor remains that of "social role." Metaphors of stage and drama have played through the history of Western thought and were consciously introduced into American sociology by George Herbert Mead and other social theorists in the early decades of this century. They thus appear to be fundamental to the traditions from which family developmental theory and symbolic interactional theories of the family emerged.[7]

The metaphor of social role has had a rich but contentious part in family sociology over the past half century, with major arguments centering on two basic questions: first, whether "role" refers to regularities of behavior or convergent expectations that are linked to social norms; second, whether "role" refers to structural regularities or to emergent processes. In contemporary family theory, these questions appear to have been more or less resolved, at least for the time being, and there seems to be general agreement that the role metaphor refers to convergent expectations linked to social norms, while increasing attention is being given to role processes, particularly those of "making roles." (See the discussion of the concept of role in Burr, Leigh, Day, & Constantine, 1979, pp. 54–60).

Clearly the role metaphor has important uses. Concepts such as role expectations, taking the role of the other, and role-playing have and will continue to sensitize analyses of both intrafamily processes and family–school, family–workplace, and other transactions. The metaphor of role, I believe, remains one of our most effective devices for describing differences between an array of interacting individuals in various times and places (e.g., in various phases of the life cycle), or between groups of contrasting character (e.g., recently immigrated Chinese compared to Mexican families), or between generalized types of persons in various settings (e.g., the parent as socializer compared to the teacher as educator). In brief, the metaphor of social role facilitates effective shorthand descriptions of differing interaction patterns.

When we ask how people "make roles," however, the role metaphor grows cumbersome, even for the purpose of description. Few of us are so persistently rational as the metaphor suggests; rarely are we so intentional. In our day-to-day lives, most of our actions are more affective and ritual than cognitive in nature. At times, of course, we focus closely on our situations; we monitor and evaluate, we calculate and bargain over what each of us should do, over what each should be expected to do, over what each thinks the other should do, or should have done, or should be. At those times we may be "making roles." But *how* are we making them? And how are we "unmaking" the roles we are discarding? By itself, the metaphor of social role is hardly adequate in the face of such questions, for it presents an image of interacting individuals who are relentlessly cognitive, lacking in affect, and self-consciously oriented toward sets of prescriptive rules or expectations.

The limitations of the role metaphor become particularly clear in the study of family–school intercontingencies. As we shall see, turning attention to intercontingent careers (cf. Farber, 1959) forces our attention back to the fundamental theories of family interaction that inform the core of family developmental theory. The sections that follow will suggest a few directions we might take in the search for a less constricting metaphor.

ROLE EXPECTATIONS AND THE "NORMALCY" OF EVERYDAY ROUTINES: MISARTICULATIONS OF HOME AND SCHOOL

In the following three sections, the challenge of family development theory that might arise from closer attention to intercontingent careers is illustrated through the example of the child's schooling. We might look with equal effectiveness at parental work careers, at church involvements, or at a host of other affiliations and commitments that individual members pursue outside the family, but the linkages of family and school offer examples that in many ways are more compelling.

In part this is because we know so little of the ways in which the child separates and interlinks familial and classroom "worlds," or how these phenomenal interlinkages influence the rest of the family. This appears to be part of an implicit presumption that children are reactive recipients of parental attention and sources of family stress, but have little ability to actively shape family relationships or influence the directions of its development. When the child's school experiences have been considered, they have been seen primarily as tensions and strains to which family members must respond.

The family has thus been seen as constrained and to some small degree shaped by the problems the child brings home from school. It also has been seen as a background variable to help explain in the child's school successes and failures. Little notice has been given, by comparison, to the family's influence on the child's day-to-day classroom behavior, or on the child's developing school career. Even less notice has been given the reciprocal influence of classroom behavior and school career on family interaction, change, and developmental transition.

The concept of intercontingent careers, then, demands a broadening of perspective, in order to consider the possibility that even the child is an active participant in both family and extrafamily interactions, and that his or her involvements and commitments in one sphere influence and are influenced by the processes of the other. The concept of intercontingent careers demands that we go even further, however, for as we consider the intercontingencies of family and school careers, we confront inadequacies in our current constructs of intrafamily processes, and in the role metaphors that inform them.

The Home–School Mismatch

The first of the illustrative examples in this paper arises from research on language and ethnic minorities, in which we frequently confront what Gallimore and Au (1979) call a "competence–incompetence paradox." The paradox is familiar to teachers: Some children who appear adept and quick to learn at home often appear slow in the classroom, are unable to grasp instructions, are easily discouraged, and are unable to complete assignments. The example is complicated by the observation that a small percentage of children essentially reverse the "paradox": they appear to do better in their classroom activities and relationships than they do at home. Further, the paradox is not limited to minorities, but is seen (though less commonly) in children from middle-class, mainstream families.

Why do some children do so well in one setting and so poorly in the other? Might it be that the two sets of performance are causally related or dialectically intertwined? This indeed seems to be so, at least in some of the more dramatic misarticulations, as stresses in school precipitate family tensions, which in turn accelerate classroom troubles, precipitating further family stress and in which the child, parents, and teacher seem to be caught in a unbreakable spiraling bind.

My research with Vicky Johnson at Berkeley offers a rich array of examples of this kind of intercontingent bind, such as the following spontaneous account by a teacher following a series of semistructured questions about homework assignments:

Teacher interview (synopsis of excerpt): [The teacher] seemed to want to say more, so I waited. After a brief pause, he said that "three or four months ago" he had sent home a note with a fifth grade child who had showed little improvement in the first half of the year. The note reported that the child rarely turned in homework, and asked the parents to come in for a visit.

The father took off from work for the conference, during which he listened quietly except to say that his son had never told him he had homework, and that he would "take care of the problem," for his son's failure was "bringing shame" on the family. The child arrived at school the next day acting repressed and angry, and [the teacher] thought he could see bruises on the child's face.

When asked for his homework, the child mumbled that he had "lost it." Over the next few weeks, the teacher continued to ask the child for homework, but made no further contact with the parents. After "two or three" similar experiences with other parents and homework, [the teacher] stopped giving homework to the entire class. (Hansen & Johnson, 1983)

This example appears to support the proposition that the competence–incompetence syndrome may rest on a mismatch of explicit role expectations. Recent research, however, suggests that the mismatch of *implicit* understandings, such as conversational discourse rules, may be even more pervasive (see, e.g., Cook-Gumperz, Gumperz, & Simons, 1981; Greenbaum, 1985). These mismatches are difficult to identify, for they are subtle and only vaguely felt by child, parents, and teacher. What is misarticulated is not explicit expectations for behavior, but rather the mostly unarticulated understandings of what is "normal."

New Zealand data (Hansen, 1986), for example, suggest that the competence–incompetence syndrome may be due in part to a misarticulation of tacit rules for interaction. The data indicate that familial influences on classroom behavior are stronger in some classrooms than in others, and that there is an interactive influence (at least in the statistical sense) of family variables and classroom variables on the child's school career; The closer the fit of family interaction rules with classroom interaction rules, the higher the child's grades both in academic subjects and on classroom deportment. These data, then, suggest that although role interpretations may help us develop adequate interpretations of misarticulations in explicit rules, they may blind us to the existence of others that are more implicit.

In the evidence of home–school mismatches, we thus confront substantive puzzles suggesting that neither the child's family career nor his or her school career can be understood unless both are understood. But in what terms are we to understand them? Does the role metaphor allow interpretations of the range of misarticulations and stresses that appear to contribute to the competence–incompetence paradoxes?

I believe the answer is a qualified "no." If role concepts are to allow such interpretations they must be complemented more fully by concepts that attend the *intersubjectivities* of family and extrafamily involvements. The metaphor of social role appears too rational, cognitive, and intentional when confronted with the richness of family living and its subtle intercontingencies with the extrafamilial careers of its members. The modifications I would urge in the role metaphor begin with a recognition of the importance of the "normalcy" of everyday life.

The "Normalcy" of Everyday Life

When we closely observe our own family involvements, we find that on occasion we do indeed consciously conform to "convergent expectations," as is presumed in the metaphor of social role. Usually, however, our behavior is not so rational. Only rarely do we first think about how we "should" act and then at in intentional accordance or defiance of the expectation. Rather, most of our day-to-day behavior in families is routine: we act in well-established manner, and think about our actions—if we think about them at all—only after the fact.

To the student of Mead, this idea will not appear new. In the flow of everyday experience, we assume some sort of normalcy, and simply interact without having to account for it continuously. In our interactions, Mead suggested, cognitive activity takes place only sporadically, and only when some difficulty or disruption of the flow of experience occurs (Mead, 1932). Our sense of a coherent past gives a sense of continuity with the present and a program for the future. Our present situation seems a reasonable extension of what has been and seems certain to flow into a reasonable future. This continuity of past, present, and future provides the sense of "normalcy" in our everyday lives, which we express in familiar interaction routines. Normalcy, then, is socially constructed.

Since it is socially constructed, normalcy may be "normal," but it is not static. It varies not only from family to family, but also from time to time, and from situation to situation. It is in process, always changing, most often slowly and imperceptibly, but at times dramatically, as family members negotiate a new normalcy or abruptly forego hopes of holding on to an old one.

Since it is socially constructed, normalcy is also arbitrary and relative. Yet each of us accepts it as "given." Our normalcy may differ from others', but it is always taken as legitimate and valid. We are at once sustained and bound by the normalcies we accept and our relationships are sustained and bound by the tacit assumption that what is normal to us is normal to the other (cf. Fish, 1979).

When the sense of normalcy is challenged by the unexpected, our relationships are also challenged. A woman who is closely familiar with the discourse rules of upper-middle-class society may comfortably fit into dinner party conversations from New York to San Francisco. But set her down at the table of a Midwestern farm family and she may find the conversational rituals baffling and frustrating. Comfortable with conversations involving quick responses and a certain competitiveness for the floor, she will have to struggle to make sense of the long silences that meet her statements and questions. To the farm family the silence is but a routine pause between comments; to the *bon vivant* it seems to mean that her question was unheard, ignored, or rejected.

The unexpected, then, may disturb our sense of normalcy, and disrupt our relationships. But this does not always happen. Even in everyday interaction the constructed sense of normalcy is continually being faulted by a "tang of novelty" in present experience. Usually, however, the novel and unexpected are readily incorporated into our understandings of the past. The "new problem of today" is resolved by interpreting it in light of the history we have constructed for ourselves. Our sense of normalcy is undisturbed. In Mead's terms:

> [W]ithin our narrow presents our histories give us the elbow room to cope with the everchanging stream of reality. . . . The past which we construct from the standpoint of the new problem of today is based upon continuities which we discover in that which has arisen, and it serves us until the rising novelty of tomorrow necessitates a new history which interprets the new future. (Mead, 1929, p. 241)

The concept of normalcy, I believe, is useful for understanding not only intrafamily processes and relationships, but also the influence on the family of schooling and other intercontingent careers. It suggests an important modification of the role metaphor when applied to family and classroom interactions. Most of the time these interactions are not role performances in response to convergent expectations, but rather *interaction routines* that take place against a background of tacit understandings based on an assumed normalcy.

Since tacit understandings are not often brought to conscious reflection, the child may feel only an emotional discomfort in one or both settings, without understanding why:

> Indian children (of the Warm Springs reservation in Central Oregon) fail to participate verbally in classroom interaction because the social conditions for participation to which they have become accustomed in the Indian community are lacking. . . . If the Indian child fails to follow an order or answer a question, it may not be because he doesn't understand the linguistic structure of the imperative and the interrogative, but rather because he

does not share the non-Indian's assumption in such contexts that use of these syntactic forms by definition implies an automatic and immediate response from the person to whom they are addressed. (Philips, 1972, p. 392)

Further, children may unintentionally engage in family interaction routines while in the classroom, and vice versa. An example is provided by a longitudinal study of the Kamehameha schools in Hawaii (Tharp & Gallimore, 1982). For almost a decade, efforts to stimulate the learning of English reading skills in young children had little effect, until the results of some 10 years of observational studies of Hawaiian family life were applied to classroom strategies.

Two forms of interaction routine common to many of the Hawaiian families were approximated in the classroom. The first was the "talk-story," a form of narrative that involves the tacit assumption that participants are to take turns in contributing to the story, which is constructed through well-established processes (i.e., the subject and content of the story may vary but the processes remain the same). The second was the interaction routines of sibling care, in which it was tacitly assumed by all involved that older children had responsibility for and authority over younger children not only in caretaking, but also in learning household tasks. When both interaction routines were introduced into the classroom processes, reading abilities improved dramatically.

Stated in other terms, these innovations reduced the disparity between classroom routines and the sense of normalcy that the child had established in the home. Classroom novelty, then, was more closely restricted to the *content* to be learned (i.e., to the lessons in reading English). By employing familiar, repetitive chains of communication and interaction that paralleled the assumed normalcy of the family interaction the children were able to confront the challenges of the lesson content with interaction routines similar to those with which they had experienced considerable emotional satisfaction and success in the home.

This perspective on normalcy and interaction routines, then, complements the interpretations of the competence–incompetence paradox allowed by prevailing role metaphors. Just as there may be a mismatch of role expectations in the family and classroom settings, so there may be a misarticulation of the tacit understandings of normalcy that underlie interaction routines. Similarly, this perspective complements a role approach to family development. Just as the movement from one stage to another involves a marked break in role content (Hill & Mattessich, 1979, p. 168), it also involves a marked break in interaction routines and in the tacit normalcy assumptions on which they rest.

PRESCRIPTIVE ROLES AND PROSCRIPTIVE RULES: THE SHIFT FROM FAMILY TO PEER ORIENTATION

To this point in the discussion, it may appear that the concept of interaction routine is nothing more than another variant of the traditional role concept. A second illustrative example of career intercontingencies, concerning the movement of the growing child from a "family orientation" and toward a "peer orientation," addresses that possibility, by focusing on the relationship of "routine" to "role."

In the preceding section, puzzles presented by home–school mismatches led to an extension of the role metaphor, to include conceptions of routine interaction, based on the assumed normalcy of everyday life. In this section, puzzles presented by the adolescent's family orientations during schooling transitions demonstrate that the concept of interaction routine focuses attention on processes that have been excluded from analysis by traditional role concepts.

The Gradual But Erratic Shift from Family to Peers

The move from family involvement and toward peer involvement generally begins in primary school and gradually accelerates through adolescence, reaching extreme rates in the later stages of high school. In one of the few studies of this movement, Bowerman and Kinch (1959, p. 208) report that the percentage of children who could be classified as most strongly influenced by parents on "normative" ideas and decisions declined from 82% in the first grade to 30% in the tenth grade. The pattern generally indicates that both parents and children are "letting go" as a reasonable response to the child's physical, emotional, and social development.

Not surprisingly, the movement is not uniform from child to child, and it appears that the pace, extent, and intensity of movement from family to cohort orientation relates to qualities of family relationship. The Bowerman and Kinch data indicate that the child's "adjustment" to the family may be more important than the child's adjustment to the peer group (Bowerman & Kinch, 1959, p. 210). On this point, role concepts provide a reasonable interpretation of the data: It is not so much that the socially adept child is pulled away into rewarding peer roles, but more that the child who is discontented with family roles pushes away from the family.

Data from New Zealand children (Hansen, 1981) complicate that explanation, however. With each year from fourth to sixth grades, the linkage of family relational qualities to children's academic grades weakened, as the Bowerman and Kinch data would suggest. Surprisingly, however. the relationship of family variables to children's grades on deportment and classroom adjustment grew stronger over the same period. Apparently, the child's family roles can influence some aspects of the child's classroom roles in one way, while they influence other aspects in other ways. But roles, it will be recalled, refer to the expectations that converge on social positions. The role metaphor suggests that the expectations converging on the child for behavior within the family have a stronger influence on some role performances (responses to expectations) in the classroom than they have on other performances. Role interpretations, then, may offer viable descriptions of these differences, but the descriptions are rather convoluted.

Another puzzle is even less readily interpreted in role terms. There seems to be a general interruption or even reversal of the shift from parent to peer orientation at transition points in a school career. The most striking interruption appears to be at points of school transfer, as the child moves from primary to junior high school and then from junior to senior high school. Bowerman and Kinch (1959) offer cross-sectional support for this view. Comparing grade cohorts of children in the same school system, these researchers found a gradual shift each year in the percentage who were most "normatively influenced by parents." By the fifth grade this percentage had fallen to 65%, but rose to 70% for sixth grade children newly transferred to middle school. The reversal of trend was only temporary, however: The percentage dropped to 52% in the seventh grade cohort and to 33% in the eight grade. For those newly transferred to high school in ninth grade, the percentage again rose to 42%, only to fall to 30% for tenth graders.

Again quality of family relations appears to be related to these undulations. For those adolescents who reported the highest level of adjustment to family, the movement away from family orientation only slowed at points of school transition. In contrast, for those who reported the lowest level of family adjustment, the movement from family orientation reversed dramatically, rising from 33% oriented toward family in eighth grade to 46% in ninth grade, then dropping to 17% in tenth grade.

Even describing these reversals in social role terms is difficult. We can readily understand that family members may accommodate their role expectations to the slow withdrawal of the maturing adolescent. As the adolescent's position in the family gradually changes, convergent expectations slowly change, at times with friction, often all but unnoticed. It is more difficult to accept the idea that discarded expectations are suddenly ractivated or that a whole array of new ones abruptly emerges in a period of a few weeks, then quickly fades over the next few months. Such undulations are theoretically possible, of course, but the interpretation is less than elegant. The problem, I believe, is that the role metaphor—emphasizing the convergence of cognitive and rational expectations for behavior in a social position—focuses attention fixidly on *pre*scriptive expectations, and virtually excludes *pro*scription.

Interaction Rules: The Central Importance of Proscription

In discussing normalcy I suggested that we do not usually first think about how we "should" act and then act in intentional accord or defiance of the expectation. This should not be taken to mean that "normally" we are simply responsive, nor that we are acting unconsciously. The concept of interaction routine, like that of social role, posits conscious, active involvement in everyday interactions. Unlike the role metaphor, however, it does not require intentionality or goal orientation. In our interaction routines, we reflexively gaze on one another, tacitly monitoring one another's behavior and emotional displays, and tacitly evaluating their appropriateness to the situation. We are alert to acts and displays that seem to violate our sense of shared normalcy, including our understandings of acceptable routines, of loyalty and commitment to one another, and of the relationship we share.

Most often, this monitoring is not accomplished in the prescriptive ways that the metaphor of role would suggest. We rarely set specific expectations for what should be done, but rather are alert for clues that we or the other person has gone beyond the range of behavior that is acceptable or appropriate to our relationship in any specific situation. This, then, is the critical and productive distinction between role and routine: whereas "social role" emphasizes prescription of certain behavior or types of behavior, "interaction routine" emphasize proscription.

Proscriptive interaction rules differ from prescriptive social roles in two critical ways. First, *proscriptive interaction rules are applied after the fact of behavior.* To be sure, we may rehearse performances ahead of time, and tell ourselves that we will "be" (display ourselves as) more polite, more respectful, kinder, stronger, more assertive. But most of the time the rehearsals and vows simply provide arbitrary standards for evaluating behavior after the fact. The rehearsal does represent some degree of conscious distancing from the everyday routines. It may represent a step toward conscious renegotiation of the relationship. More often, however, it is a rehearsal of the *content* of interaction, which may lead to variations in the routine but do so within the established guidelines of the routines. Even in these moments of content rehearsal, then, we are employing statements of what we "should not do" in order to stay within the security of the established routines.

Second, *proscriptive interaction rules permit a relatively broad range of behavior within a situated relationship.* Whereas prescriptive roles shape and direct behavior by specifying convergent expectations (i.e., they identify what specific things should be done), interaction rules constrain behavior through restriction (i.e., they identify what kinds of things should not be done). Within the established constraints and restrictions, however, they place few limitations on individual creativity and innovation. The interaction routines of everyday life free us from the need to continuously reflect on what we should do, allowing us to interact in ways that seem familiar and legitimated, even when they are somewhat novel. The content of our interaction may vary enormously. Within the limits set by the proscriptive rules, we have considerable license in terms of the specifics of what we do. What we actually do is monitored and evaluated, tacitly and after the fact, only for situational and interpersonal appropriateness.

As long as the proscriptions of interaction rules are honored, all is well. Interaction rules may not even be articulated, but rather remain tacit, and even resistant to formal statement. But when an individual appears to violate or go beyond the acceptable limits, the rules may be invoked. We may say: "Don't talk to your mother that way," "That's not fair," "We don't do things like that in this room." Or we may simply raise an eyebrow. The rule itself may remain unspecified, and usually the "violator" alters subsequent behavior to fit within the acceptable range. Given continued violation, however, the rule may be articulated. Then further violation of the articulated rule may lead to an explicit renegotiation of proscriptive rules.

In this process—the negotiation of proscriptive rules—the relevance of an enlarged metaphor of social role/interaction routine to family development theories is most clearly seen. For it is through such negotiations that the most profound and lasting family changes occur, including developmental transitions to new phases of family life. These negotiations, then, are the subject of the following section.

AFFECT AND THE NEGOTIATION OF RULES AND ROLES: SCHOOL TRANSITIONS AND FAMILY STRESS

Negotiation of proscriptive interaction rules is seen as a consequence of continued and severe violation of the accepted interaction rules or continued and severe emotional discomfort within the restrictions of the interaction rules. When the persisting violations and unrest are less severe, they may be handled less dramatically, even by tacit or subtle means, such as a slight relaxation of the implicit rules (e.g., the growing child is allowed to question a parental decision). When the violations and unrest grow severe, however, interaction routines give way to negotiation, even though the proscriptions remain tacit and unarticulated.

Usually, it is not proscriptive interaction rules that are negotiated, but rather prescriptive roles. On those rare occasions when proscriptive rules are renegotiated, the family is immersed in dramatic change, not only of what is done by whom, but of how it is done. Normalcy itself is being negotiated. And even more may be changing. Since proscriptive rules also govern negotiations, the rules for negotiation are themselves being negotiated—including the rules for negotiating normalcy.

To elaborate, let us consider a case in which the child's school transitions precipitate fundamental changes in the family. The example demonstrates how sudden a family transition can be, when proscriptive rules are discarded as irrelevant or no longer valid. It also calls attention to another aspect of interaction that is relatively neglected in prevailing role metaphors: the affective core of family life.

School Transitions and Family Disruptions

The examples presented in the two previous sections both concern the intercontingent influences of family and school on the child. The third example, drawn from clinical data, concerns an influence that most parents, and particularly parents of teenagers, accept as part of everyday life: the child's school career, which can often does affect family life profoundly, at times even altering family careers irreversibly.

The most dramatic influences often are seen at points of major schooling transitions. The eldest child's entry to kindergarten and later to junior high school, for example, often are periods of familial stress and adjustment. At best the tension is absorbed into the shared excitements of growth and unfolding possibilities. At worst it is accentuated by a resistance to changing relationships and responsibilities, by a struggle for control, by fears of the known and unknown that await.

Usually the tensions and changes converge most clearly on the child-in-transition. Now he is allowed to stay up later; now she can go out on dates; now they are ready to help in the family business. Where once the child was allowed or even encouraged to cry openly when upset, now crying is met with anger, derision, or inattention.

In some situations, however, it is other family members who are affected most dramatically. In one pertinent case a middle-aged woman, who (according to her own report) had been a "model mother" and "loyal wife," transformed over a few months into a rather independent "gadabout," going to movies and plays with female friends, leaving notes for her husband instead of dinner, even planning a tropical holiday without any of the family. The changes both exhilarated and frightened her:

> *Clinical synopsis (excerpts):* Where once she had carefully controlled her feelings of frustration, anger and disappointment in her marriage, now she openly expresses them. She believes that she had "unconsciously" been waiting for her youngest son to finish junior high school. Conflicted in her fam-

ily situation, she feels she "owes" feelings of happiness and loyalty in her marriage, but her continuing disappointments with her husband have left her depressed and bitter. Now, in displaying her feelings to the maturing child, she recognizes that she was saying to her child, in essence, "You're in high school now; you're old enough to know about this."

. . . *[A few sessions later.]* She now recognizes that she is saying even more: "Now that you're in high school, I can admit *to myself* that this is the way I feel." (Excerpted from author's case files.)

It appears that this woman's earlier denial of anger was something more than a role performance, involving an effort at impression management (cf. Goffman, 1969), in which she was protecting the child from knowing what she knew. Many parents, of course, do carefully manage the expression of their emotions around young and dependent children. But the clinical report indicates that this mother was not simply "managing" her emotional displays. Rather, she believed that "responsible" parents of young children do not have the *right to feel* alienated from their marriage.

This rupture between her feelings and the proscriptions she implicitly accepted did not simply lead her to act as if she were happy in front of her children, in a surface display that covered her real definition of her situation. Rather, she coped with the discrepancy by "deep acting" or trying to feel happy in her marriage (cf. Hochschild, 1979). When the child was young, it appears that the mother tried to feel only in those ways that were legitimated by the tacit proscriptive rules in her family. Telling herself that she really felt those ways, she persuaded herself that her feelings of loyalty were genuine. However, the strategy worked only as long as she was the mother of young children.

With the school transition of her youngest child, the proscriptive interaction rules she had accepted against appearing unhappy with her marriage no longer held. Thus the schooling transition precipitated not only a dramatic change in the relationship of mother to the maturing child, but also in the relationship of wife to husband. The proscriptive rules of the interwoven relationships no longer applied, and it was the career transition of another member of the family that had occasioned the change between husband and wife.

From one perspective, the woman was "negotiating" a role change within her family. Freed from the proscriptions that had constrained her in earlier years, her strategy was to dismiss unilaterally the role expectations that converged on her, and to innovate new behaviors that others might come to accept. Parallel examples are familiar in research on the effects of "child-launching" on marriages (see Aldous, 1978, ch. 9). This woman's strategy was more dramatic and risky than most, but it was highly effective in bringing changes both in family roles and in interac-

tion routines. Not surprisingly, the changes were neither fully anticipated nor fully appreciated, even by the innovator.

Adding the concept of proscriptive interaction rule to the prescriptive role metaphor permits a level of description of family change that is
otherwise unavailable, and broadens our approach to the study of family stability, change, and developmental transitions. But the metaphor
becomes even more useful when it is joined to the concept of negotiation. In that linkage, we see that negotiation, too, is somewhat more
complex and varied than has been suggested in the more restricted metaphor of prescriptive roles.

Negotiation in Familial Routines and Roles

The concept of negotiation, involving such things as bargaining, collud-
ing, mediating, compromising, acquiescing, innovating, and demanding, has developed in recent years alongside the social role metaphor in
interactional theory (see, Hall & Spencer-Hall, 1981; Scanzoni & Szinovacz, 1980; Strauss, 1979). While it is compatible with social role
analysis and allows us to retain the utility of the prescriptive role metaphor, it has the advantage of directing our attention more closely to the
social processes of family change.

Theorists who adopt the negotiation metaphor are usually quick to
add that it does not imply that everything is always being negotiated,
nor that interacting individuals are at all times intentional or in rational
control of their acts and messages. In practice, however, attention has
focused on negotiations of prescriptive role expectations. Negotiations of
the proscriptive rules of everyday life have been ignored.

In a nutshell, this chapter suggests that we not only recognize the
importance of proscriptive rule negotiation, but that we also view negotiation as one "moment" of a continuing dialectic, interaction routine as
another, role performances as still another.[8] Negotiation, routine, and
role must be understood as part of a single metaphor in our theories of
family process. The utility of one depends on utilization of the others.

Perhaps one reason that the negotiation of proscriptive rules has
been overlooked is that it makes little difference in analyses of everyday
life. Only rarely does negotiation concern proscriptive rules or interaction routines. More commonly, in the day-to-day life of the family, it is
explicit expectations—role prescriptions—that are negotiated. Usually
the negotiation is over minor points, and the "convergent expectations"
slowly change, bit by bit. On rare occasions the change is abrupt and
dramatic, and involves a "wholesale" negotiation of convergent expectations, as one or more individuals move into distinctly different family
roles, or out of the family altogether.

This process of "making roles," of course, is readily described with the prevailing role metaphor. But the concept of interaction routine suggests a critical addition: These prescriptive role negotiations take place within the constraints and restrictions imposed by the proscriptive rules of normalcy, that is, those that underlie interaction routines. It is the proscriptive rules that keep the role negotiations within tolerable bounds, as family members continue to accept a shared but tacit agreement on the limits of acceptable conduct. These proscriptive constraints—which may be loosened somewhat in the course of the role negotiation—permit the innovative flexibility (but within acceptable bounds) so necessary to negotiation.

The moments of most profound change, then, are those in which the proscriptive rules of normalcy are themselves renegotiated, for these are the rules that constrain not only the interaction routines of the family, but also its negotiation processes. In other words, the negotiation of proscriptive rules is also the negotiation of negotiation rules.

Elaboration of this point leads to consideration of the place of emotion in interaction routines and in the "normalcy" of everyday family life.

Emotion, Routine, and Negotiation

I have suggested that the prevailing metaphor of family role is overly cognitive and rational. Another way to put this is that it directs attention away not only from tacit understandings, but also from the emotional qualities of interaction. The metaphor, then, reflects a neglect that is endemic to role theory and to modern social theory in general: Affect is given at most only passing attention. Although its centrality to the dynamics of social interaction may be implicitly acknowledged in constructs such as "role satisfaction," "values," "goal orientations," and "status discontent," it is explicitly ignored. When the concept of interaction routine is added to the role metaphor—bringing with it an emphasis on a shared sense of normalcy—explicit and continuing attention to affective processes is unavoidable.

Interaction routines maintain their vitality only so long as they feel satisfying to the participants. When they have become affectively neutral, interaction routines may be far more vulnerable to extinction or disruption than are prescriptive roles. When they grow irritating or frustrating, interaction routines help generate the energies of their own change. For when negative affect grows strong enough and endures long enough, the established continuities on which the interaction routines rest are disputed; the sense of normalcy fades, and the proscriptive rules that underlie the routines are called into question. The stage is set for tacit or explicit negotiation, which may be precipitated by any of a great range of minor or major changes in the life of any family member.

Affect, then, is seen as a critical element in both interaction routine and negotiation, in both stability and change.

Family members may be deeply upset when they perceive threats to established routines and commitments, as when the adolescent announces that she or he would rather go to a school party than on a family picnic or a parent arranges to spend weekends away from home. For disturbance of the continuity and coherence of past, present, and future is essentially a disturbance of the sense of self.

The self, Mead (1936) demonstrated, is rooted in the groups with which the individual is affiliated and to which he or she is committed. Among other things, these commitments and affiliations give us our sense of who we are, and are the sources of our feelings of well-being, of worthiness and confidence, as well as pride, vanity, guilt, shame, and embarrassment (cf. Shott, 1979, especially pp. 1324–1330). Group affiliations, then, involve far more than rational negotiation or cognitive monitoring of convergent expectations. Even the "reflexive gaze," which for Mead (1934) was the primary mechanism of monitoring affiliation, involves assessment not only of our cognitive perceptions of one another, but also one another's affective states.

Collins (1981) goes so far as to suggest that emotional monitoring is the *essential* mechanism whereby social structures are upheld and changed. Human cognition, he argues, is extremely limited, and is hardly up to the task of monitoring the complex lines of authority and sets of associations and coalitions in the social world. The world may be negotiated, but the negotiations are implicit and are conducted with something other than consciously manipulated verbal symbols.

> I propose that the mechanism is *emotional* rather than cognitive. Individuals monitor others' attributes towards social coalitions, and hence toward the degree of support for routines, by feeling the amount of confidence and enthusiasm there is towards certain leaders and activities, or the amount of fear of being attacked by a strong coalition or the amount of contempt for a weak one. (Collins, 1981, p. 994)

One need not accept Collins' full thesis (which he in any case offers tentatively) to recognize its utility in the study of family stress, change, and development. Whether "affective monitoring" is the central mechanism of social structure and change or simply an important process of individual and group life, it sensitizes us to further subleties in the intercontingencies of family and other careers.

As a child moves through a school career, forming and maintaining coalitions and affiliations with varied and changing groupings of peers and teachers, new ways of feeling as well as acting may be learned. Other family members, continually and subtly monitoring one another's behavior and emotional displays, may sense a weakening of affiliative bonds within the family. As the sense of disaffiliation grows, understandings once implicitly shared may be questioned, leading to a loss of the sense of shared normalcy within individuals and increased negotiation between them, first of role prescriptions, eventually perhaps even of proscriptive rules.

The important point is this: it is not just family relationships that are disturbed as the child forms new coalitions and loyalties in his or her school career. It may also be that family members' senses of continuity, their feelings of well-being, security, and confidence are upset. Both role allocations and established routines no longer quite work, and until new ones are negotiated and established, family members feel confused and upset with one another, with their relationship, and with themselves. Normalcy itself is in question, and normalcy itself is being renegotiated.

This renegotiation is central to the processes whereby accommodation and change in family relationships take place, and through which family members move to new phases in their family careers. These negotiations alter the boundaries of legitimacy and appropriateness within which established routines can mutate and new ones emerge. But they also alter the boundaries of legitimacy and appropriateness within which negotiation itself is conducted. In extreme cases, such negotiations may concern the very right of certain individuals (e.g., the child in school transition) to participate in negotiations.

In this enlarged metaphor, both family stability and family change are manifestations of a dialectic process involving routine, role, and negotiation: stability in the exercise of proscriptive routines and prescriptive roles, and change in their negotiation. It is a dialectic that itself is normally constrained by the restrictions set by the proscriptive rules of family interaction. Family change, then, is most dramatic and profound when it is those proscriptive rules—in essence, normalcy—that are being negotiated. In this perspective, the negotiation of normalcy may be recognized as the vital process in the transition from one phase of family development to another.

SUMMARY AND DISCUSSION

In family developmental theory, Reuben Hill and his colleagues have constructed a conception of the family that goes far beyond the image of a "unity of interacting personalities" (cf. Burgess, 1926). Generations of family sociologists have been sensitized and constrained by that image, linked to an increasingly elaborate array of concepts based on the metaphor of "social role." Family developmentalists have continued effectively to employ role analyses, at times linking it to the metaphor of "social systems," while freeing themselves of the "unity" of personalities commitment.

With a time frame that moves far beyond the short-term processes attended by most interactional theories, and an implicit imperative to extend space perspectives beyond the small group, Hill's developmental theory offers a unique range of interrelated perspectives. Stability and change in the family over the life span are seen as responses to the changing sociobiology of the family and the changing social coalitions, situated commitments, and career involvements that are part of the extrafamily involvements of its members, all of which are contextually situated within historically specific macro processes.

Developmental and cognitive psychologists have traditionally attended the first of this array of developmental concerns, and interactional sociologists are now engaged in linking their theories of social-psychological process to macro processes. Yet the linkages of extrafamily involvements to family processes and development, which are central to the family developmental perspective, continue to be ignored. The exploration of these career intercontingencies thus offers a promising priority for family development research.

Closer attention to the careers and affiliations of members outside the family need not distract us from a fundamental concern for intrafamily processes, if we recognize the intercontingencies of these extrafamily involvements with family processes. When we consider the child's school career, for example, we confront an array of puzzles that force attention not only to the interplay of the child's family and school careers, but also back to family processes and the intersubjectivity of familial interaction.

Faced with such puzzles, traditional role concepts appear to be useful but unduly limited. The role metaphor, particularly when used to express a convergence of expectations and generalized norms, is an effective shorthand for describing our sense that individual expectations and behavior decisions are influenced by conditions beyond the present time and situation. When we enter the realm of individual and interpersonal processes, however, (a move that we make when we discuss "making roles") role concepts grow burdensome. Given that we do accept roles, given that we "take" the roles of others, given that we define situations, given that we participate in normative understandings, the basic question is whether these understandings, agreements and expectations guide our actions and define our interactions.

The answer may be that they do, but only now and then. Although we can and do act with the intentionality and cognitive control suggested by the metaphor of role, we do not normally do so in our day-to-day family lives. Our day-to-day family lives are characterized not so much by role performances as by interaction routines, based on an assumed normalcy that frees us from continuously having to account for our behavior. Even in familial negotiations we are rarely guided by prescriptive roles (or role expectations). Far more commonly, we are constrained and restricted by the same proscriptive rules that constrain and restrict our interaction routines.

This does not mean that we act unconsciously, or that we are simply responsive most of the time. Like the concept of prescriptive roles, that of interaction routine posits conscious, active, sentient involvement. In our everyday life we consciously monitor and evaluate our own and other's behavior, after the fact, employing the often tacit proscriptive rules of interaction that are unique to our relationships. Only when the assumed normalcy of everyday family life is challenged do we become intentionally involved in negotiations of new roles and routines, and in the modification of existing ones.

Emotion is an important and neglected aspect of interaction routines, monitoring, and evaluation. The assumed normalcy of everyday life rests in part on a sense of affiliation and commitment. Thus when a family member is perceived to be forming new loyalties outside the family, established routines no longer seem to apply; until new ones are negotiated and established, all members may feel disoriented, frustrated, and insecure, not only with one another and their relationships, but also with themselves. In this emotional turmoil, accommodation and change in family relationships take place.

The processes of family life, then, involve an affect-laden interplay of routine, role, and negotiation, in a dialectic that occurs within the constraints and restrictions of the implicit proscriptive rules that are unique to each family. When it is these proscriptive rules that are being negotiated, change may be profound, for the negotiation of proscriptive rules is at the same time the negotiation of the rules of negotiation. These negotiations—virtually, negotiations of normalcy—are rare in day-to-day living, but they may mark the most fundamental changes in the family, including the transition to a new phase in the family career.

ADDENDUM: ON RESEARCH METHODS

For family developmental theory the basic argument of this essay can be put simply: It is the negotiation of normalcy—the negotiation of proscriptive rules for evaluating acts and displays—that is at the core of developmental transitions. This argument rests on an expanded metaphor of rules, roles, and negotiation in a dialectic process. It is offered with the hope that it will precipitate discussion and exploration of issues both in theory and in methods of inquiry.

In this addendum, two issues raised by the expanded metaphor are discussed. The first concerns research foci. If each family has its own, unique "normalcy," then each must undergo transitional or "systemic" changes somewhat idiosyncratically. Does this mean that family developmentalists have been misguided in their efforts to identify sequential stages or to predict when families will move from one developmental phase to another? I believe not.

Questions of transition and sequence predictability have troubled developmental theory from its inception. This paper does little to resolve those questions, since the routine/role negotiation metaphor (to the point it is herein developed) refers to familial processes, not the biosocial realms on which predictive statements about transitions have been grounded. The family developmentalists' hard-won generalizations—for example, those that relate changes in familial composition to developmental transitions—are neither more nor less valid when the process of change is couched in terms of an expanded metaphor involving a proscriptively constrained "normalcy."

In the long run, the expanded metaphor may actually increase the possibilities for anticipating and even predicting developmental transition. In turning attention to the *situated* processes involved in the maintenance, disruption, and reconstruction of normalcy, we may discover stress factors, growth potentials, and transition points for interpersonal development that currently escape our notice. In addition to generalizations about the relationship of family development to changes in its biosocial/material composition, we then might more actively explore the utility of generalizations that focus on situated processes.

For example, we might observe that heightened ambiguity of family role expectations elicits the kinds of proscriptive rule negotiations that attend developmental transitions. Drawing on developmentalists' generalizations, we might then situate this observation, in propositions that link ambiguity-precipitated negotiations to situations and events such as changes in biosocial composition, parental unemployment, sudden wealth, the onset of substance addiction, or schooling transitions. We might then identify those situated developmental states of family life in which ambiguity-precipitated negotiations generate not only role and rule changes, but more profound developmental transitions. In short, the expanded metaphor suggested in this paper is not only compatible with the kinds of generalizations about situations and events that developmental theorists have sought (e.g., propositions about the relationship of compositional change to developmental transitions), but also adds the possibility of linking these generalizations to others based on process (yielding more subtle and sensitive propositions about the relation of "situated processes" to transitions).

These possibilities bring us to the second, and more troublesome, issue. Given that proscriptive rules and the sense of normalcy most often are *tacitly* understood by family members, is research even a possibility?

At one conceptual level, it is more than a possibility; it is already underway in the work of diverse family researchers. This is the familiar level of research that employs what Schutz (1962) terms "second-level constructs": that is, concepts that the researcher derives from the research subject's constructions or typifications of his or her world. For example, the study of proscriptions is implicit in research on ambiguity in family boundaries (cf. Boss, 1977); the study of the negotiation of proscriptive rules is suggested in work on family stress and in studies of responses to public "rule violation" (cf. Garfinkle, 1967; Hansen & Johnson, 1979); the study of "affective monitoring" is implied in work on communicative pragmatics (cf. Watzlawick, Beavin, & Jackson, 1968). These, of course, are only representative of the many possibilities that have already been opened, but they clearly suggest that researchers already have theoretical and methodological tools that apply to the metaphor suggested in this paper.

There is little doubt that theory-stimulating research could be generated in coming years, if family developmentalists chose to explore the potentials of that metaphor. Initial advances in theory might be made quickly, through systematic and imaginative surveys of the various literatures that are relevant to the metaphor. The effort would demand the special combination of intellectual capacities that we came to recognize in Reuben Hill's life-long work: an encyclopedic command of the literature, a passionate creativity, and a relentless rigor. In most academic disciplines only a rare few individuals are prepared for such an effort, but to a great extent through Reuben Hill's encouragement and inspiration an unusually large number of family theorists today possess the capacities and the discipline that are necessary to the challenge.

At another conceptual level, however, the issue of research possibilities is even more difficult to address, for the expanded metaphor raises a seemingly unanswerable question. How can anyone know another's phenomenology, or even what another person experiences? The research difficulties of confronting subjectivity (even one's own) are further compounded in this metaphor by the assertion that self and other are inextricable from one another. Subjectivity is by its very nature social. Hence, it can be understood only as intersubjectivity, and in relation to its specific historical time and place as well as its future possibilities.

Subjectivity-based metaphors have suffered sharp and continuing criticism for failing to answer this unanswerable question. The criticism, for the most part, has been correct. What critics often fail to adequately consider, however, despite social philosophers' persistent reminders, is that the unanswerable question is in fact shared by *all* social research. It is a condition of human existence. Put simply, we can ignore the question in our research, but the question does not go away. In attempting to understand human life, we face a frustrating choice. The more successfully we avoid (or pretend to avoid) the problem of subjectivity, the less relevant are our theories to human life. Yet the more fully our theories confront the problems posed by subjectivity, the more difficulty we have in pursuing our research.

It is exceedingly difficult to systematically observe, categorize and correlate overt behaviors and verbalizations. It is far more difficult to identify the motives that lie beneath these observables, or to discern the subjective meanings that they may express or mask. How, then, are we to fathom the intersubjective understandings and agreements between family members, much less their affective monitorings and unarticulated evaluations of one another? And what of the tacit assumptions and emotional infusions that are so much a part of the family's sense of shared normalcy? Ultimately, questions of intersubjectivity may equally affect all theories of human life, but it is tempting to conclude that, if clear and consistent research strategies are the goal, the questions are best left to a later date.

Through most of the short history of social science in this country, research has been conducted as if avoiding those questions was not only essential to effective social research, but was also the best strategy for eventually approaching an "answer" to them. However elusive they may be, answers might be roughly approximated through scientific methods, and with ingenuity and effort, the approximations could slowly improve. The presumption gave a priceless energy to research, and contributed to the development and elaboration of powerful conceptual and procedural tools for human inquiry.

One price of these accomplishments, however, was an institutional and professional discouragement of alternative and even complementary approaches to research. Some theorists actively explored subjectivity and few would fully ignore it, but when it came to research, the theory had to be expressed in ways appropriate to ratioempirical methods. Even Mead, passionately involved in the intellectual ethos of his time, closely linked his intersubjective theories to the procedures of behavioral psychology. In recent decades, as recognition of the limitations of the ratioempirical approach has spread, theorists have begun to explore and develop more actively metaphors of individual and social life that are less neglectful of affective and intersubjective qualities. Such metaphors are less constrained by the presumption of a "reality" that need only be discovered and understood, through increasingly accurate approximations. (See, especially, McLain & Weigert, 1979.)

The search, however, for appropriate research procedures has not kept pace. In part, this reflects the inherent difficulty of intersubjective inquiry. In part it also reflects a residual presumption that ratioempirical methodologies are *the only* legitimate approach to human inquiry. The search for a method of inquiry based on subjectivity and intersubjectivity has been rarely joined, despite repeated warnings that methods that neglect the subjective and intersubjective are "doomed to failure" (cf. Habermas, 1979, p. xi). Without such a method, "absolutely no one . . . writes or speaks a sentence or word about us and our contemporaries that is not a gross error" (Sartre, 1963, p. 111).

It is not likely that a "subjectivity adequate" theory will emerge in our time. We first may have to develop a new language for addressing and representing the intersubjective, and such a language may be attainable only in a transformed culture. As a beginning, we might find clues in the more intersubjectivity-focused novels. Yet even the most gifted novelist, working under the same linguistic constraints as the social theorist, falls short of expressing the "multidimensional unity" of a single act, much less of a social person:

> The novelist will show us first one, then the other of [the multiple] dimensions as thoughts alternating in the "mind" of his hero. But the novelist will be lying. It is not thoughts which are involved (at least not necessarily), and all are given together, not one at a time. . . . Each signification is transformed, continues to be transformed, and its transformation has repercussions on all the others. (Sartre, 1963, pp. 110–111)

The search for a subjectively adequate method and for the forms of language it requires will demand an effort that may be endured by only a few in each generation of scholars. Yet those whose gifts are more modest are also involved, for we can chose whether to encourage those few to take up and persist in the effort. We can also attempt to use our own capacities more flexibly, in ways that extend our own efforts in directions that are less inadequate to the multiple dimensions of intersubjectivity. In this, again, we may turn to those novels that detail the "intersections of biography and history" (cf. Mills, 1959), and the works of the more historically aware psychotherapists such as Erik Erikson (1958). We might also consider more closely the relevance of clinical methods of individual and group therapy (e.g., Haley & Hoffman, 1967; Minuchin & Fishman, 1981; Yalom, 1980) to the exploration of shared patterns of perception and other dimensions of intersubjectivity. An example of this sort of relevancy is demonstrated in anthropologists' recent applications of the Thematic Apperceptions Test (see De Vos, 1983; Scheper-Hughes, 1979; Suarez-Orozco, 1988).

One of the more challenging dimensions of intersubjectivity (and one in which the relevance of intersubjectivity to family development theory is clearly seen) is its infusions of present with past and future (cf. Mead, 1929, 1934). This dimension demands that the phenomenological be located temporally, as well as structurally, that is, located within the specific society's sociohistorical structures, linked to its "structures of the future" (those structures its members anticipate and imagine are possible). Again, new vocabularies will be required to represent these interfusions, but even those we already have allow us to approach more closely the phenomenological/sociostructural/temporal multidimensionality of human life.

Richard Bernstein (1978, 1986), for example, offers one workable suggestion: To move toward a more adequate metaphor, we must transcend the arbitrary divisions among current methodologies. Quantitative empiricism, interpretive phenomenology, and critical theory are not alternatives, but three moments in the internal dialectic of social theory.

Within the limitations of our current languages, then, the most adequate theory of family development would be at once empirical, interpretive, and critical. This, too, is a demanding challenge, but one that we can effectively address if we so choose.

NOTES

1. The metaphor of "discovery" lies at the heart not only of classical anthropology, but also of classical social theory, as exemplified in Marx and Weber. In 20th-century United States social research, however, it was eclipsed by the powerful methodologies that attended the ratioempirical metaphor of "theory verification." "Theory discovery" has gained some degree of acceptance in social psychology in the past 2 decades (particularly since Glaser & Strauss, 1969, linked qualitative discovery methodologies to the quantitative analytic techniques of Lazarsfeld [see, for example, Lazarsfeld & Barton, 1951]). It remains somewhat suspect among family theorists, in part because it has often been used to mask an absence of method, and in part because the metaphor, "at its extreme, verges on indeterminism to such a degree that it would be impossible to make it the basis for systematic theory" (Klein & Hill, 1979, p. 512).

The Klein and Hill caution is quite valid. Theory exploration is not an adequate methodology for systematic theory development. It can open new possibilities for systematic development, by suggesting possibilities beyond the system-limited capacities of prevailing thought. Systematic theory development, through goal-oriented puzzle solving, has been highly productive in the study of family stress, change, and development, as it has been pursued by Hill and his most productive students. In studying family stress, change, and development, however, there is also the need for exploration, creativity, and discovery. The need exists not in the service of systematic theory development and verification, but as an equally important moment in the emergence of more adequate understandings (or metaphors) of family life.

2. My approach, of course, is consistent with the more restricted symbolic interaction perspectives of Herbert Blumer (1969), Manfred Kuhn (1964), and Arnold Rose (1962). In its concerns for subjectivity and intersubjectivity, it is also basically compatible with the more persistently phenomenological approaches of Alfred Schultz (1969) and Harold Garfinkle (1967), though it differs in terminology and emphases (cf. McLain & Weigart, 1979). As will be seen below, it might also be consistent with reformulations based on the social systems theories of Buckley (1967), if those theories were carefully followed.

3. See particularly, Aldous, 1978; Duvall and Hill, 1948; Hill, Foote, Aldous, Carlson, & McDonald, 1970; Hill and Rodgers, 1963; Rodgers, 1973.

4. A notable exception is Aldous's use of Buckley's (1967) concepts to describe the family as a social system. In Aldous' treatment, the systems concepts appear to offer a useful shorthand in describing the interlinkages of family and other associations, such as social welfare agencies and educational systems (Aldous, 1978, pp. 25–50).

5. The compatabilities of Buckley's (1967) systems concepts and those of symbolic interaction are no accident. Buckley, who had been one of the sharpest cri-

tics of the functionalist's approaches, completed his own systems theory at the University of California, Santa Barbara, at a time when that school was still a stronghold of symbolic interactionism and other interactional theories. Tomatsu Shibutani led the collegial and congenial challenge to incorporate concepts of self-generative change, (which Buckley met brilliantly with his concepts of "morphogenesis"), while (then) younger "interactionists" such as Peter Hall and myself provide a supportive cheering section.

6. The inattention of family development theories to "historical contexts and events," identified by Hill and Mattessich (1979, p. 170), might also be redressed by aggressive attention to the "intercontingent careers" of family members. Adequate study of these intercontingencies virtually demands that attention turn to the social, economic and political contexts both of the family as a unit, and of its individual members. In considering intercontingent careers, then, the individual members are revealed to be the agents who import the historically specific understandings and events of the larger society into the internal processes of family life.

7. Through their development, the conceptual core of these research areas has remained the interactional philosophy of George Herbert Mead and W. I. Thomas. That conceptual core was brought into the family area by Ernest Burgess, and was developed by generation after generation of researchers and theorists, notably Robert Angell, Willard Waller, Reuben Hill, Sheldon Stryker, and Wesley Burr (see, particularly, Burr et al., 1979; Stryker, 1964; Waller & Hill, 1951). The enduring strength and pertinence of family developmental theory are rooted in the fundamental viability of this perspective.

8. I believe that family development theory, as well as the study of family stress and change, could benefit greatly from closer attention to the rich traditions of dialectical approaches to social and cultural change. In this paper, however, I use the term *dialectic* in a rather "de-philosophized" and general sense, as is the current fashion in sociological literature. It refers to the interactive influence of routine, role, and negotiation. Tensions within any one, or discontinuities between them, generate change, and changes in one occasion changes in the others.

   In this general sense, dialectical analyses are implicit in our literature on family processes and change. See, for example, Scanzoni's (1979) discussion of social process and power, and Hansen and Johnson's (1979) family stress theory. But dialectical perspectives have a far greater potential than is even suggested in such discussions. Unfortunately, recent social and cultural inquiry in this country offer little to build upon.

   When they have been explicitly used in United States sociology, dialectical analyses have taken an "immanent development" variant of dialectical development. It is expressed in the adage, "Success breeds its own failure." This variant is reflected in a variety of concepts that have enjoyed popularity in United States sociology, such as in Merton's (1936) "unanticipated consequences of social action," Pareto's (1935) "circulation of elites," and Weber's (1948) analysis of the ways the Protestant virtues of thrift, frugality, and industry are eroded by the very wealth they create. This productive variant is described by Schneider (1964):

The dialectic approach to change as taken here exploits the possibilities of understanding change . . . suggested by notions that may be crudely rendered as follows: the very "factor" that brings strength or viability or success to a system will also bring its downfall; 'elements' at work in a system are likely to engender their own 'opposites' (the intention–outcome discrepancy being a special case of this). (p. 385)

Though this is a fruitful approach, a far more elaborate array of tools is available for dialectal analysis than is suggested in contemporary social research. One relatively neglected statement is seen in Sartre's (1963) "progressive–regressive" method for understanding both person and history. Surveying European social and political thought, Gurvitch (1962) identified five distinct approaches to dialectic analysis: dialectic complementarity; mutual dialectic implication; dialectic ambiguity; dialectic polarization; and dialectic reciprocity of perspective. I suspect that family development theory would be considerably enriched by a careful consideration of this generally neglected tradition.

REFERENCES

Aldous, J. (1978). *Family careers: Developmental change in families*. New York: Wiley.
Bernstein, R. (1978). *The restructuring of social and political theory*. Philadelphia: University of Pennsylvania Press.
Bernstein, R. (1986, May). *Interpretation of its discontents*. Paper presented at the Conference on Critical Interpretation, California State University, Hayward, CA.
Blumer, H. (1969). *Symbolic interactionism: Perspective and method*. Englewood Cliffs, NJ: Prentice-Hall.
Boss, P. (1977). A clarification of the concept of psychological father presence in families experiencing ambiguity of boundary. *Journal of Marriage and the Family, 39*, 141–151.
Bowerman, C., & Kinch, J. (1959). Changes in family and peer orientation of children between the fourth and tenth grades. *Social Forces, 37*, 206–11.
Buckley, W. (1967). *Sociology and modern systems theory*. Englewood Cliffs, NJ: Prentice-Hall.
Burgess, E. (1926). The family as a unity of interacting personalities. *Family, 7*, 3–9.
Burr, W., Leigh, G., Day, R., & Constantine, J. (1979). Symbolic interaction and the family. In W. Burr, R. Hill, F. Nye, & I. Reiss (Eds.), *Contemporary theories about the family: Vol. 2. General theories/theoretical orientations* (pp. 42–111). New York: Free Press.
Collins, R. (1981). On the microfoundations of macrosociology. *American Journal of Sociology, 86*, 984–1012.
Cook-Gumperz, J., Gumperz, J., & Simons, H. (1981). *Final report on school/home ethnography project*. Washington, DC: National Institute of Education.
De Vos, G. (1983). Achievement motivation and intra-family attitudes in immigrant Koreans. *Journal of Psychoanalytic Anthropology, 6*, 25–71.
Duvall, E. (1971). *Family development* (4th ed.). Philadelphia: Lippincott.
Duvall, E., & Hill, R. (1948). *Report of the Committee on the Dynamics of Family Interaction*. Paper presented at the National Conference on Family Life, Washington, DC.
Elder, G. H., Jr. (1975). Age differentiation and the life course. In A. Inkeles, J. Coleman, & N. Smelser (Eds.), *Annual Review of Sociology* (Vol. 1, pp. 165–90). Palo Alto, CA: Annual Review.
Erikson, E. (1958). *Young man Luther*. New York: Norton.

Farber, B. (1959). The family as a set of mutually contingent careers. In N. Foote (Ed.), *Household decision-making* (pp. 276–97). New York: New York University Press.

Fish, S. (1979). Normal circumstances, literal language, direct speech acts, the ordinary, the everyday, the obvious, what goes without saying, and other special cases. In P. Rabinow & W. Sullivan (Eds.), *Interpretive social science: A reader* (pp. 243–65). Berkeley: University of California Press.

Gallimore, R., & Au, K. Hu-Pei (1979). The competence/incompetence paradox in the education of minority children. *The Quarterly Newsletter of the Laboratory for Comparative Human Cognition, 1,* 32–37.

Garfinkle, H. (1967). *Studies in ethnomethodology.* Englewood Cliffs, NJ: Prentice-Hall.

Glaser, B., & Strauss, A. (1969). *The discovery of grounded theory: Strategies for qualitative research.* New York: Aldine.

Goffman, E. (1969). *Strategic interaction.* Philadelphia: University of Pennsylvania Press.

Greenbaum, P. (1985). Nonverbal differences in communication style between American Indian and Anglo elementary classrooms. *American Educational Research Journal, 22,* 101–15.

Gurvitch, G. (1962). *Dialectique et sociologie.* Paris: Flammarion.

Habermas, J. (1979). *Communication and the evolution of society* (T. McCarthy, Trans.). Boston: Beacon.

Haley, J., & Hoffman, L. (1967). *Techniques of family therapy.* New York: Basic Books.

Hall, P., & Spencer-Hall, D. (1981, April). *The school as negotiated order?* Paper delivered at American Educational Research Association meetings, Los Angeles, CA.

Hansen, D. (1981). Family structures and the effects of schooling in a New Zealand suburb. *Journal of Comparative Family Studies, 12,* 63–80.

Hansen, D. (1986). Family–school articulations: The effects of interaction rule mismatch. *American Educational Research Journal, 23,* 643–59.

Hansen, D., & Johnson, V. (1979). Rethinking family stress theory: Definitional aspects. In W. Burr, R. Hill, F. Nye, & I. Reiss (Eds.), *Contemporary theories about the family: Vol. 1. Research-based theories* (pp. 295–316). New York: Free Press.

Hansen, D., & Johnson, V. (1983). *Locating learning: The social contexts of second-language acquisition.* Washington, DC: National Institute of Education.

Hill, R. (1970). *Family development in three generations.* Cambridge, MA: Schenkman.

Hill, R. (1971). Modern systems theory in the family: A confrontation. *Social Science Information,* October 7–26.

Hill, R. (1981). Theories and research designs linking family behavior and child development: A critical overview. *Journal of Comparative Family Studies, 12,* 1–18.

Hill, R., Foote, N., Aldous, J., Carlson, R., & MacDonald, R. (1970). *Family development in three generations.* Cambridge, MA: Schenkman.

Hill, R., & Mattessich, P. (1979). Family development theory and life-span development. In P. Baltes & O. Brim, Jr. (Eds.), *Life-span development and behavior* (Vol. 2, pp. 161–204). New York: Academic Press.

Hill, R., & Rodgers, R. (1963). The developmental approach. In H. Christensen (Ed.). *Handbook of marriage and the family* (pp. 171–211). Chicago: Rand-McNally.

Hochschild, A. (1979). Emotion work, feeling rules and social structure. *American Journal of Sociology, 85,* 551–74.

Hodgson, J., & Lewis, R. (1979). Pilgrim's progress. III: A trend analysis of theory and methodology. *Family Process, 18,* 163–89.

Klein, D., & Hill, R. (1979). Determinants of family problem-solving effectiveness. In W. Burr, R. Hill, F. Nye, I. Reiss (Eds.), *Contemporary theories about the family: Vol 1. Research-based theories* (pp. 295–316). New York: Free Press.

Kuhn, M. (1964). Major trends in symbolic interaction theory in the past twenty-five years. *The Sociological Quarterly, 5,* 61–84.

Lazarsfeld, P., & Barton, A. (1951). Qualitative measurement in the social sciences: Classification, typologies, and indices. In D. Lerner (Ed.), *The policy sciences* (pp. 155–192). Palo Alto, CA: Stanford University Press.

Maines, D. (1977). Social organization and social structure in symbolic interactionist thought. *Annual Review of Sociology, 3,* 235–59.

McLain, R., & Weigert, A. (1979). Toward a phenomenological sociology of family: A programmatic essay. In W. Burr, R. Hill, F. Nye, I. Reiss (Eds.), *Contemporary theories about the family; Vol 2. General theories/theoretical orientations* (pp. 160–205). New York: Free Press.

Mead, G. H. (1929). The nature of the past. In J. Coss (Ed.), *Essays in Honor of John Dewey* (pp. 235–42). New York: Holt.

Mead, G. H. (1932). *Philosophy of the present.* Chicago: University of Chicago Press.

Mead, G. H. (1934). *Mind, self and society.* Chicago: University of Chicago Press.

Mead, G. H. (1936). *Movements of thought in the nineteenth century.* Chicago: University of Chicago Press.

Merton, R. (1936). The unanticipated consequences of purposive social action. *American Sociological Review, 1,* 894–904.

Mills, C. W. (1959). *The sociological imagination.* New York: Oxford.

Minuchin, S., & Fishman, H. (1981). *Family therapy techniques.* Cambridge, MA: Harvard University Press.

Morgan, G. (1980). Paradigms, metaphors, and puzzle solving in organizational theory. *Administrative Science Quarterly, 25,* 605–22.

Pareto, V. (1935). *The mind and society* (Vol. 4) (A. Bongiorno & A. Livingston, Trans.). New York: Harcourt, Brace.

Philips, S. (1972). Participant structures and communicative competence: Warm Springs children in community and classrooms. In C. Cazden, V. John, & D. Hymes (Eds.), *Functions of language in the classroom* (pp. 370–94). New York: Teachers College Press.

Rodgers, R. (1973). *Family interaction and transaction: The developmental approach.* Englewood Cliffs, NJ: Prentice-Hall.

Rose, A. (Ed.). (1962). *Human behavior and social processes.* Boston: Houghton-Mifflin.

Sartre, J. (1963). *Search for a method* (H. Barnes, Trans.). New York: Knopf.

Scanzoni, J. (1979). Social processes and power in families. In W. Burr, R. Hill, F. Nye, & R. Reiss (Eds.), *Contemporary theories about the family; Vol. 1. Research-based theories* (pp. 295–316). New York: Free Press.

Scanzoni, J., & Szinovacz, M. (1980). *Family decision-making: Sex roles and change over the life cycle.* New York: Sage.

Scheper-Hughes, N. (1979). *Saints, scholars and schizophrenics: Mental illness in rural Ireland.* Berkeley: University of California Press.

Schneider, L. (1964). Toward assessment of Sorokin's view of change. In G. Zollschan & W. Hirsch (Eds.), *Explorations in social change* (pp. 371–400). Boston: Houghton-Miffling.

Schutz, A. (1962). *Collected papers; Vol 1. The problem of social reality.* The Hague: Martinus Nijhoff.

Schutz, A. (1969). *The phenomenology of the social world.* Evanston, IL: Northwestern University Press.

Shott, S. (1979). Emotions and social life: A symbolic interactionist analysis. *American Journal of Sociology, 84,* 1317–1334.

Strauss, A. (1979). *Negotiations: Contexts, processes and social order.* San Francisco: Jossey-Bass.

Stryker, S. (1964). The interactional and situational approaches. In H. Christensen (Ed.) *Handbook of marriage and the family* (pp. 125–70). Chicago: Rand-McNally.

Suarez-Orosco, M. (1988). *In pursuit of a dream: New Hispanic immigrants in American* schools. Palo Alto: Stanford University Press.

Tharp, R., & Gallimore, R. (1982). Inquiry process in program development. *Journal of Community Psychology, 19,* 103–11.

Waller, W., & Hill, R. (1951). *The family: A dynamic interpretation.* New York: Dryden.

Watzlawick, P., Beavin, J., & Jackson, D. (1968). *Pragmatics of human communication.* New York: Norton.

Weber, M. (1948). *The Protestant ethic and the spirit of capitalism.* (T. Parsons, Trans.). New York: Scribners.

Weick, K. (1971). Group processes, family processes and problem solving. In J. Aldous, T. Condon, R. Mill, M. Strauss & I. Tallman (Eds.), *Family problem solving: A symposium on theoretical and methodological concerns* (pp. 3–54). Hinsdale, IL: Dryden.

Wentworth, W. (1980). *Context and understanding: An inquiry into socialization theory.* New York: Elsevier.

Yalom, I. (1980). *Existential psychotherapy.* New York: Basic Books.

4

A *Feminist Look at Family Development Theory*

LERKE GRAVENHORST
Deutsches Jugendinstitut, Munich, West Germany

FAMILY SOCIOLOGY VERSUS FAMILY-RELATED FEMINIST SOCIOLOGY

Competing Claims, Separate Communities

The basic differences between family sociology and feminist sociology have long been part of the social science enterprise (cf. Habermas, 1968). For the last 10 to 15 years in the United States and somewhat later in West Germany, where this chapter was written, these differences have been expressed in a new historical form. A feminist-oriented science has developed that opposes or attempts to be independent from the established social sciences.[1]

The different types of knowledge sought and philosophies of social science underlying family sociology and feminist sociology have obtained their legitimacy within two different "universes of discourse." This is most apparent when examining the social and societal content and form of gender relationships, an object of analysis for both sociologies. To be sure, there is some amount of overlap and exchange between the two. But there is no denying the fact that within each of the respective social science communities there is a different major thrust in defining and tackling social scientific problems.[2]

The differences are most apparent on the level of discourse. Taking the feminist vocabulary as a frame of reference, one has only to look at those ideas and concepts providing the core identity of feminist research. It is a research program intended to promote the interests of women and to do so by opposing patriarchy as a social system. The patriarchal system puts men and not women into positions of direct power and influence in society, particularly by maintaining a social division of labor and stratification of political, economic, and cultural resources along gender lines. Therefore, concepts such as patriarchy or the hierarchical division of labor based on gender are indicative of a feminist perspective that will hardly be found in family sociology as an established academic discipline.

Not every piece of research and writing has to refer explicitly to "patriarchy" to demonstrate its feminist nature. (The rhetoric of the illustrative case study presented below may be a case in point.) But regardless of how difficult it may be to define and observe patriarchy, if it is not made the guiding issue for a community of social scientists, this community can hardly be said to be feminist in orientation. For this reason, family sociology as an established academic discipline is judged here not to be feminist.[3]

The concept of patriarchy may be inappropriate for capturing essential characteristics of present societal structures that produce and shape the family as we know it. It has been argued, for instance, that patriarchy is so pervasive and universal a form of social organization as to be useless for explaining concrete events and constellations (Joan Aldous, personal communication, 1983). However, such a judgment would equally hold for other terms used without hesitation by the community of family scholars. It would seem that it is not so much the substantive inadequacy of the concept of patriarchy that explains its rare use in family sociology but rather its threatening connotations.[4]

It is my contention that the relative discontinuity in the development of family-relevant sociology that can be observed in the cases of nonfeminist and feminist family sociologists reveals the existence of two social science guilds. In this chapter, I would like to comment on what I see to be some of the organizing elements in the two different approaches to social and specifically family reality. In this comparison, Reuben Hill's version of family development theory[5] is taken to stand for a non-feminist-inspired orientation in family sociology, with an emphasis on universality and objectivity. The comparison primarily relies on Hill's most recent statement of the theory in an article examining the gains for family development theory from the literature on life-span development (Hill & Mattessich, 1979).[6] A case study of a housewife that the reader will find below represents a feminist orientation with an emphasis on particularity and subjectivity.

Differing Interests and Standards

As stated earlier, family sociology and feminist social science, abstractly speaking, have overlapping subject matter: the structure and dynamics of gender relationships. Nevertheless, it is no matter of chance that, on a concrete level and for the present comparison, it is difficult to identify the commonality of the subject matter. The feminist-inspired case study analyzes the account of the individual development of a female family member, taking the sensitizing perspective of the family as the prime organizing factor of a female life context in modern industrial, patriarchal societies.[7] In family development theory, the emphasis is placed elsewhere. It is the family's development that is of prime interest, and individual development is conceptualized in terms of its being prerequisite to the dynamics and the organization of the development of the family.

These different foci on knowing about the individual as family member on the one hand, and the family as such on the other, are here taken to be one reflection of the feminist contention that the social whole is conceived inappropriately if some of its parts do not have a chance of being adequately integrated into the whole. "Adequately" would mean that their motives, interests, and life trajectories would not have to be repressed, distorted, or left unsaid but could be expressed and find reasoned consideration according to standards of universality.

Feminist social science thus looks at women as particular members of a social system and only then asks what the social system does not (or does) do for them. It does not look at a social system and the input of its female members into its functioning, structure, and development over time, as would be expected from the family development framework.

Even though, in the family development perspective, the family is conceptualized as an organization responding to developmental tasks of its members, it is the development of the family unit as such that provides the focus of interest and the organizing questions. This is best expressed in a recent working definition of family development:

> Family development refers to the process of progressive structural differentiation and transformation over the family's history, to the active acquisition and selective discarding of roles by incumbents of family positions as they seek to meet the changing functional requisites for survival and as they adapt to recurring life stresses as a *family system*. (Hill & Mattessich, 1979, p. 174, italics added)

The explicit formulations of this framework stress the family system as an object of inquiry in its own right and subordinate to it questions about the social structuring of the lives of family members as individuals.

Feminist research that aims at achieving due legitimacy for social particularity cannot do so without relying on the subjective. It is not by chance that in the case study presented below, particularity is expressed in its subjective form. Subjectivity is the realm of experience in which intuitions and interests in life, life trajectories or fragments of them, as well as their fulfillment and failures are molded, recognized, and expressed. Only women's subjective accounts have effectively told about the exclusion, negation, and domination directed against them that are in need of abolition. Therefore, it is subjectivity and not objectivity that receives prime attention in feminist research.[8] However, it is well to note that these accounts are of processes and events that have objectively occurred as reported by women.

The subjective orientation of feminist research is intended to lead to a description of the social world that much more specifically and adequately represents the problematic situation of women in patriarchal society, and consequently much more specifically and adequately represents that of men too. In terms of research methods favored in the beginning phase of feminist social science, this interest has meant a renaissance of qualitative, historical, and literary approaches (cf. McRobbie, 1982; Zentraleinrichtung, 1984).[9] The case study presented at the end of the chapter is intended to illustrate an approach to the social reality that is of specific relevance to a female family member, thus differing from family development and other perspectives in family sociology.

There is another angle in comparing the family development approach and the feminist-inspired case study: the different interests in knowing about individuals in each of the two types of inquiries. Mention has been made of the fact that the two approaches differ in the priorities assigned to the individual members on the one hand and the family system on the other. In family development theory, individuals are perceived in their function as family members without the social structurally induced differences among them being considered. In contrast, in the feminist-oriented case study, it is the particular social existence of a woman that is of interest, with the family considered to be the central element in her life context.

A more conspicuous difference can be identified if one looks at the modes of conceptualizing the development of family members in each of the two approaches. Family development theory looks at the "movement through time of individual family members" (Hill & Mattessich, 1979, p. 190) or the age-dependent "sequentially normative regularities" (Hill & Mattessich, 1979, p. 185) of individual behavior. The illustrative case study with its feminist interpretation looks at the content and the realization of subjectivity of a woman over her life span, that is, at her self-fulfillment and self-alienation within the family context.[10]

The family development perspectives makes use of a number of value-laden concepts. Such concepts include, for instance, "needs" of individual family members (Hill & Mattessich, 1979, pp. 163, 167), "individual autonomy" and "growth" experiences (p. 172), or the "dictate" of societal expectations (p. 180, and *passim* in Hill, 1971; Hill & Rodgers, 1964). However, the most recent systematic formulations of the approach do not build on the existential-evaluative potential of its concepts and problem definitions. They rather attempt to render them marginal. This can best be seen when members of the family are described, as well as when the state of the family is evaluated.

With regard to the members of a family, the formulations view social existence and social organization of individuals in terms of social roles. On the evaluation level, the systematic formulations use formal standards such as structural differentiation and structural complexity (Hill & Mattessich, 1979, pp. 187, 199), rather than substantive standards, which point up the inadequacy or adequacy of a given social system in relation to a member's interests.

Neither the concepts of roles and their arrangements nor the concepts of complexity and differentiation sufficiently represent family life and its social organization. Family life, from the feminist point of view, also means visions and hopes of people, realistic possibilities and legitimate beliefs in their coming true, and the illegitimacy of their prevention and suppression. The quality of the family, it is argued, has also to be judged according to subjectively and intersubjectively validated images and concepts for a dignified life of individuals living together. Such images today refer to the notions of absence of domination, reciprocity of interactions, or equality of rights.

Different Views of Development

Family development theory and the feminist analysis of a woman's life differ in their conceptualization of "development." Again, it is not so much on the phenomenal level that the two approaches deviate from one another. Rather the distinctions are located on the level of the basic organizing interests and principles that apply to family development as well as to individual development. As was seen above, these differences amount to whether or not existential issues of the "good" and "just" life should be considered to be *within* the province of the social sciences. As pointed out already, family development theory, as examplified in the writing of Reuben Hill, has taken a definite stance against incorporating such issues. A feminist-inspired analysis, however, takes the stance in favor of their inclusion.

Both conceptual approaches agree on the definition of general developmental tasks of families as stated by Hill and Mattessich (1979, p. 195): "Families will need to develop patterns of interaction suitable to meet the developmental demands of their members." But the approaches differ as to the kind of categories that are to reflect organizational states of family systems and their changes. From a feminist perspective, family organization comes into view as "organization for subjectivity." This perspective looks at organizational change in terms of the extent to which such change gives room to significant subjective interests of all family members, specifically to those of female family members.

The case study below, for example, focuses on the biographical process in which a social world, with the family at its center, forms the subjectivity structures of a particular woman. It documents the history of how the woman's societal chances for subjectivity are prevented or supported, neglected or acknowledged. Thus, the case study depicts the family organization and its changes as it is reflected in a woman's "process of subjectivity," or, as Hegelian language would refer to it, her life-long "struggle for recognition" (Prewo, Ritsert, & Stracke, 1973). The woman's experience of alienation and neglect, of adjustment and resistance, of assertion and of being acknowledged and accepted are interpreted as experiences in reference to patriarchal social organizational structures and their changes.

In contrast to the existential-evaluative concepts of feminist inspired research, family development analysis utilizes formal categories. By means of these categories, it characterizes the state of the family system and its changes. From psychological development theories there appear the following formal issues:

- where the locus of the development dynamic lies;
- whether the change is qualitative or quantitative, continuous or discontinuous, unidirectional or polydirectional;
- whether the regulatory principles are similar or dissimilar across stages of the life cycle (Hill & Mattessich, 1979, pp. 197–198).[11]

Characterizing family development in terms of a change in structural complexity and differentiation seems to move the analysis of family development closer to fulfilling the norm of universality for social science knowledge. The pattern of empirical change in these variables along the time axis impresses one as being intrinsic and noncontingent.

> Yet despite all the dissimilarities among cohorts there are undeniably rhythms to family life which all cohorts have shared since the earliest days of the human species. In fact, perhaps no other rhythmic social processes possess the universality of those which are associated with family formation, growth, and dissolution. (Hill & Mattessich, 1979, p. 197)

In the case of existential descriptions of family development, universality would be much more difficult to establish. It seems more than doubtful that it does exist at all. The quest for realizing subjectivity may be assumed to form a lifelong and constant motive. Yet its realization hardly follows an intrinsic and universal pattern of change over the life span of an individual family member or the family as a whole. Rather, it seems essentially contingent upon particular social arrangements and organizational structures as well as on situational interpretations of individuals (Dannefer, 1984).

This does not mean that the course of subjectivity or the organizational opportunities for subjectivity do not follow a coherent logic. The coherence of the development of subjectivity may become visible by identifying the consequences of one life phase for the next or else by identifying the linkages between them. These linkages most likely will be "limited linkages." This is a term Aldous (1978) has applied to the reduction of a family's behavioral options in one stage due to events occurring in a previous stage. The case study contains ample instances of such limited linkages between biographical phases.

Subjectivity is formed by a dialectical process. It only develops in response to social opportunities and constraints. It is the advantage of subjectivity that it can transcend social structural probabilities and proclivities. Yet that which is socially accepted and in order is constantly measured and monitored in terms of how well it agrees with intuitive expectations and standards about one's own life. The discrepancy between the social being an individual would want to be in terms of her or his intuitions and images and the socially accepted being she or he actually is makes for the struggle for recognition.

Feminist-inspired research joins in this struggle. It sides with those subjective interests, particularly those of women, that have been unduly restricted and constrained by social limitations. The attention of feminist researchers is on the family because it has been considered to be a decisive instrument limiting and narrowing women's lives.

It is important to keep in mind that the "Gestalt" that patriarchy gives to a woman's struggle for recognition and to the development of her subjectivity is not straightforward. When analyzing the concept of patriarchy, one can neither deduce a clear-cut identification of women with patriarchal values and norms nor a clear-cut opposition to them (Becker-Schmidt, 1980; Gravenhorst & Jurczyk, 1983; Ostner, 1983). Take for instance the value of motherhood. In patriarchal society, the legitimate existence of women is reduced to the role of mother.[12] Yet, however much this reduction may indeed occur, one cannot deny that for many women the label "mother" is likely to be part and parcel of their authentic identity. Thus, for women in patriarchal society, the struggle for recognition reflects a basic structural contradiction due to an intense ambivalence regarding the roles, and social possibilities of women, as the case study illustrates.

CASE STUDY: THE SOCIAL BIOGRAPHY
OF A HOUSEWIFE AND MOTHER

An account of a woman's life and the problems faced is documented on the following pages.[13] Helga Hanftl, as the woman is called for purposes of publication, participated in an investigation designed to make public parents' views and subjective perspectives on the everyday life of child-rearing. The research took place during the years 1977 to 1979 among lower-class families with young children in a large West German city (Wahl, Tuellmann, Honig, & Gravenhorst, 1980; Wahl, Honig, & Gravenhorst, 1982).

The biographical reconstructions are based on material taken from extensive conversations with the woman and the man with whom she lived. The series of eight conversations, each of which lasted between 3 and 4 hours, was carried on in the home of the family. There were both joint and individual conversations. All possible topics of parents' lives with small children were discussed. Very few parts of the talks were structured. The taped conversations were taken down in note form with frequent quotations, and in a few cases complete transcriptions were made. In the following descriptions, names, occupations, and sometimes also place names have been changed, so that the family cannot be identified. (For details on research procedures see Gravenhorst, Honig, & Wahl, 1979).

At the time of the investigation, Helga Hanftl was 27 years old. She lived with her family in a three-room apartment provided by the state, in a new suburb of Munich. In addition to Mrs. Hanftl, the members of the family included her husband (aged 30), the two children they had together—a girl of 4 and a boy of 3—as well as Mrs. Hanftl's oldest child, an 8-year-old boy. Helga Hanftl's work was in the home and with her family. She had also begun to work as a cleaning woman by the hour. Her husband, Heini Hanftl, worked for the German railways as a manual laborer. In 1978 his salary was about 1,800 German marks a month, after taxes and deductions. Helga Hanftl earned about 400 DM in addition.[14]

Childhood and Adolescence: Development Despite Constraints

The connection between the past and the present for Helga Hanftl exists subjectively as well as objectively. Childhood and adolescence live in her consciousness as "recent history." They determine the images and ideas which she uses in her present attempts to live her life satisfactorily. They are images of restriction and suffering, disappointment and humiliation, but also of hope and fulfillment. Yet the latter are counter-images of actual deficiencies and deprivations rather than direct images of "good" experiences.

Mrs. Hanftl has expressed this connection clearly. A large part of the energy which she musters to do her work in her present life comes from the negative image of the family left over from her childhood and adolescence: "If only things weren't so lousy for us so much of the time that I say I'm going to chuck it all—but you can't do that. I'm telling you. I just don't want it to be like it was before."

"Before" is a reference for Helga Hanftl to the lasting experience of having been shut out from chances and recognition in life. It was mainly her own parents who cast her off rather than encouraging and supporting her. There is nothing in her family situation to which Mrs.

Hanftl can positively relate. "Everything was wrong," she says in looking back. The father—an alcoholic—tried to earn money as a peddler in
the country. Eight of them lived together in one room.

> Helga had to do the shopping and buy on credit: "As a child I was often so
> down that I was afraid to go [into the store]." When she was 7 years old,
> she got tuberculosis of the lungs and had to stay in a sanatorium for 2
> years. During this time, each of her parents visited her once. But stronger
> than this indifference, Mrs. Hanftl still feels today the social deprivation
> caused by her mother: "As a child I had tuberculosis. She told everyone
> about it who wanted to hear. I was always shamed to death when she said
> that. I remember it even today."

It is as if her mother would transfer to her daughter the social contempt
that she herself experienced. This contempt was most acutely and
violently acted out by her own husband. The mother herself suggested
her own handing down of the contempt to which she was exposed: "She
once told me, 'I hope your husband beats you as much as mine has
beaten me.'"

The parents prevented Helga Hanftl as an adolescent from acquir-
ing her own independent life. Most of all, she could not train herself for
a job. When she finished elementary school, she had first to take care of
her brothers and sisters.

> "As a girl you are stuck with housework and children. Children and house-
> work, nothing else." She experienced this drastic restriction of her future as
> a personal fault. On her first contact with colleagues at work, she felt like a
> "real country hick . . . At home and in my village I didn't learn anything
> else."

The process of neglect and being held back from opportunities continued, and she experienced it in the way in which she was forced to
enter the job market: "One day my father comes home drunk . . . 'I
have a job for you.'" Her father had arranged a job for her as a poorly
paid worker in a restaurant. He in no way considered her possible
interests and ideas. The job was the price for one of his peddler's deals.

> Now she did not actually have an apprenticeship, but this job must have
> seemed a lot better to her than the one she had at home. She was actually
> very happy. She said to herself: "It can't be so hard that you won't be able
> to do it. . . . I wanted to get away at any cost. But, how we worked, 65
> marks a month and no days off."

Shortly after the end of her obligatory vocational schooling, she got
the opportunity for the first time to direct her life toward social recognition and being her own person. Now the legal restrictions were gone,
and a favorable accident made it possible for her to free herself from her
parents, especially her mother. She could not do it in an open
confrontation but secretly: "I secretly put an ad in the 'Sueddeutsche

Zeitung' so that I could get a job in Munich . . . My mother did something crooked and was in jail . . . I left right away."

She was 17 when she escaped to the big city, hoping for more opportunities and self-determination. For her, these were primarily attached to the kind of work available. Then and later, she prized jobs "above all, where I can work independently, where no one can watch me."

In Munich she again worked in a restaurant, but she had reason enough to feel "like God in France." She had to work only from 8:00 to 3:00 and earned 400 marks per month! She also got along well with the other girls and women who lived and worked there. But, in spite of everything, she was not able to come nearer to her goal, to train for a job and to do work that was important and recognized by society.

Helga Hanftl was just beginning to take the first steps toward an independent and positive life when something happened that made no more than survival possible for the next few years. She became pregnant, unwillingly and unknowingly. Her relationship with the father of the child must have been unsatisfactory and of a transitory nature. Mrs. Hanftl does not want to talk about it much and says only: "It was all very complicated." Her pregnancy was not confirmed until she was already 5 months pregnant.

> "I was astonished! My God! At the moment I wasn't completely aware of my situation, or at all of the problems, or of everything that lay ahead of me. I just knew that I was to have a child now. What then? I didn't know what was going to happen the next day. When I think about it today, boy! I didn't even know that there were nurseries where I could have put my child, where I could have had it every day."

She felt completely overpowered, deserted and in despair—and at the same time she fought for her child.

> "And when I had the baby then . . and I didn't know what was going on, and I was all alone, and all the other women were sitting around and having labor pains. Of course, I felt terrible there—on the one hand, I was ashamed, and, on the other hand, I wanted somebody to be there for me. And when he arrived, the little boy, my mother made it complete when she asked me if the child was dead. But otherwise—I was very happy then. . . . They always told me, that was still before the birth, 'Have it adopted and you'll be free of your worries.' I said, 'That is out of the question.' I know today that if the boy weren't there, I would move heaven and hell . . . I would never be at peace, never, if I gave a child of mine away."

There is something very strange about the way in which Mrs. Hanftl experienced this first pregnancy and this first child. Ignorance about abortion or the barriers against it cannot be what motivated her to give birth to her child. Helga Hanftl up to this time, in dealing with the problems of her life could only rely on her own personal resources and on the abilities she developed in spite of all the adverse influences. Now, her female body became the instrument of a further, even total, reduction. The pregnancy destroyed her chance to continue with her own conscious shaping of her life, when she had just begun. But her body also became a resource. It gave existence to something that not only had to be completely her own (no one besides her accepted responsibility for the child), but that also could be completely "my own flesh and blood."

Her life subjectively took a dramatic turn with her first pregnancy, and at the same time it can be interpreted objectively as the fully logical story of a girl and woman of the lower class. Her life now revolved around creating conditions under which she and her child could merely survive. To reach this goal she was at the mercy of her female place in society and her knowledge of that same society. Her initiatives to find an arrangement in which she and her child could stay together, for example, in a home for mothers and children, were without success. She felt forced to accept her mother's invitation to come to her for a few months following the birth. But a day before she had planned to leave to find new arrangements, the mother threw her and her child out. In this emergency she had quickly to find a foster placement for her son. She found such a place with great difficulty in the next city. She herself took a job in Munich.

It was in this situation of despair that she met her future husband. On her first day at her new job, a colleague tried to cheer her up and dragged her to a bar. She was actually too tired to say no to the man when he asked her to dance. But she was angry with him and only talked about her child. Yet he was quiet and listened to her and she noticed how much good this did her.

> "He . . . understood me. And so that . . . made me like him very much, and he also helped me with my problems . . . in every case when I needed him. I only knew him a short time then. He helped me with everything, and when there was something with the child, helped me and the child. . . ."

The start of her relationship with this man must have been a completely extraordinary experience for Helga Hanftl. She was cut off from the objective means by which she could arrange her life with her child so that it was really livable for both of them.

In our culture, a woman typically finds the nonobjective, nonplannable, and yet constructive features of life in erotic friendship, normally with a man. Her meeting this man now resulted in a rare coming together of experiences, which must have been good for her sense of erotic closeness. These experiences provided understanding for her as a woman with a child and, moreover, as a woman in a hopeless situation, as well as recognition through the relationship with a man. It was a solution to the problem that took the form of a personal miracle.

Marriage: The Only Resource for Mother and Child

The event that began and hastened the spiral of solutions to problems leading only to new problems, was the loss of the foster home for her son, who was then 1½ years old. In this situation, it was natural that marriage seemed to be the best of the few possible solutions available to her. She recalls the situation:

> "The foster mother gave back the child all of a sudden. We had no other foster home, we had no apartment. We were only engaged, so we wanted to get married. We had already spoken about marriage before. We needed someplace for the child now."

Marriage to her husband assumed extraordinary importance in Helga Hanftl's life. What at that time seemed the only reasonable possibility in looking back has retained its decisive importance for her. Subjectively experienced as a necessity, marriage functioned as the gateway to a materially and socially secure life. Mrs. Hanftl returns to the initial issue of feeling grown up.

> "I asked myself the question consciously when we had to sign the papers at the marriage registry office. I was 21, and the official there said to me, 'Here, sign your name, then from now on you are the only guardian for your boy.' And, at that moment I said to myself, 'Now nobody can tell me what to do, now I'm responsible for the child and everything.'"

But Mrs. Hanftl could not break out of the vicious circle of problem solutions leading to new sources of problems. Opportunities to take charge of her own life resulted again and again in existential bottlenecks.

> She got married, but for half a year they had no apartment. Then they got one, but in horrible condition and without any possibility of contact with neighbors. Now she had a legal family, but her husband, who was a great help in her earlier difficult situation, failed her now. In the family situation he could not face the demands of shared work and communication. In the first year of the marriage, he got drunk every evening. Then he had difficulties at work when others took advantage of his good nature. He was transferred for disciplinary reasons. As a result, he returned to heavy drinking. In the meantime they had a new apartment. But again "something happens at work" and her husband attempted suicide. They had their first baby together, one they had wished for, but they could afford neither the additional expenses nor to work more. Then Mrs. Hanftl became pregnant for the third time. "Bad luck" and the indifference of a doctor resulted in a catastrophe for Mrs. Hanftl. "I was at my wit's end," said Mrs. Hanftl. "I

said I'll kill myself. I did not want to have it at all. I had already inquired."

They were in constant need of money. They never would have managed if it had not been for Mrs. Hanftl's ingenuity and care in the household. In spending money, as well as in the borrowing of money, which they were forced to do, she was the responsible one. When it was at all possible, Mrs. Hanftl went out of the house to earn money. But now it was almost impossible to manage the family in a reasonable way and to give the children what they were entitled to. And out of the circle of problems which already existed before the marriage, they had to take on as an inheritance a serious developmental problem in the oldest son. This problem, as far as the Hanftls were able to explain it, came into existence as a result of neglect in one of the foster homes. Both parents say that the other two children would never have been born if they had known how much worry and work they would have to do in doing justice to the oldest. Finally, the care of and conflict with Mrs. Hanftl's divorced mother was also important. It absorbed an enormous amount of Helga Hanftl's energies.

One's Own Family: A Place of Particular Ambivalence for a Female Member of the Lower Class

In this chronicle of the events of the life of Helga Hanftl, the "lows" appear in the foreground. As events, they were more numerous and easier to tell about than the "highs." The latter did exist, however, and even if they were rarer, they could create a balance against the "lows" for her.

> "You know, there have been many highs and lows. I don't know if it's the same in every marriage, but with us there have actually been only highs and lows. There has never been a steady, good family life. . . . With us, it just wasn't there."

For Helga Hanftl the difficulties and catastrophes were not final, and, in the long run, they did not dominate her experience of family life. This is because, in spite of everything, there were also productive and happy events, the "highs." Such events had a strategic value, in giving the character of reality to her ideal of family life. It is "overdetermined," because it must "heal" so many injuries and limitations to which she was exposed as a female member of the lower class. These included the destructive influences of the family of her childhood and adolecence, her failure to train and qualify for a profession, and her exclusion from the world of gainful work. The ideal must also make tolerable the boundaries that limit her personal development in family life.

For the time being, the scope of Helga Hanftl's life is limited to her family. She uses the conventional, normative images of fulfillment. Marriage and family are the precise institutionalized places of fulfillment. Mrs. Hanftl takes their promises literally and wants them to work for her.

The utopian ideas for which she struggles are facets of an idea of "true" community that can be derived from a number of her "should" and "should not" images and norms. She appeals to the family as a community in which the members are together and care for each other.

In spite of all the low points in her family life, she has experiences that do her good and that confirm for her the rightness of her family ideals. "Happy" and "together" can be joined. A very important source of such experiences is her life with her children.

> To the question "What does your family mean to you? What is the meaning of the family?" Mrs. Hanftl answers, "That means sticking together and the pleasures and the worries, and I like that very much! Or when a child is sick, *you are all mother for him there*, and I know that I am needed. *That makes me very, very happy.* Or when they just like something that I've cooked or ice cream that I've made. You have so many joys, even when you have so many worries again. But you have so much happiness with it all." (Italics added)

Such experiences confirm for her, therefore, that her ideal of the family, in spite of everything, is valid and right, that her family context can be a good life context. This family ideal, however, is still very fragile and could easily be broken.

The reality of the Hanftl family is, as a whole, far from the utopian claims often associated with family life. Massive disappointments catch up with Helga Hanftl again and again. Her life in and with her family is the embodiment of a principle of ambivalence. Helga Hanftl's surprising strength and at the same time great vulnerability stem from the fact that she does not suppress this ambivalence. Respecting herself and her role in her family, she says,

> I have the feeling of being somebody just through being able to have my way, and my family and such. I can honestly say that I really achieve a lot. I am often proud of myself. But I could just as well pull my hair and say, . . . "Why did I do this, why did I do that?" When I was nasty to my husband, that follows me around for days . . . I saw that at home. And why am I like my mom? She did exactly the same thing with my dad. . . . You've already been through a family like that. But otherwise I'm actually content with myself.

WHAT FAMILY DEVELOPMENT AND FEMINIST PERSPECTIVES CAN CONTRIBUTE TO EACH OTHER

The exposition so far has been biased in favor of a feminist-inspired analysis, but the weak points of this approach have not been equally made the object of examination. The feminist analysis could benefit from the family development perspective, in particular from a version of the perspective that does not attach prime importance to obtaining truly nomothetic and universal knowledge.

A feminist approach is interested in the neglected particular and subjective. It also works with the basic assumption of the individual as social actor disposed to construct her or his world. These orientations raise the value of local and historical knowledge for a feminist analysis. Such knowledge makes it easier to identify specific structures of domination and struggles for recognition. An approach that defines development as the response to a chronological sequence of specific critical events challenging an existing family organization, and that focuses on what happens at each critical point of an individual or family career is better able to provide this kind of knowledge. It seems more useful than an approach that tries to focus on what is universal about these events and the sequence of their changes. Such a direction of working within the family development framework would also be consonant with recent calls for historical reorientations in family research (cf. Aldous, 1981; Elder, 1981).

Let us now look at what the family development perspective, in keeping with its own essentials, could learn from the case history with its feminist interpretation. It points up two broad issues: (1) the limits to necessary changes of family organization; and (2) the extent to which patterns of change are generated by patriarchal social structures of prevention and constraint.

Limits to Necessary Changes in Family Organization

Hill and Mattessich (1979, p. 195) characterized families as social systems that "will need to develop patterns of interaction suitable to meet the developmental demands of their members." Applying this standard of accomplishment to the case history, it becomes evident that it contains a number of instances where a family organization remains totally unresponsive to the developmental needs of at least one family member, that is, the girl and then the woman of later years. In other instances, the family organization changes only insufficiently. The case history also suggests as an important source of inadequate organizational change the existing patriarchal social structure.

Patriarchal structures are by no means the only limits to necessary change. They interact primarily with social class factors, yielding the structural dispositions of the final subject matter of experience. Yet, the structures of patriarchy give a particular form and content to the exclusion and neglect that women have to confront (cf., most recently, Becker-Schmidt, 1984; Ferree, 1984). In the case of the particular woman under discussion, her parental family was a lower-class family, yet the violent events and destructive dynamics within it cannot be explained only by the lower-class characteristic. In the final analysis, these events and dynamics were permeated by a patriarchal logic. As many destructive experiences as the husband/father may have had to endure as a member of the lower class, and as much power as the wife/mother may have exerted over her husband and her children, it was still the father more than the mother who terrorized the other family members. The gender asymmetry observed in this family is consistent with what the literature has to say on the relationship between gender, class, and marital violence (cf. Fagan, Stewart, & Hansen, 1983; Gravenhorst, 1984b; Strauss, Gelles & Steinmetz, 1980).

Structural patriarchy, which assigns women primarily to the family and therefore to financial and social dependence, must also be considered partly responsible for the impossibility of the woman's organizing a joint life with her child when she became a young single mother. Clearly, that situation was prevented by the lack of a social support system other than a husband that would exist if women's rights to an economically and socially independent life were acknowledged and taken seriously by the society at large. The impossibility of a family organization that could take sufficient account of the woman's needs for a paid occupation outside the home continues into her married life. The hierarchical division of labor between the two genders must be seen as the prime reason for the fact that a combination of parental and occupational roles was next to impossible for the women to achieve, at least as long as her children were young.

Finally, it should be noticed that the woman had come to internalize part of a patriarchal value system. Clinging to this value system may well have presented a hindrance to a change in family organization toward greater equality that would have been more responsive to the developmental needs of her husband. The husband could not become the "good patriarch" his wife wanted him to be but instead had a social and mental breakdown.

Patterns of Change and Structural Constraints

Family development scholars have stressed the fact that family changes follow a social chronology. The chronology is a specific social time sequence embedded in a broader one that encompasses larger social systems. The case study demonstrates that social chronologies, to a considerable degree, are generated by social structures inimical to women. It suggests that family scholars should not only look at events and expectations that directly constrain and reduce women. It also suggests they should look at the extent to which sequential patterns of family change are generated by patriarchal structures in the family's life context.

The fact that the woman became a mother when she still was almost a girl must be seen in relation to living in a patriarchal culture. She did not have at her disposal sufficient knowledge and interactive strategies to handle the reproductive capabilities of her body when she became involved in a sexual relationship. She was totally overwhelmed when she learned late in her first pregnancy that she was indeed pregnant. Afterwards, she may have seized the opportunity of becoming a mother because she had no other alternative way of asserting an independent and recognized identity. The situation of her first sexual relationship and pregnancy is consistent with what the literature has to say about the heterosexual contacts of girls, at least in Western European countries.

For girls, and this also holds for lower-class girls, there exists a seemingly contradictory, complex set of social conditions which eventually lead to a high probability of girls getting pregnant against their will and plans. The structure of the early heterosexual interactions still is such that girls are expected to be the passive and waiting ones; usually, they are younger and therefore have less knowledge than their male counterparts. Yet, responsibility for pregnancies and contraception is generally assigned to them and not to their male partners (cf. Pagenstecher, 1985).

Later in her life, the woman entered marriage not only because she loved a man, but also because marriage was the only social institution of survival possible for her and her child. The love for her husband arose in a lower-class situation of female despair essentially shaped by a patriarchal context that does not generate equivalent negative experiences for lower-class biological fathers. Her future husband, who was not the father of her child, was the only one to listen to all her worries and troubles. He alone accepted her with her child when her own mother had thrown her out before she could find a foster place for the child.

Moreover, the timing and advent of her second child, the first in the marriage, can best be explained by a patriarchal life context. The beginning years of marriage were full of problems. The woman chose to solve the problems by having a child with her husband. She very quickly reduced the number of solutions that theoretically would have been possible alternatives to this "child solution." She thus followed the normative familial and patriarchal imperative for solving the problems she had with the marriage. All in all, the impact of the patriarchal gender division and hierarchy of labor or the establishment of a heterosexual relationship and the advent and timing of children that permeates lower-class conditions is readily visible.

The pattern of change in the woman's "family of procreation" reflects the energies and boundaries of her life interests. Thus, they also reflect the linkages that give coherence to the sum of her life phases.

And these linkages cannot only be understood as "limited linkages." More specifically, they must be thought of as a series of constraints set by patriarchal society in which the woman continuously makes a virtue of necessity. Her "career" is doubly burdened by her being a member of both the lower-class and the female gender. She proceeds from the neglected, uninformed, and untrained girl to the young unskilled worker and single mother. Her next step is to married woman and caretaker of her child, and further to the mother of still more children and to the cleaning woman paid by the hour.

And yet, as much as this female life is constrained and narrowed by patriarchal and lower-class conditions, it is not without promising possibilities and gratifying fulfillments. All in all, it can best be described as a result of an intensely dialectical process, a continuing and partly successful struggle *against* hindrances and preventions and *for* realizing the promises attributed to living with and for a family. It shapes the woman's subjective experience of her life as one of encompassing ambivalence (Gravenhorst, 1984a; cf. also Becker-Schmidt, 1980, 1984; Becker-Schmidt, Brandes-Erlhoff, Rumpf, & Schmidt, 1983; Ferree, 1984).

CONCLUSION

The meeting and separating of two approaches to studying families has been interpreted as an indication of historical changes of interest in knowing about the family. An attempt has been made to make visible the principles that govern the two approaches. Family development theory as espoused by Reuben Hill responds to an interest in understanding family life as well as to a demand for universal and unbiased knowledge of the family. The feminist-interpreted case history documents a particular form of the existence of an individual woman. Her life context with the family at its center is characterized as reflecting systematic neglect and subsequently an intense struggle for recognition. It is suggested that the patriarchal form of social organization, with its gender-specific and hierarchical division of labor that shapes both the lower class and female limitation, lies at the bottom of this neglect.

Applying a feminist perspective to social and family analysis could have at least two consequences. First, attention to the feminist perspective could promote fulfilling the norm of universality for social science knowledge. By attempting not to neglect or distort the social existence of women, social science in general and family social science in particular come closer to a "true" picture and a "truly universal" knowledge of society and of the family therein.

Second, going beyond the norm of the universality of knowledge, the feminist approach to family analysis reintroduces the basic issues of how to conceptualize the subject matter of family science and family theory. The development of a feminist social science suggests that the issues of subjectivity and of subjective interests, and of their adequate formation and organization, if excluded from the established body of scientific knowledge, will reappear and make their claims apparent. The emergence of what may be called a feminist sociology of subjectivity may encourage family development scholars again to reflect on the potential scientific significance of those of their assumptions, premises, and norms that implicitly or explicitly refer to values and interests.

Family development theory as shaped by Hill implies the necessity of relying on the realm of subjectivity. The subjectivity of the social system members who are focused on in research (as well as the subjectivity of the researchers) is bound to be one of the important sources of providing standards of adequacy of family functioning. Determining the adequacy of family functioning, in turn, has been defined as a "service function" and as such as one of the major purposes of family development theorizing (Hill & Mattessich, 1979, p. 162; Hill & Rodgers, 1964, p. 209). It remains a central issue whether this service function of the theory can be accomplished if the related standards of adequacy do not refer to the social context of subjectivity.

Some thoughts of Christa Wolf, the great contemporary German philosophical poet, may be apt to bring this essay to a close. Wolf points to a dilemma that poets and scientists alike have to confront and that may well describe a dilemma of sociologists pursuing family-relevant social analyses. But she also suggests that those days poets, those experts of subjectivity, may be closer to resolving the dilemma than scientists, and that scientists may well profit from a poetic mode.

> Quite clearly one senses the resistance within oneself, but at the same time the pressure to push forward into that still unresearched area. There the structure of the moral world of socially living individuals is at issue—a feeling perhaps similar to the cautious groping of nuclear scientists when they dare to develop provisional, figurative ideas about the processes in the inside of the atom. It is not without reason that we are fascinated by their adventure. From the outside, it appears in the form of extremely exact, subtle and most likely, by their constant repetition, monotonous measurements. Thus, they are, from all one can hear, at the point where the old language of classical physics does express nothing pertinent, and where "one [has], for the description of the smallest parts of matter, alternately to use different, figurative pictures contradicting one another." Heisenberg calls them "word paintings." He assigns them the task "of evoking in the mind of the listener, by image and parable, certain relations pointing towards the intended direction without wanting to force upon him, by definite formulations, the precise development of a certain train of thought . . . as [do] the poets." (Wolf, 1980, pp. 34–35)

NOTES

1. Reuben Hill has referred somewhat ambivalently to this difference. In previewing the developments of family research in the 1980s, he comments: "Countering these pressures for continuity in emphasis and direction are the negative evaluations of critics of contemporary family research who characterize it as *sexist*, adult-centered, ahistorical, and limited by the conventions of the white middle class. These critics will press, although *not too successfully, I suspect*, for new emphases and directions in the 1980s" (Hill, 1981b, p. 265, italics added).

2. As a quantified indication of the existence of two essentially separate "guilds" of social science—to take up a fitting term used by Hill in a similar context (Hill, 1981b)—compare the cross-referencing of the two leading journals of the respective academic communities, the *Journal of Marriage and the Family (JMF)* on the one hand, and *Signs: Journal of Women in Culture and Society* on the other. During 1977, *Signs*, published since 1975, was not among the journals referenced in *JMF* more than ten times. Conversely, even though *JMF* was cited in *Signs* more than ten times, in *JMF* there were 14 other journals with higher citation frequencies than *Signs* (Bayer, 1982, p. 535). At the same time, it has been noted that the topic of "sex roles," a possible abstract expression of the common subject matter of the two social science guilds, was the most frequently appearing topic in the family research literature during the 1970s (Bayer, 1982, p. 536).

3. If headings and subject indexes tell anything about the conceptual mappings and priorities of a community of scientists and their discourse, then they also tell about the overall nonfeminist orientation of the established discipline of family studies. In general, the explicit term "patriarchy" is not often used in the titles of articles in the leading journals of the two communities, neither in *JMF* nor in *Signs*. In *JMF*, it was not used once in the volumes published from 1975 to 1982. During the same period, it appeared in *Signs* five times. Yet the substantive topic of patriarchy as a social organization of power disproportionately benefiting men is significantly more often referred to in *Signs* than in *JMF* titles. Counting all explicit references to women's inferior and men's superior social position including such concepts as "rape" or "feminism," patriarchy as a substantively organizing concept appears 135 times in the *Signs* titles and 34 times in the *JMF* titles.

4. The assumption that patriarchy is threatening appears when one looks at the language used when reference is made to so-called family violence and to the gender of the persons involved. As if breaking a conceptual and moral taboo, the discourse of family research does not treat men as dominant and violent. Certainly, family researchers in the course of their work have to take note of the men involved. However, battering, abusing, or raping men do not provide the organizing perspective when researchers analyze events in which men play the greater or the exclusive immoral part. It is almost as if battering males have to be covered up by using such concepts as "family violence," "violence against women" or the balance-preserving "husband–wife violence." To get an impression of the camouflaged language masking the specific male dominant and des-

tructive part in marriage and family violence, one only has to scan titles of articles, subject indexes or abstracts of relevant publications.

5. Deviating from terminology used previously, Hill has referred to his most recent efforts at understanding family development using the term "theory." Since the present work relies on these explications, I will often use the term "theory" and do so interchangeably with "framework" and "perspective" when referring to Hill's thinking about family development.

6. The use of this article is complemented by Hill's earlier formulations of the theory (eg, Hill & Rodgers, 1964), his application of modern systems theory for family analysis (Hill, 1971) and other examinations of the family development approach (Hill, 1981a). For the purpose of the present comparison, works on family development by other authors—notably Aldous' (1978) most comprehensive presentation—have been omitted.

7. The concept "female life context" has been developed by Prokop (1976) in a book that became one of the foundations of a feminist social science in West Germany.

8. With regard to the central role of subjectivity, it should be pointed out that feminist research is one of a number of strands of critical research in support of underprivileged groups in society and in social theories. An analysis of the structures and politics of subjectivity-oriented research is contained in Wahl *et al.* (1982).

9. For an ironic treatment of the gender bias in granting scientific dignity to the contrasting methods in the established social science community, see Benard and Schlaffer (1981).

10. Since it is fulfillment *and* alienation that feminist research addresses, it does not coincide with a conflict perspective on the family as described by Aldous (1978, p. 13). Even though, as pointed out there, the "darker side" of (female) life constitutes the roots of a feminist social science, it is not restricted to it.

11. The reader is asked when examining the social biography of the woman to pay attention to the different meanings the woman attaches to her three pregnancies and births as well as to the different interpretations she gives to one and the same pregnancy in different communication contexts.

12. "The capability of delivering children is a female biological potency—that much is evident. Up to our time women, for their life perspectives, almost totally were reduced to this capacity and to the social relationships with their children and the children's procreator. In our world in which individuals are in need to go far beyond their hereditary predispositions, *reduction* to biology always is a repressive postulate. There are massive interests behind the thesis of motherhood as the female purpose in life in removing women from the male domains of professional and public spheres. This may be illustrated by the fact that up to now nobody has demanded that men concentrate their aims in life on their procreative power and give second priority to everything else" (Sichtermann, 1983, translation, italics in the original; cf. also Gravenhorst, 1983).

13. The case study was originally written as part of an analysis prepared for the Sixth Youth Report to the Government of the Federal Republic of Germany

(Gravenhorst, 1984a). It was translated into English by Eleanor Dormack, whose language competencies I could trust more than my own. The case study has been abbreviated for purposes of the present paper. With regard to the value of case studies in subjectivity-oriented research, compare the section in Wahl *et al.*, 1982, pp. 204–210: "Was erzaehlt ein Fall und wieviel zaehlt er? Zu Fragen von Reichweite und Verallgemeinerbarkeit."

14. Given an exchange rate of 2:1 in 1978, this income amounted to $10,000 per year for the husband and $2,400 for the wife, after taxes and deductions.

REFERENCES

Aldous, J. (1978). *Family careers; Developmental change in families.* New York: Wiley.
Aldous, J. (1981). Second guessing the experts: Thoughts on family agendas for the eighties. *Journal of Marriage and the Family, 43*(2), 267–270.
Bayer, A. E. (1982). A bibliometric analysis of marriage and family literature. *Journal of Marriage and the Family, 44, 3*, 527–538.
Becker-Schmidt, R. (1980). Widerspruechliche Realitat und Ambivalenz: Arbeitserfahrungen von Frauen in Fabrik und Familie. *Koelner Zeitschrift fuer Soziologie und Sozialpsychologie, 32*(4), 705–725.
Becker-Schmidt, R. (1984, August). *Women between factory and family: Work at home and participation in the labor force.* Paper presented at the 79th Annual Meeting of the American Sociological Association, San Antonio, TX.
Becker-Schmidt, R., Brandes-Erlhoff, U., Rumpf, M., & Schmidt, B. (1983). *Arbeitsleben–Lebensarbeit: Konflikte und Erfahrunngen von Fabrikarbeiterinnen.* Bonn, West Germany: Neue Gesellschaft.
Benard, C., & Schlaffer, E. (1981). Maennerdiskurs und Frauentratsch. *Soziale Welt, 32*(1), 119–136.
Dannefer, D. (1984). Adult development and social theory: A paradigmatic reappraisal. *American Sociological Review, 49*(1), 100–116.
Elder, G. H., Jr. (1981). History and the family: The discovery of complexity. Journal of Marriage and the Family, 43(3), 489–519.
Fagan, J. A., Stewart, D. K., & Hansen, K. V. (1983). Violent men or violent husbands? Background factors and situational correlates. In D. Finkelhor, R. J. Gelles, G. T. Hotaling, & M. S. Straus (Eds.), *The dark side of families* (pp. 49–58). Beverly Hills, CA: Sage.
Ferree, M. M. (1984, August). *German feminist approaches to working class women and work.* Paper presented at the 79th Annual Meeting of the American Sociological Association, San Antonio, TX.
Gravenhorst, L. (1983). Konservative Tendenzen in der Frauenbewegung. In W. Schaefer (Ed.), *Neue soziale Bewegungen: Konservativer Aufbruch im bunten Gewand?* (pp. 80–86). Frankfurt, West Germany: Fischer.
Gravenhorst, L. (1984a). Die ambivalente Bedeutung von "Familie" in den Biographien von Maedchen und Muettern. In L. Gravenhorst, M. Schablow, & B. Cramon-Daiberl: *Lebensort: Familie* (Vol. 2 of the series *Alltag und Biografie von Maedchen*, Sachverstaendigenkommission Sechster Jugendbericht, ed., pp. 9–48). Opladen, West Germany: Leske and Budrich.
Gravenhorst, L. (1984b). *Empirische Ergebnisse zum Zusammenhang von Erwerbslosigkeit, sozio-oekonomischem Status und familialer Gewalt* (unpublished manuscript). Munich, West Germany: Deutsches Jugendinstitut.
Gravenhorst, L., Honig, M. S., & Wahl, K. (1979). Forschungsmethod des Projekts "Erziehungsalltag in der Unterschict." In *Beitraege zur Familienforschung:*

Arbeiten aus dem Forschungsprojekt *"Erziehungsalltag in der Unterschicht"*: Problemsicht und Problemverarbeitung von Unterschichtseltern mit kleinen Kindern (Chapter VII). Munich, West Germany: Deutsches Jugendinstitut.

Gravenhorst, L., & Jurczyk, K. (1983). Familie. In J. Beyer, F. Lamott, & B. Meyer (Eds.), *Frauenhandlexikon*. Munich, West Germany: Beck.

Habermas, J. (1968). *Erkenntnis and Interesse*. Frankfurt, West Germany: Suhrkamp.

Hill, R. (1971). Modern systems theory and the family: A confrontation. *Social Science Information, 10*(5), 7–26.

Hill, R. (1981a). Theories and research designs linking family behavior and child development: A critical overview. *Journal of Comparative Family Studies, 12*(1), 1–19.

Hill, R. (1981b). Wither family research in the 1980s: Continuities, emergents, constraints, and new horizons. *Journal of Marriage and the Family, 43*(2), 255–257.

Hill, R., & Mattessich, P. (1979). Family development theory and life-span development. In P. Baltes & O. Brim, Jr. (Eds.), *Life-span development and behavior* (Vol. 2, pp. 161–204). New York: Academic Press.

Hill, R., & Rodgers, R. H. (1964). The developmental approach. In H. T. Christensen (Ed.), *Handbook of marriage and the family* (pp. 171–214). Chicago: Rand McNally.

McRobbie, A. (1982). The politics of feminist research: Between talk, text and action. *Feminist Review, 12*, 46–58.

Ostner, I. (1983). Kapitalismus, Partiarchat und die Konstruktion der Besonderheit "Frau." *Soziale Welt* [Special Volume], *2*, 277–297.

Pagenstecher, L. (1985). Sexualitaet—Versuche and Tabus. In Deutsches Jugendinstitut (Ed.), *Immer diese Jugend! Ein zeitgeschichtliches Mosaik: 1945 bis heute*. Munich, West Germany: Koesel.

Prewo, R., Ritsert, J., & Stracke, E. (1973). *Systemtheoretische Ansaetze in der Soziologie: Eine kirtische Analyse*. Reinbek, West Germany: Rowohlt.

Prokop, U. (1976). *Weiblicher Lebenszusammenhang: Von der Beschraenktheit der Strategien und der Unangemessenheit der Wuensche*. Frankfurt, West Germany: Suhrkamp.

Sichtermann, B. (1983). Mutterschaft. In J. Beyer, F. Lamott, & B. Meyer (Eds.), *Frauenhandlexikon: Stichworte zur Selbstbestimmung*. Munich: Beck.

Straus, M., Gelles, R., & Steinmetz, S. (1980). *Behind closed doors: Violence in the American family*. Garden City, NY: Anchor/Doubleday.

Wahl, K., Honig, M., & Gravenhorst, L. (1982). *Wissenschaftlichkeit und Interessen: Zur Herstellung subjektivitaetsorientierter Sozialforschung*. Frankfurt, West Germany: Suhrkamp.

Wahl, K., Tuellmann, G., Honig, M. S., & Gravenhorst, L. (1980). *Familien sind anders: Wie sie sich selbst sehen: Anstoesse fuer eine neue Familienpolitik*. Reinbek, West Germany: Rowohlt.

Wolf, C. (1980). Lesen and Schreiben. *Sammlung Luchterhand 295*. Darmstadt/Neuwied, West Germany: Luchterhand.

Zentraleinrichtung zur Foerderung von Frauenstudien und Frauenforschung an der Freien Universitaet Berlin (Ed.) (1984). Methoden in der Frauenforschung. *Symposium an der Freien Universitaet Berlin vom 30.11–2.12 1983*. Frankfurt, West Germany: R. G. Fischer.

5

Problem Solving in Families: A Revisionist View

IRVING TALLMAN
Washington State University

INTRODUCTION

Reuben Hill's ability to chart new regions of investigation and to inspire others to pursue and amplify his ground-breaking efforts may be among his greatest contributions to the scientific study of the family. His pioneering work on family crisis and stress, developmental theory, family planning, systems analysis, and three generational cross-sectional analysis are cases in point. The one area where his scholarly activity has failed to produce this generative effect is the study of family problem solving (Klein, 1983; Klein & Hill, 1979). In many ways this is surprising. Problems are clearly a salient aspect of family life. Few doubt that families face a broad array of problems or that problem solving is a relevant indicator of family functioning. As Klein and Hill (1979, p. 493) indicate, "Virtually anything can become problematic in families." In fact, they claim "it seems appropriate to view family problem solving as a broad perspective from which to analyze many facets of family life" (p. 493). Clearly the subject matter offers the potential for confronting virtually every type of family situation from dating to widowhood. Why then has this particular area of investigation failed to capture the imagination of most family scholars?

I suggest two possible reasons for this failure. The first pertains to the definitional ambiguities associated with the key concepts of "problems" and "problem solving," the second, to the lack of a clearly developed and parsimonious theory. The two issues are related. The failure to differentiate "problems" from similar concepts such as "trouble," "dilemma," "stress," and "crisis" and to distinguish problem solving from such behavioral processes as coping and goal attainment contributes significantly to the difficulties of building an adequate theory. The prevailing tendency to try to build such a theory by drawing principles directly from experience and/or empirical research with families has led

I wish to express my appreciation to my colleagues Sandra Ball-Rokeach, Viktor Gecas, Louis Gray, Marilyn Ihinger-Tallman, Milton Rokeach, and the editors of this volume for their suggestions and criticisms of an earlier draft of this chapter.

to a plethora of propositions but no systematic explanation. This is due, in large part, to the phenomenon itself. Its very ubiquity makes classification unwieldy. If virtually everything in families can be seen as problematic, than it becomes difficult to specify those special characteristics or events that constitute a family problem or the processes through which it is resolved. What seems necessary is that we adapt greater precision in our definitions while, at the same time, removing the constraints of tying our concepts directly to empirical referents and to the temporal and spatial limitations those referents place on our generalizations.

This chapter presents key assumptions and propositions from a deductive general theory of problem solving behavior and explores some of the implications of this theory for problem solving in families. In the process, the concepts of problem and problem solving will be defined and differentiated from related concepts. The theory presented here is abstracted from a larger work being prepared by my colleague, Louis Gray, and myself. Because of space limitations, it is not possible to develop fully the foundations for the various definitions, assumptions, and propositions that make up the theory. Nor can I provide the formal proofs demonstrating the theory's internal logic, although such proofs are available to the interested reader. The theory seeks to establish general principles that we want to apply to the family. It is conceivable that these principles may also be relevant to groups other than the family. Although this is not the purpose of the paper, it does not distract from it. My purpose is to contribute to an understanding of problem solving in families, not to explain or understand what is unique only to families. The latter focus seems less important than the former from either a scientific or a practical perspective.

Theories cannot be eclectic. They are closed logical systems that are either true or false, useful or not useful. Consequently, this presentation is of necessity somewhat polemical. This holds for the definitions as well. They are not proposed with the intention of being included within a lexicon of possible definitions or merely to represent a particular viewpoint. Rather, they are offered as the basis for establishing essential meanings and operations and eliminating extraneous meanings. At the very least, I hope the definitions presented in this paper can stimulate debate dedicated to rearching some consensus as to the essential components in the definition of problems and problem solving. A shared set of definitions is not only important for facilitating communications among researchers in the field, it is a necessary condition for building a cumulative body of knowledge (Cohen, 1980, pp. 134–36; Freese, 1980, p. 19).

I assume that building a cumulative body of knowledge is the goal of all science. It is with this goal in mind that the theory presented here was developed. In fact, its principles can be traced through a gradual progression of theoretical development from classical conditioning, to operant conditioning, to Bandura's (1977) social learning theory, to some formulations of social exchange theory (Emerson, 1972, 1976; Homans, 1961, 1974). Its basic postulates have probably received more consistent empirical validation than any other body of theory used by social scientists. The theory relevant to this paper is an extension of these principles to account for decision making processes, group formation and group problem solving, with special reference to the family.

SCOPE CONDITIONS FOR THE THEORY

The focus of the theory will be on explaining generic aspects of human problem-solving behavior. The essential operations involved in solving problems are considered to be the same, whether the problem-solving unit is an individual, group, or institution. The principles to be employed in the theory to be presented here are essentially social-psychological. That is, they pertain to how individuals or groups interact with one another for the purpose of solving problems. Biological, physical, ecological, political, cultural, and social-structural conditions are relevant in this theory only to the extent that they contribute to the type of problem that is created, or they influence the individual's or group's abilities to solve the problem.

Drawing on basic assumptions of human motivation and interaction, the theory seeks to identify the essential perceptual, cognitive, and behavioral components involved in engaging in problem-solving behavior. Thus, its focus is limited to a particular type of means–ends behavior. It is not concerned with all types of goal attainment or outcome-oriented behaviors, nor does it seek to account for the processes through which actors adjust to difficult or troublesome situations and conditions. Rather, its emphasis is on designated types of decision making and information search that guide actions intended to change an existing situation in a desired direction.

The aspect of change most relevant in this theory, pertains only to changing the situation confronting the actor and need not imply fundamental or permanent changes in the elements of the situation. For example, an individual faced with a tree in his or her path may find a way around the tree, thereby changing the situation for the individual without altering its essential structure; the tree is still in the path. Similarly a family living in an economically depressed area may have a member who finds employment; this accomplishment, however, will not alter the basic economic situation in the area. On the other hand, under certain conditions, the individual may find it necessary to remove the tree from the path, or the family member may need to participate in efforts to change the basic social and economic conditions producing unemployment in the area. The point is, although a theory of problem solving may have implications for understanding such phenomena as goal-oriented behavior, processes for adjusting to misfortune, or even social change, these are not the criteria upon which the theory should be judged. The theory's scope is limited to the question of how actors, be they individuals, groups, families, or family subgroups, interpret and seek to solve the problems with which they are confronted.

There is another question that, although it is outside of the scope of the theory, must be addressed. Assuming for the moment that the general theory to be developed applies to all human problem-solving units, however organized, the question for those of us interested in the family is under what conditions will the family function as a single problem solving unit. The question implies several related questions pertaining to the changing problem-solving orientations of individual family members and the problem-solving consequences produced by internal family conflicts. Although space will limit a full discussion of these issues, the final section of this chapter will propose a set of antecedent conditions, derivable from the same principles upon which the theory is developed, that establish when families function as problem-solving units.

The key to developing the theory and all that follows is the definitions of our central concepts. We begin by attempting to answer the most fundamental questions posed in this paper: What are problems, and how do actors go about solving them?

DEFINING PROBLEMS, PROBLEM SOLVING, AND DECISIONS

The Problem

Despite innumerable treatises on problem solving in the fields of science, education, psychology, sociology, politics, and philosophy, the concept designated by the term *problem*, in its generic sense, is rarely defined. Most writers who deal with this issue pay some homage to Dewey's (1910) classic work, *How We Think*, but Dewey did not systematically set about to define problems, referring to them rather vaguely as "felt difficulties." His interest lay primarily in identifying the thinking processes involved in problem solving (Agre, 1982). This emphasis on problem solving without considering the nature of the term problem seems to have set the course for subsequent writers and scholars. The problems to be solved seem to be anything the investigator designates. This is clearly not a situation conducive to building a general theory.

In the past decade, however, there have been a few attempts to provide a general, abstract, and real (in the sense of empirically based) definition. It is surprising, and somewhat reassuring, to note that these attempts have produced a considerable amount of consensus. There seems to be general agreement that a problem represents an impediment to the attainment of some desired goal, and that some uncertainty exists as to whether the impediment can be overcome. (Agree, 1982; Bourne, Ekstrand, & Dominowski, 1971, p. 9; Hattiangadi, 1978; Klein & Hill, 1979, p. 495; Newell & Simon, 1972, p. 72; Tallman *et al.*, 1974, p. 4). The essence of a problem, then, is the notion of an impediment (barrier or obstacle) that potentially can be circumvented, eliminated, hurdled, or overcome to achieve a goal. An impediment is any psychological, interpersonal, social, economic, environmental, or physical condition that interferes with an actor's opportunity to attain a desired goal. Overcoming the obstacle may facilitate the actor's goal attainment efforts as, for example, in passing an examination, or it may involve eliminating some troublesome or noxious condition such as an illness that, once eliminated, restores a prior state of affairs enabling the actor to go about his or her business.

Implicit in the above conceptualization is the idea that a problem represents an undesirable state of affairs. As Agre (1982) points out, a problem cannot be a desirable state since any problem, including mathematical or theoretical problems, calls for some condition to be changed or eliminated. Thus, although it may be satisfying to solve a mathematical problem, as long as the problem exists it must be considered as an undesirable state. The desirable state occurs if and only if the problem is solved. Similarly, the fact that a problem may be viewed as a challenge and, therefore, attractive to some actors, does not mitigate its undesirable characteristics. The attraction lies primarily in the potential of mastering, setting right, or overcoming an undesirable condition.

If an impediment or barrier is to be overcome, some kind of activity is required. Such activity can be either mental or motor, depending upon the desired outcome. For some actors or in some situations, knowledge or understanding is all that is required, whereas in other situations the desired change requires some form of physical or verbal action. Suppose a father has suddenly changed his manner, becoming moody and thereby upsetting the family equilibrium so that other family members become strained and tense with one another. Under such conditions the family might seek to return to its earlier state of affairs. In some families this can be brought about by gaining an understanding of the father's mood. Knowledge that the father "has had a hard day" may be enough to restore normal relationships. In another family, such restoration may require taking some action to change the father's mood such as showing him affection, joking with him, or getting him to talk about his problems

In summary, the definition of a problem is as follows:

Definition 1: A problem is an intrusion in an actor's state of affairs that has the following characteristics:
    a.   It impedes, blocks, or interferes with the actor's efforts to attain a particular goal.
    b.   It creates an undesirable situation for the actor that is alterable if and only if the actor engages in mental and/or motor activities that will eliminate, bypass, or overcome the impediments, obstacles, or barriers that are interfering with goal attainment efforts.
    c.   There is some degree of uncertainty that the activities listed in the second statement can be successfully completed.

Thus, a problem is a situation that calls for analysis and action to produce a specific desirable change; in other words, a solution is possible. The components of required activity and solution distinguish "problems" from such related concepts as "dilemma," "trouble," and "crisis"— concepts that do not necessarily imply either actions or solutions.

Statement 1b in the above definition stipulates that a problem is an undesirable situation and that it is conceivable that something can be done to change the situation. The statement, however, does not indicate that these conditions need necessarily be perceived by the actor for the problems to exist. The ommission is deliberate and is contrary to much of the family problem-solving research. Much of this research has proceeded on the assumption that if an actor does not perceive a situation as a problem, it is not a problem, at least for that actor. Without becoming overly involved in the philosophical question pertaining to the nature of reality, I suggest that this assumption is unnecessary and, in fact, muddles the picture for the investigator. A member of the family may be suffering from cancer without any of the family members being aware of the problem. Agre (1982) concludes that a problem may be experienced without the actors being able to define it, locate it, or formulate it. At times the awareness that a problem exists may slowly dawn on the actors involved. Moreover, as Hattiangadi (1978) points out, "even when we are aware of it, we may mistake its nature, and the problem would not be the problem-as-we-see-it but rather as it is" (p. 347). Nevertheless, the problem as defined above is empirically identifiable and therefore perceptually identifiable if the perceiver knows where to look. In other words, a problem can be said to exist as long as it is identifiable and, once recognized, it is possible to get some agreement concerning its existence. Such recognition may come at any time during a problem's existence, or it may come even after the problem has ceased to exist. It is, as we shall see in our discussion of problem solving, even possible for actors to engage in solving problems without consciously labeling their activity as such.

Statement 1c in the above definition implies that all problem solving involves some risk of failure. The statement also suggests that the level of risk (or the probability of success) is one indicator of a problem's degree of difficulty. Other indicators are the effort required to solve the problem, the complexity of the problem, and the degree of coordinated effort it takes to reach a solution.

Although the problem is defined as an "intrusion" in an actor's state of affairs, this does not imply that all problems are generated outside of the individual or group. Clearly, many problems are exogenous, such as, for example, those created by unemployment or a life-threatening disease. But many others, such as tensions between family members or parent–child conflicts, are generated within the group itself. Still others may be generated by an individual actor, as when a family member becomes unhappy with his or her job or falls into unrequited love. The term "intrusion" is deemed appropriate in the definition because in each of these examples an ongoing state of affairs is altered in a way that interferes with an individual's or group's goal-seeking activities.

Problem Solving and the Problem-Solving Process

Our definition of problems implies our definition, and indeed much of our theory, of problem solving. Problems are situations that require action to produce change. More specifically, the actions taken must deal with a nonroutine situation in which there is some level of uncertainty as to the outcome. Thus, we can infer that problem solving requires nonroutine activities that are undertaken at some risk. It also follows that the more difficult the problem, the greater the risk.

The combination of risky and nonroutine action necessarily produces a change in a normal state of affairs. Such changes can often foster instability in situations and relationships (Hansen & Hill, 1964; Smelser & Smelser, 1981, p. 638). Thus, it is possible that efforts to solve problems may produce additional problems. Consider a family in which the mother has a serious illness requiring bed rest. The family, if it wants the mother to return to health, must remove her from her various roles and find ways to fill in the gaps she previously filled. This may require that the various family members play unfamiliar roles. If the mother is employed, the family may also be forced to accept a lower income for some period of time. Loss of income, as well as uncertain or incompetent role performances are likely to affect adversely the family's day-to-day operations, thereby contributing to confusion and increasing the level of tension. Thus, by attempting to bring an end to the mother's illness, family disequilibrium and tension is increased. Similar role shifts and strains may occur if the family seeks to compensate for a member's unemployment, assist a family member when he or she is facing a difficult examination, increase its collective income, face the need for relocation, and so forth. In sum, the process of problem solving creates, at least in the short run, conditions of instabillty. We have an apparent paradox; an attempt to eliminate disequilibrium results in the creation of disequilibrium. In essense, solving the problem creates the same kind of problem.

The resolution of his paradox lies mainly in unraveling the meanings attached to the verb, *solve*. The term can be used to refer to an activity that is successfully completed. "To solve the problem" is to have found a solution. Another use of the term refers to a type of ongoing activity that is not necessarily completed. To be "problem solving" can mean to be engaged in the activity or process of seeking a solution, regardless of whether the solution is ever obtained or discovered. For some scholars no confusion exists; only the first explanation is acceptable. For example, Agre (1983) maintains, "An hour's worth of solving is entitled to the title of 'solving' if and only if the job has been completed and if and only if a solution has been generated" (p. 94). If we were to adopt these criteria, we could only determine if an actor was engaged in problem solving after the action had been completed.

To accept such a limiting definition would, in my view, not only eliminate important areas of investigation, it would also diverge from the main stream of available research. But the difficulty remains. How can we reconcile these two divergent meanings? It seems to me reasonable to accept them both as referring to different behavioral phenomena. In this paper I shall adapt the convention of using the phrase "problem solving" to refer to the completed act of reaching a solution and I will append to that phrase words such as "action," "behavior," or "process" when referring to the activities involved in seeking solutions. However, it is the *process* of problem solving that seems most relevant to students of the family, and it is this process that will receive major attention in this paper. We can now state our definition of problem solving:

Definition 2: Problem solving occurs when some barrier, obstacle, or impediment to attaining a goal is removed, ended, or overcome.

As we have seen, the essential component of a problem is in the barrier that lies between the actor and his, her, or their attempts to attain a goal. Thus, the outcome of successful problem solving is a change in the problem situation that enables the actor to proceed on his or her route toward a given goal. It follows that problem solving cannot be viewed as synonymous with goal attainment. Consider the goals involved in career planning. A couple may be oriented toward achieving status and income by having the wife earn a degree in electronic engineering. They may surmount all of the educational, financial, and sexual discrimination barriers involved in earning the degree only to find that the market has fallen out of the electronics industry and there are no jobs available. In this example we have no basis for inferring that the family depicted was anything but a successful problem solver despite the fact that its goal was not obtained.

Conversely, successful goal attainment need not imply successful problem solving. The scion of a wealthy and famous family whose goal is to be wealthy and famous may achieve that simply as a matter of birth without overcoming any serious obstacles to that end. In a similar sense, the adjustment of family members to a tired or moody father may be automatic and routine. Family members may know that when the father gets into this mood he will soon recover his good humor if they are quiet and do not disturb him. A situation that at one time may have required problem solving behavior now requires a routine adjustment.

The distinction between problem solving and goal attainment requires emphasis here primarily because it is frequently obfuscated in the family problem-solving literature. Almost universally, problem solving is measured in terms of goal attainment. I include in this criticism much of my own work (e.g., Tallman & Miller, 1974; Tallman, Marotz-Baden, & Pindas, 1983), as well as the work of others (Klein & Hill, 1979; Oliveri & Reiss, 1981; Straus, 1968). Klein and Hill (1979) make this orientation explicit: "The purposive character of problem solving, its goal-seeking orientation, suggests that outcomes or products of family interaction can be evaluated not only by family members but by outsiders as well. How well goals are achieved and problems solved then becomes the focus of attention" (p. 499). Family problem-solving effectiveness is thus designated as the appropriate dependent variable. It is defined a *"the degree to which family problems are solved—to the mutual satisfaction of family members"* (p. 499; italics in original). Goal achievement is designated as one of the key criteria for the first part of the definition; the second part includes satisfaction with both the solution and the process by which the problem was solved. This linking of problem solving with goal attainment and subjective feelings of satisfaction accurately reflects the prevailing orientation in family problem-solving research. It is an orientation that I believe deserves reexamination.

If problem solving pertains to the overcoming of barriers rather than to the achievement of goals, then satisfaction (either expressed or experienced) may not be a necessary or sufficient indicator of problem-solving effectiveness. The question arises as to what we mean by the term satisfaction. The term *satisfaction* according to the *Brittanica World Language Dictionary* implies complete gratification or satiation.

Can the subjective experience of a driver whose quick response avoids an accident be considered to bring satisfaction? Is the appropriate term for the feelings of a family whose activities made it possible for the mother, through sufficient bed rest, to return to health, satisfaction? The most reasonable answer to both of these questions is "not necessarily." The response might be as much relief as satisfaction. In fact, one can imagine a multitude of emotional responses to positive problem-solving outcomes, including anger at being delayed in one's efforts at seeking a goal, or a lack of any awareness that a problem has been solved but merely a renewed determination to go about one's business. Conversely, problem-solving failures may not be manifest by disappointment or dissatisfaction. The well-documented tendency of actors to want to present themselves in the most positive light possible (Brown, 1979; Goffman, 1959; Jones, 1964) suggests that people may respond to such failure by denial and indifference (Janis & Mann, 1977, p. 364).

Later, in developing the formal aspects of our theory, I use the term satisfaction in a different context and different manner from its use in the above discussion. Rather than considering satisfaction as an empirically identifiable outcome, I use it as an assumption pertaining to human motives for engaging in any choice behavior. Satisfaction, in this usage, does not refer to an assessment of goal attainment but to a motive by which the actor seeks to attain benefits *and* avoid costs.

If goal attainment and satisfaction are not appropriate indicators of effective problem solving, the obvious question is what behaviors would provide such indicators. One answer to this question should by now seem abundantly clear: The outcome of successful problem solving changes a situation so that the actor is able to proceed on his or her route toward a given goal. But what of the emotional and psychological reactions to such successes? If satisfaction is not a necessary reaction to effective problem solving, what effects can we expect on individuals or groups who are successful or unsuccessful in their problem-solving endeavors? There is evidence indicating that continued successful performance in a given activity leads to a sense, not necessarily articulated, of mastery and efficacious expectations (see Bandura, 1977, p. 78–85). This outcome may allow us to identify the factors that enable some families to face severe problems with strength and assurance while others, with the same resources, react with panic and disorganization. (See Elder, 1974, and Liker & Elder, 1983 for data relevant to differential reactions in families facing economic deprivation during the Great Depression). We shall examine self-efficacy in greater detail in later sections of this chapter.

Our discussion thus far suggests the following criteria for assessing effective problem solving: (a) the elimination of identified barriers to goal attainment when such elimination can be directly attributed to an individual's or group's actions; (2) the readiness of actors to commit themselves to attempting to solve problems similar to the one's they have previously faced; and (3) the actor's level of effort and persistence when engaged in attempting to solve difficult problems.

We are now ready to examine the types of activities that are oriented toward producing such outcomes. The following definition is derivable from our earlier definition of a problem:

Definition 3: The problem-solving process involves nonroutine mental or physical activities in which the actor attempts to overcome a condition that impedes his or her goal attainment efforts. These activities always entail some degree of risk that the problem may not be solved.

The specific type of activity undertaken depends upon the nature of the barrier. Agre (1983) claims that "When solving something one completes, ends or removes one thing or another, and/or brings about some sort of stability or permanence" (p. 93). This suggests four general types of barriers: (1) there are tasks that require completion such as puzzles, examinations, specific "jobs" such as fixing the car, cleaning the house, and so forth; (2) noxious, taxing, or debilitating events that need to be ended or stopped for actors to proceed toward their goals; (c) literal or figurative blockages, like an accident on a highway, that must be removed; and finally, (4) threatening or disruptive conditions or situations that upset the actor's equilibrium or stability. (In this last case, solving the problem may be equivalent to attaining the goal.) Therefore, a problem-solving activity entails one of the following four possible orientations: (1) completing a task; (2) bringing an end to a noxious situation; (3) removing a blockage; and (4) restoring an unstable situation to its previous state of stability.

The Relevance of Decisions

Problems, as we have seen, may occur in an individual's or group's environment without the individual or group being aware of them. Problem-solving activities, however, require that the actor is aware of the problem's existence. By "aware" I do not mean an ability or readiness to identify a "problem," as I have defined it. It is not likely that most people engaged in problem-solving activities describe their behaviors in such terms. What is necessary is a conscious interpretation of a situation requiring change. Once such an interpretation is made the actor must make a decision as to whether or not to engage in problem solving. Given the nonroutine nature of the actions involved in problem solving, a decision must also be made as to the type of action to take. take. The decision need not take a long time to make, as when a driver swerves his automobile in order to avoid a collision. But regardless of the time involved, a problem-solving activity is always initiated by a decision on the part of the actor to undertake an action oriented toward eliminating a perceived undesirable state of affairs.

The initial decision an actor must make is whether or not to attempt to solve the problem (Newell & Simon, 1972, pp. 88–104; Simmons, Klein, & Simmons, 1977, pp. 272–274; Tallman *et al.*, 1983). If this decision is made in the affirmative, then subsequent decisions must be made as to the course of action to take, and in given situations, whether or not to continue or to alter a given course of action (Tallman *et al.*, 1983). We define a decision as follows:

Definition 4: A decision is a conscious and non-routine process of comparing alternative objects or courses of action, selecting one of the alternatives and making a commitment to that alternative until a subsequence evaluation is made.

The above definition is designed to differentiate decisions and decision making from choice behavior. The latter is the more generic concept. The selection processes in choice behavior include conditioned, automatic, and reflexive responses. They do not require either conscious awareness or nonroutine reactions. Decision making is considered here as a special case of choice behavior.

The hub of the problem-solving process is decision making. It is the mechanism that triggers all subsequent problem-solving activity. An essential component of this process is information search and information processing. All decisions are based on processing available information. How much information is sought and how it affects the decision process will be discussed below after we examine the basic elements of the problem-solving theory. The terms defined above—*problems, problem solving, problem-solving activity,* and *decisions*—are the cornerstones for such a theory.

BASIC ASSUMPTIONS AND PROPOSITIONS

Our theory derives from two assumptions that are accepted by most social scientists.

Assumption 1: Human actors are satisfaction seekers.

This assumption is explicit or implicit in virtually every major principle or proposition in the social sciences. It speaks to an essential motive and is the premise for predicting what and how actors will learn and the choices they will make. Walster, Walster, and Berscheid (1978, p. 6), who begin their theory of equity with the similar assumption, "Individuals will try to maximize outcomes," claim that "even the most contentious scientist would find it difficult to challenge . . . [this] proposition". For our purposes, satisfaction seeking serves as the underlying motive for determining (1) whether or not actors decide to engage in problem-solving activities, and (2) the type of problem-solving action to be undertaken.

The second assumption amplifies the first:

Assumption 2: Satisfactions are sought by attempting to attain highly valued benefits (rewards, gains, and so forth) and by attempting to avoid high costs, (losses, punishments, and so forth) at the least possible risk (i.e., the greatest probability that the desired outcome will be accomplished).

The assumption suggests that actors will behave in ways that they believe or have learned will offer them the best chance of obtaining satisfactions (i.e., the greatest benefit for the least cost). This statement is consistent with behaviorist theories, social learning theory and social exchange theory. It has also been empirically verified in thousands of studies over the past 60 years (Herrnstein, 1970).

The two assumptions are directly applicable to the process of decision making. Thus,

Proposition 1: (Given Assumptions 1 and 2). Decisions are made by comparing alternatives in terms of the actor's subjective estimates of the probable costs and benefits associated with each alternative and selecting the alternative that provides the best assurance of attaining the best expected satisfaction.

The phrase "expected satisfaction" refers to the actor's estimates of his or her expected cost/benefit ratio for each alternative. It also includes the actor's subjective estimate as to the probabilities that a given alternative will produce a given outcome. Thus, the actor makes an estimate of the risk involved for each available alternative.

Not all problem situations provide the opportunity for choosing a high-benefit/low-cost alternative (see Gray & Tallman, 1984). This is frequently the case in problematic situations. On some occasions actors may be confronted with circumstances in which they are faced with only high cost alternatives—as when a family confronted with economic hardship must decide between removing their child from college or selling their home. In such a case, on the basis of assumptions 1 and 2, we can expect that the actor will select the alternative that is perceived as least costly. In brief, "expected satisfactions" are the best outcomes perceived as available in a particular decision situation.

Since solving a problem requires time, effort, and the risk of failure, it is always costly to the actor. The degree of cost, of course, varies with the type of problem. Thus, one of the questions that the actor must answer is whether solving the problem is worth the costs involved. The answer to this question depends upon how actors weight and relate the three key variables of benefits, costs, and probability of outcomes. We will consider first the relationship between benefits and costs.

Proposition 1a: The higher the value an actor places on a particular benefit, the greater the cost he or she is willing to pay for that benefit.

And,

Proposition 1b: Proposition 1a will hold if and only if the magnitude of the costs are perceived as lower than the magnitude of the benefits.

The above principles derive from our basic assumptions and are keystones of social exchange theory (see, e.g., Homans, 1961, p. 55) as well as economic theory (Kuhn, 1974, p. 120–124). More generally, they seem to fall into that group of principles that are disregarded because they are simply "common sense."

Although the assumptions seem to state the obvious (i.e., "People will engage in problem solving when it is worth their while"), they nevertheless provide an analytic framework for explaining which problems families (and their individual members) will attempt to solve and which they will ignore, or acknowledge and do nothing about. For example, Proposition 1b provides one explanation for inaction in a problem situation even when the goal is highly desired, the actor has the resources to solve the problem, and the problem is viewed as particularly unpleasant. Consider parents who are faced with the excessive use of drugs by their offspring. They feel that the adolescent's drug use is destroying his or her chances of leading a productive life and therefore that it would be highly desirous to break the adolescent of his or her drug use habit. At the same time, they may believe any action they take in this regard will very likely result in the adolescent's permanent rejection of them. If the cost of losing their son or daughter's affection and loyalty is sufficiently high, we can predict that these parents would not take action, even if they felt their actions would be efficacious.

Propositions 1a and 1b also have implications for the level of risk an actor will consider acceptable.

Proposition 1c: Other things being equal, the more highly valued a benefit, the greater the risk an actor will take to obtain the benefit.

And,

Proposition 1d: Other things being equal, the greater the magnitude of anticipated costs confronting an actor in a given situation, the greater the risk the actor will take to avoid the cost.

It follows from Propositions 1c and 1d that the more highly valued a goal the greater the willingness of the actor to engage in problem-solving behavior relevant to attaining that goal. Similarly, the more the problem is perceived as a salient and serious threat to goal attainment, the more willing the actor will be to engage in problem-solving attempts.

But what can we say about the relative strength of the three key variables affecting the decision process? What carries greater weight for the actor—the attainment of a benefit, the avoidance of a cost, or the level of risk involved in the activity? To answer this question we turn to the theoretical work and research carried out by Tversky and Kahneman (Kahneman & Tversky, 1979; Kahneman & Tversky, 1982; Tversky & Kahneman, 1981). In a series of studies they demonstrate "the certainty effect," showing that subjects will prefer a certain payoff even though the payoff is considerably less then they could expect from the alternative with a relatively high probability of success. These findings run contrary to the predictions that would be made on the assumption that the subject is a rational actor seeking to maximize his or her outcomes. However, their research also shows that when problems are posed in terms of costs or losses to be avoided rather than benefits to be gained, subjects are much more likely to choose the probabilistic or risky alternative. In essence, actors will tend to make a risk-avoiding choice when benefits are involved, whereas they will tend toward risk-seeking behavior when costs are involved. Given the "certainty effect," it appears that the subjective value placed on every additional cost unit is greater than the value placed on a gain or benefit unit. As Tversky and Kahneman (1981) note, "The displeasure associated with losing a sum of money is generally greater than the pleasure associated with winning the same amount" (p. 454).

The following principles derive from this body of theory and research:

Proposition 2: Whenever a choice is possible, actors will prefer courses of action that promise certain outcomes over courses of action in which the outcomes are probabilistic (the "certainty effect").

With regard to problem solving, which always involves some risk, the "certainty effect" can be interpreted as an inertia effect. That is, we can assume that any actor will show some resistance to engaging in problem-solving activities.

From Tversky and Kahneman's research, we also conclude that,

Proposition 3: Other things being equal, for any given good or service, a unit of loss (cost) of that good or service will be given greater weight than a unit of gain (benefit).

Therefore (from propositions 1c and 1d),

Proposition 3a: Actors will take greater risks to avoid a loss (cost) than to obtain a gain (benefit).

Thus, on the basis of Propositions 3 and 3a we can predict a greater tendency for families to attempt to avoid losses, excessive costs, or pain-situations than to achieve desired success goals. In fact, this premise seems to be the basis upon which insurance companies make their appeals to families. Families tend to invest considerable amounts of money to protect themselves against low probability events such as loss of life or fire, theft, or house damage. It is unlikely that similar high investments would be made at the same outcome probabilities to attain a positive payoff. In general, family members will not invest the same amount of money for the same payoff at the same probabilities of outcome in a lottery as they would for insurance.

Extending this principle to problem-solving situations, we would predict that, other things being equal, families will be more likely to engage in problem-solving activities if the problem to be solved enables the actor to avoid costs, losses, or punishments, than if it facilitates the attainment of a given benefit, reward, or gain. Thus, a family is likely to decide more quickly to repair a second car whose breakdown would disrupt its usual patterns of transportation than to make the same investment of effort, time, or money to obtain a desired and needed piece of furniture.

Given our definition of a problem, it follows that engaging in problem-solving activities requires that the actor alter his or her usual behavioral patterns and select a relatively novel, or at least, infrequently used set of behaviors in an attempt to change the current state of affairs. Also, since, by definition, there will be some degree of uncertainty about any course of action designed to solve a problem, we can infer from Proposition 2 (the certainty effect) that the actor will seek to find that course of action that is perceived as offering the least risk. These two conditions–the need for a new course of action and the desire to limit the risk—suggest that actors will seek information about the alternatives available to them before they select a course of action. Therefore,

Proposition 4: (from Definitions 1 and 3 and Proposition 1). *Actors who are confronted with a problem will engage in a search for information about the alternative courses of action available for solving the problem.*

And,

Proposition 4a: (from Propositions 1, 2, and 4). *The information gathered in the search will provide the basis for estimates of the expected satisfactions associated with each course of action and for reducing as much as possible the uncertainty associated with adopting a particular course of action.*

"Expected satisfactions," as noted above, refers to the subjective probability estimates of the occurrence of designated benefits and costs

for each alternative course of action. These estimates depend on two
types of information: (1) the actor's assessment of his or her ability to
carry out a given course of action to solve the problem and (2) an
appraisal of the courses of action that may conceivably solve the problem. The latter appraisal requires information about the problem's
characteristics, especially its complexity and difficulty.[1]

Information searches are both external and internal. They involve:
(1) evaluations of problem characteristics; (2) estimates of the opportunities or lack of opportunities available in the environment for solving the
problem (eg., access to information and necessary resources); and (3)
estimates of the actor's skills, knowledge, and dispositional state relevant
to a particular course of action.

An actor will probably seek to determine how long it would reason-
ably take to solve the problem, as well as how much time he or she has
available for dealing with the particular problem. It would also be
important to know the degree of temporal flexibility associated with the
problem (i.e., whether or not there is a deadline). Both Aldous (1971)
and Weick (1971) have noted that families differ from most other groups
in that they cannot easily isolate or control the problems with which
they are confronted. In fact, they are overrun with problems and frequently must set aside one problem in order to deal with a more pressing one. Under these conditions the time elements become critical.

It is equally important to be able to determine whether the source
of the problem is internal or external. If the barrier or obstacle is not
appropriately located, problem-solving efforts will be in vain. Similarly,
the actor will want to know if there are available rules for solving the
problem. How many component parts make up the problem? How
many actors must be brought to bear in the problem-solving effort? And
how does one know when the problem is solved?

For some problems, the relevant information can be determined,
registered, and processed in a split second; for others, this phase of the
information search may be long and costly. The driver of an automobile
faced with an oncoming truck knows instantaneously that her required
and allotted time is short and specific, that the source of the problem is
externally located in the oncoming truck, that she must undertake a set
of complex maneuvers to avoid the onrushing truck, that she can rely
only on herself and that there is no question about how to evaluate the
solution—her actions will either be right or wrong. Consider, however,
the problem faced by a family member who has been fired from his job
and cannot find another one. There are many unanswered issues
relevant to the allotted or required time he has to find another job.
Moreover, it is not altogether clear without further examination whether
the actor's job problems lie within himself or in the job situation,
whether finding a job is the sole responsibility of the actor or whether it

is best accomplished by the actor's family and community agency coordinating efforts, what rules must be followed in the job search, and so forth. In brief, information search concerning problem characteristics is highly variable depending in part on the time parameters and the problem's specificity and complexity.

Access to both subjective and objective information about alternative routes for solving problems varies with positions in the social structure (Freedman & Sears, 1965; Piker, 1968; Wade & Schramm, 1969; Wilson, 1963). For families, access varies not only with the position in the social structure but with the type of family structure. Family structure, in turn, partially reflects the larger social structure (Tallman & Miller, 1974; Tallman *et al.*, 1983, p. 63–77). Not only are people in certain social positions able to have greater access to relevant and sometimes privileged information; they also have the additional advantages of training, work that involves the manipulation and management of symbols and people, and language skills, all of which make it easier for them to assess the dispositional states of key actors that influence possible courses of action. Similarly communication channels, hierarchical structures, value orientations, language styles, and so forth influence the information opportunities available to family members (see Tallman, 1970).

Self-assessments of an actor's problem-solving abilities, like other estimates of problem-solving outcomes can never be reduced to certainty. This is not only because the actor cannot control extraneous events affecting problem solving, it is also because the behaviors necessary to solve a problem may evolve and change as the problem unfolds. Thus, the effort to fix the family car may begin with an assessment of the family members' mechanical skills. The discovery that parts are worn out, however, may require skills in financial budgeting and manipulation to make the necessary purchases. Or it may become clear that the task requires more than one person, and therefore certain interpersonal skills are necessary to obtain the desired assistance. If information about the skills necessary to solve a problem is not always available at the time actors must commit themselves to a problem-solving effort, what criteria can they use to form a judgment concerning those skills? The most likely source for such a judgment is the actor's general self-evaluation of his or her efficacy in such situations. This is linked with the actor's sense of confidence, which is based on past experience. If one is confronted by a malfunctioning automobile, the willingness to deal with the problem is partially determined by one's general sense of self-efficacy as related to repairing cars.

What determines this sense of efficacy? The work of Albert Bandura (1977, p. 81) suggests three types of experience that are relevant to the development of such self-evaluations. They include past performances, the observations of others who serve as models, and the opinions of others. Of the three types of experience, the most dependable, according to Bandura, is performance. Performances have a demonstrable and reinforcing influence on the actor. Actual performance is not subject to the multiple interpretations associated with observing the behavior of others with whom one can identify, or to the verbal information and/or assurances of others. Very often, however, the three types of experience are correlated and it is reasonable to infer that they have an additive effect.

As we have previously noted, information searches can be costly in time, energy expended, and effort. Therefore, on the basis of Propositions 1 and 3a, we conclude:

Proposition 4b: Actors will engage in an information search only up to the point at which they believe additional information will not sufficiently reduce their level of uncertainty about what course of action to select, or that the benefits to be attained from selecting a better course of action will not outweigh the costs entailed in seeking more information.

Clearly problem characteristics play a critical role in the amount of information search that takes place. Simmons and her colleagues (1977) report that kidney donors spend little time considering their action. This may be due in part to the clear-cut alteratives available to them. From the perspective of the donor, the problem is relatively simple. The choice is dichotomous. The outcome is clearly assessed in moral "right" or "wrong" terms. Thus, the actor is in a position of either doing or failing to do "the right thing." Simon's (1976) conception of "satisficing" is also relevant there. He suggests that rarely will actors seek the last ounce of available information before making a decision; rather, they are more likely to gather information only until they can settle on a course of action that is "good enough." The basis for the "good enough" solution may lie in the last phrase of Proposition 4b. That is, seeking additional information to improve the choice eventually becomes more costly than the benefits to be gained in solving the problem.

In brief, the theory proposed here focuses on decisions and information processing as the key behaviors involved in problem-solving activities. The decision making model developed in the above propositions differs from the more common "utility" models (Camilleri & Connor, 1976), in that it considers costs and benefits as independent and separately weighted variables (Gray & Tallman, 1984). By considering costs and benefits independently, it is feasible to recognize the general tendency of people to place greater value on avoiding costs than on attaining benefits. This has implications for specifying the salience of different problems for families. Generally speaking—and holding a variety of conditions and values constant—we would expect families to be more involved in attempting to solve problems in which there is the potential threat of loss, pain, or cost than to focus on problems that require overcoming barriers to attaining some valued benefit. The former tends to be experienced with more immediacy than the latter.

Actors faced with a problem will decide whether or not to engage in problem-solving activities on the basis of a subjective estimate of their chances for success. This requires an information search. In this paper, I have examined three sources of such information—the problem, the opportunity structure, and the actor's self-evaluation of ability. In the course of this examination, we determined that successful problem solving influences the actor's sense of self-efficacy. A strong sense of efficacy is manifest in the actor's readiness to engage in problem-solving activities, a greater willingness to devote effort to the problem-solving activity, and a high degree of persistence in the face of discouraging results (Bandura, 1977, p. 80).

It follows that the collective experience of the family and its members in dealing with problems will either facilitate or inhibit its readiness and the readiness of its members to engage in subsequent problem-solving behavior. Thus, we have a spiraling effect. Efficacy breeds effort, effort contributes to problem-solving success, and problem-solving success breeds efficacy—and so it goes.

Not all family members need always to be involved in these activities. Through the process of identification and the sense of shared fate, the experience of the family as a group or as individuals representing the group may be generalized and internalized. In this way, family experience of success or failure may become part of every family member's sense of self-efficacy. Our cross-cultural study of adolescents' socialization in Mexico provides support for this claim (Tallman *et al.*, 1983, pp. 138–140). We found that sons of Mexican and United States families who experienced failure while engaging in a problem-solving activity as part of their family group were significantly less likely than boys whose families had performed effectively to take reasonable risks in subsequent problem-solving activities.

In sum, this theory of problem-solving behavior suggests a criterion for assessing problem-solving effectiveness—the individual, group, or family's sense of *efficacy*. This sense of efficacy is measurable not only in terms of self-reports but also in behavioral terms by gauging the actor's readiness to take on new problems and to persist in the problem-solving process. Moreover, a sense of efficaciousness does not require goal attainment. Bandura (1977, p. 79) draws a distinction between efficacy expectations and outcome expectations. An actor may realize that he or she has the ability to achieve a particular goal but also understands that extraneous factors interfere with attaining that end. Thus, a sense of efficacy does not imply that the actor will attempt the impossible, nor will his or her self-concept be damaged by failures that are beyond that actor's control. It should follow that the family with a history of problem-solving success would be active, confident, and more ready to confront the internal and external problems with which it is faced. Conversely, the family with poor problem-solving experiences would be more likely to be passive and less likely to consider situations in problematic terms.

Summary

The assumptions and propositions presented above constitute a framework for a general theory of problem solving. Like all general principles, they operate in the empirical world only under specified antecedent and initial conditions (see Cohen, 1980). For our purposes, we must recognize that these principles are operative within social and psychological contexts. The available space does not allow for a discussion of these conditions here. I have identified some antecedent conditions in a longer version of this chapter, available on request.[2]

I have placed primary emphasis on the decision-making aspects of problem solving, because I think it is central to understanding and explaining the problem-solving process. Once decisions are made, performance becomes the important component in the process. I have not considered the mental and physical processes or the organizational and structural elements involved in problem-solving activities in any detail. Principles relevant to these aspects or problem solving are discussed elsewhere (Klein & Hill, 1979; Newell & Simon, 1972; Tallman, 1970; Tallman et al., 1974; Tallman et al., 1983). I must add, however, that I would alter my earlier work to conform to the essential elements of the framework developed in this paper. Within this framework, problem solving can be viewed as a decision and learning process, mediated through the actor's genetically determined abilities and environmental opportunities.

DO FAMILIES SOLVE PROBLEMS?

I have used the term "actor" to apply to any human individual or group capable of acting as a single unit. The family represents such a unit. Indeed, there seems to be considerable agreement among scholars that the family is among the most likely social groups to function in this unitary manner (Kuhn, 1974, p. 416; Turner, 1970, p. 65–95). There is a growing body of research and theory that can be broadly categorized within the social exchange tradition that describes a process of deepening human relationships beginning with individuals seeking to maximize personal benefits in the relationship. The process results in commitments in which the calculation of costs and benefits is transformed from a focus on individual outcomes to a concern for the relationship (cf. among others, Backman, 1981; Huston & Burgess, 1979; Leik & Leik, 1977; Scanzoni, 1979; Walster *et al.*, 1978). As the relationship between the partners develops, alternative sources of need and want fulfillment are rejected, and the actors make joint investments in a shared future (Backman, 1981). Thus, the time frame within which positive payoffs are expected to occur is greatly extended (Kelley & Thibaut, 1978).

The key factor in this developing process of bonding is the growing interdependence of the individuals involved. For families, this interdependency leads to a shared identity and sense of shared fate (Tallman *et al.*, 1983, p. 27–29; Turner, 1970, pp. 94–96). The mutual influences that derive from high levels of interdependency make it more likely that family members will maintain the same perceptual orientation toward the world around them and therefore perceive problems or alternative courses of action in a similar way. This premise is the underlying theme in the extensive body of research carried out by David Reiss and his co-workers (Reiss, 1981; Reiss & Oliveri, 1983).

The above discussion, of course, does not imply that all families act as a unit or that any family will always function in a unitary manner. Families are made up of individuals who have personal careers and aspirations as well as those that are shared with the family as a whole. It is possible, as Klein and Hill (1979) indicate, that family members may perceive problems quite differently, and one member's solution may become another member's problem. In fact, as Kelley and Thibaut (1978) illustrate, interactions in which individuals are completely oriented toward beneficial shared outcomes at the constant cost of their personal outcomes could not result in long-term, mutually satisfying relationships. What occurs within families is an ongoing process of internal problems arising and being resolved.

If families vary in their tendency to function as a unit, what variables influence this tendency? The answer to this question may be found in the level of interdependency among the family members. This level, in turn, influences the degree of commitment family members make to the family, and the collective level of commitment among family members determines its potential for operating as a single unit. Louis Gray and I have developed a framework within which to measure the commitment of members in a given group and consequently to determine the level of group cohesion. It derives in part from the research of

Michaels and Wiggins (1976) and Molm (1980) on the relationship between power/dependency and social exchange. It is based on the assumption that an individual's dependency on a group is a function of two factors: his or her reliance on the resources and services resulting from exchanges with other group members (mutual dependence) and a reliance on the products produced by the group as a whole (interdependency). Thus, family members may be dependent on each other for love and affection (mutual dependence) and dependent on the family as a group for the income or status it produces (interdependence). The level of mutual dependence and interdependence is a function of how much the individual values the resources involved, the opportunities he or she has available to attain the resources elsewhere, and the person's access to those resources without the aid of the group or group members.

We can infer that the greater the individual's dependencies on the group, the greater the commitment to the group. Moreover, commitment should also be a function of the total number of valued resources the individual is dependent on the group to provide. In brief, commitment for an individual can be summarized in the following form:

$$\prod_{j=1}^{N} \left(\frac{MD_i + INT_i}{IND} \right)$$

where *MD* refers to mutual dependency, *INT* to interdependency, *IND* to the individual's level of independence, and *N* to the number of resources being exchanged. Π is a product term used to indicate that all of the dimensions are multiplied with one another. Thus the dependency term would be multiplied by each of the resources involved in the exchange situation. Group cohesion is measured as the mean commitment of all members of the group. We hypothesize that the greater the individual's commitment to the group, the greater the group's power over the individual, and thus the more the actor will defer his or her individual desires to group desires. It follows that the greater the group cohesion (i.e., the average of the individuals' commitments), the more likely the group will function as a single decision unit.

The limitations on space do not allow for a full discussion of the uses to which this formulation can be put. For example, the level of symmetry or asymmetry between the commitment quotients of the family members is an indicator of the power distribution within the family with regard to key resources. It should therefore provide an indication as to how family members will deal with internal problems requiring cooperative solutions.

The formula also provides us with a means for evaluating changes in family cohesion over the family life cycle. The denominator in the formula, independence, is likely to change, as family members have the opportunity to attain desired resources from nonfamily members, or as those resources are denied them within the family. Therefore, we would expect less family cohesion when children are adolescents. Since youngsters are striving for greater independence from their families, they will seek such resources as status, approval, and affection outside of the family. Similarly, periods of high cohesion when the members' independence from the family tends to be low might occur in the establishment, child-rearing, and retirement stages of the cycle. More generally, the level of cohesion within the family may be one factor in predicting the kinds of problems that the family will seek to solve. For example, cohesive families may be more sensitive to external pressures and group-threatening temptations than noncohesive families.

CONCLUSION

There is little doubt that problems and problem solving are a pervasive part of ordinary family life. There are quarrels to be settled, illnesses to be overcome, unforeseen expenses that wreak havoc on budgets, and economic conditions that upset career plans. There are disruptions in school, in the home, and in the community. The list of possible problems families face seems interminable. How good families are at solving their problems should have a profound effect on the family members' sense of competence and well-being. This degree of efficacy differentiates between those who are oriented toward action, who can take control of their destinies when possible, and those who passively wait for events to overtake them.

The way families go about dealing with their problems is likely to be an important aspect of children's socialization. Patterned family problem-solving orientations and behaviors are transmitted across generations. Thus, family members may be placed on trajectories that unknowingly can have profound effects on their lives and plans. Clinicians and therapists know this. Their task is often explicitly stated as helping family members to identify their problems and learn to solve them. It is difficult to see how we can accomplish our goals of helping families solve problems unless we know the basic processes involved in problem solving, and how those processes apply to the family.

Reuben Hill and his colleagues were right in identifying problem solving as a critical area of research and theory for family scholars. It has proved more difficult to deal with than many had anticipated, but such difficulties make problem solving no less important. We may be able to move faster if we make our knowledge incremental and build on each other's work. To accomplish this, we have to be able to communi-

126

cate to our colleagues, using unambiguous concepts whose meanings are shared and whose measurement is clearly derivable from those meanings. This chapter is intended to contribute to that end.

NOTES

1. Elsewhere my colleagues and I have developed a taxonomy of problems that provides a framework that suggests the problem components that would be the subject of information search (Tallman *et al.*, 1974). In the interests of saving space, I will not discuss the elements of the taxonomy here. It nevertheless forms a basis for the discussion that follows.

2. Requests can be sent to Irving Tallman, Department of Sociology, Washington State University, Pullman, WA 99164-4020.

REFERENCES

Agre, G. P. (1982). The concept of problem. *Educational Studies, 13*, 121–141.
Agre, G. P. (1983). What does it mean to solve problems? *Journal of Thought, 18*, 92–104.
Aldous, J. (1971). A framework for the analysis of family problem solving. J. Aldous, T. Condon, R. Hill, M. Straus, & I. Tallman (Eds.), *Family problem solving: A symposium on theoretical, methodological, and substantive concerns* (pp. 265–81). Hinsdale, IL: Dryden Press.
Backman, C. W. (1981). Attraction in interpersonal relationships. In M. Rosenberg & R. Turner (Eds.), *Social psychology: Sociological perspectives*. New York: Basic Books.
Bandura, A. (1977). *Social learning theory*. Englewood Cliffs, NJ: Prentice-Hall.
Bourne, L. E., Ekstrand, B. R., & Dominowski, R. L. (1971). *The psychology of thinking*. Englewood Cliffs, NJ: Prentice-Hall.
Brown, B. R. (1970). Face-saving following experimentally induced embarrassment. *Journal of Experimental Social Psychology, 6*, 255–271.
Camilleri, S. F., & Conner, T. L. (1976). Decision making and social influence: A revised model and further experimental evidence. Sociometry, 39, 30–38.
Cohen, B. P. (1980). The conditional nature of scientific knowledge. In L. Freese (Ed.), *Theoretical methods in sociology: Seven essays*. Pittsburgh, PA: University of Pittsburgh Press.
Dewey, J. (1910). *How we think*. New York: D. C. Heath.
Elder, G. H., Jr. (1974). *Children of the Great Depression*. Chicago: University of Chicago Press.
Emerson, R. M. (1972). Exchange theory, parts I & II. In J. Berger, M. Zelditch, Jr., & B. Anderson (Eds.), *Sociological theories in progress* (Part I, pp. 38–57; Part II, pp. 58–87). Boston: Houghton Mifflin.
Emerson, R. M. (1976). Social exchange theory. In A. Inkeles (Ed.), *Annual Review of Sociology* (pp. 335–362). Palo Alto, CA: Annual Reviews.
Freedman, J. L., & Sears, D. L. (1965). Selective exposure. In L. Berkowitz (Ed.), *Advances in experimental social psychology* (vol. 2, pp. 58–97). New York: Academic Press.
Freese, L. (1980). The problem of cumulative knowledge. In L. Freese (Ed.), *Theoretical*

methods in sociology: Seven essays (pp. 13–69). Pittsburgh, PA: Pittsburgh University Press.

Goffman, E. (1959). *The presentation of self in every day life.* Garden City, NY: Doubleday.

Gray, L. N., & Tallman, I. (1984). A satisfaction balance model of decision making and choice behavior. *Social Psychology Quarterly, 47,* 146–159.

Hansen, D. A., & Hill, R. (1964). Families under stress. In H. T. Christiansen (Ed.), *Handbook of Marriage and the Family* (pp. 782–819). Chicago: Rand McNally.

Hattiangadi, J. N. (1978). The structure of problems (Part I). *Philosophy of Social Science, 8,* 345–365.

Hattiangadi, J. N. (1979). The structure of problems (Part II). *Philosophy of Social Science, 9,* 49–76.

Herrnstein, R. J. (1970). On the law of effect. *Journal of Experimental Analysis of Behavior, 13,* 243–266.

Homans, G. C. (1961). *Social behavior: Its elementary forms.* New York: Harcourt Brace and World.

Homans, G. C. (1974). *Social behavior: Its elementary forms* (rev. Ed.). New York: Harcourt, Brace, Joanovich.

Huston, T. L., & Burgess, R. L. (Eds.). (1979). *Social exchange in developing relationships: An overview.* New York: Academic Press.

Janis, I. L., & Mann, L. (1977). *Decision making.* New York: Free Press.

Jones, E. E. (1964). *Ingratiation: A social psychological analysis.* New York: Appleton-Century-Crofts.

Kahneman, D., & Tversky, A. (1979). Prospect theory: An analysis of decision under risk. *Econometrica, 47,* 263–291.

Kahneman, D., & Tversky, A. (1982). Variants of uncertainty. In D. Kahneman, P. Slovic, & A. Tversky (Eds.), *Judgment under uncertainty: Heuristics and biases.* Cambridge, England: Cambridge University Press.

Kelley, H. H., & Thibaut, J. W. (1978). *Interpersonal relations: A theory of interdependence.* New York: Wiley.

Klein, D. M. (1983). Family problem solving and family stress. In H. I. McCubbin, M. B. Sussman, & J. M. Patterson (Eds.), *Social stress theory and the family: Advances and developments in family stress theory and research* (pp. 85–112). New York: Haworth Press.

Klein, D. M., & Hill, R. (1979). Determinants of family problem solving effectiveness. In W. Burr, R. Hill, F. I. Nye, & R. Reiss (Eds.), *Contemporary theories about the family* (Vol. 1, pp. 493–548). New York: Free Press.

Kuhn, A. (1974). *The logic of social systems.* San Francisco: Jossey-Bass.

Leik, R., & Leik, S. A. (1977). Transition to interpersonal commitment. In R. L. Hamblin & J. H. Kunkel (Eds.), *Behavioral theory in sociology* (pp. 299–322). New Brunswick, NJ: Transaction Books.

Liker, J. K., & Elder, G. H., Jr. (1983). Economic hardship and marital relations in the 1930's. *American Sociological Review, 48,* 343–359.

Michaels, J. W., & Wiggins, J. A. (1976). Effects of mutual dependency asymmetry of social exchange. *Sociometry, 39,* 368–376.

Molm, L. (1980). The effects of structural variation in social reinforcement contingencies on exchange and cooperation. *Social Psychology Quarterly, 43,* 269–282.

Newell, A., & Simon, H. A. (1972). *Human problem solving.* Englewood Cliffs, NJ: Prentice-Hall.

Oliveri, M. E., & Reiss, D. (1981). A theory-based empirical classification of family problem-solving behavior. *Family Process, 20,* 409–48.

Piker, J. (1968). *Entry into the labor force: A survey of the literature on the experiences of negro and white youths.* Ann Arbor, MI: Institute of Labor and Industrial Relations.

Reiss, D. (1981). *The family's construction of reality.* Cambridge, MA: Harvard University Press.

Reiss, D., & Oliveri, M. E. (1983). The family's construction of social reality and its ties to its kin network: An exploration of causal direction. *Journal of Marriage and the Family, 45,* 81–91.

Scanzoni, J. (1979). Social exchange and behavioral interdependence. In R. L. Burgess & T. L. Huston (Eds.), *Social exchange in developing relationships* (pp. 61–98). New York: Academic Press.

Simmons, R. G., Klein, S. D., & Simons, R. L. (1977). *Gift of life: The social and psychological impact of organ transplantation.* New York: Wiley.

Simon, H. A. (1976). *Administrative behavior: A study of decision-making processes in administrative organization* (3rd ed.). New York: Macmillan.

Smelser, W. T., & Smelser, N. J. (1981). Group movements, sociocultural change and personality. In M. Rosenberg & R. H. Turner (Eds.), *Social psychology: Sociological perspectives* (pp. 625–652). New York: Basic Books.

Straus, M. (1968). Communication, creativity, and problem solving aility of middle and working class families in three societies. *American Journal of Sociology, 73,* 417–420.

Tallman, I. (1970). The family as a small problem solving group. *Journal of Marriage and the Family, 32,* 94–104.

Tallman, I., Klein, D., Cohen, R., Ihinger, M., Marotz-Baden, R. Torsiello, P., & Troost, K. (1974). *Problems and implications for a theory of group problem solving* (Tech. Rep. No. 3). Minneapolis: University of Minnesota.

Tallman, I., Marotz-Baden, R., & Pindas, P. (1983). *Adolescent socialization in cross-cultural perspective: Planning for social change.* New York: Academic Press.

Tallman, I., & Miller, G. (1974). Class differences in family problem solving: The effects of verbal ability, hierarchical structure and role expectations. *Sociometry, 37,* 13–37.

Turner, R. H. (1970). *Family interaction.* New York: Wiley.

Tversky, A., & Kahneman, D. (1981). The framing of decisions and the psychology of choice. *Science, 211,* 453–458.

Wade, S., & Schramm, W. (1969). Mass media as sources of public affairs, science and health knowledge. *Public Opinion Quarterly, 33,* 197–209.

Walster, E., Walster, G. W., & Berscheid, E. (1978). *Equity: Theory research.* Boston: Allyn and Bacon.

Weick, K. E. (1971). Group processes, family processes, and problem solving. In J. Aldous, T. Condon, R. Hill, M. Straus, & I. Tallman (Eds.), *Family problem solving: A symposium on theoretical, methodological, and substantive concerns* (pp. 3–54). Hinsdale, IL: Dryden Press.

Wilson, A. B. (1963). Social stratification and academic achievement. In M. A. H. Pansow (Ed.), *Education in depressed areas* (pp. 217–35). New York: Columbia University Press.

PART TWO

STRESS IN HISTORICAL AND FAMILY TIME

6

The Significance of Time in the Study of Families Under Stress

PHYLLIS MOEN
Cornell University
and the National Science Foundation

CARLA B. HOWERY
American Sociological Association

Two issue areas have been prominent in the study of the family. The first concerns family stress and adaptation, and the second incorporates the notion of time and timing into the explanatory process. Emphasis on both the temporal aspects of families and on family stress owes much to the work of Reuben Hill (1949, 1964, 1970), beginning with his classic study of families in wartime America. Hill's elaboration of concepts such as "family development" and "family life-cycle stage" (see also Hill & Mattessich, 1979; Hill & Rodgers, 1964) brought fresh attention to issues involving the timing and scheduling of events, a focus, as we shall show, that is particularly salient for researchers addressing family issues in the 1980s.

This chapter investigates the implications of time for studying families under stress. We first explore the more general significance of time and timing in the broad area of family studies, with temporality seen as encompassing concepts such as age, cohort, stage of the life cycle, and historical context. Then the role of time as a set of variables in relation to family stress is addressed, examining the timing of adversity as well as the process of managing stress. We conclude with some current issues in family research, suggesting the continuing significance of time as a cluster of variables of both theoretical interest and explanatory power.

Sensitivity to time underscores the dynamic aspects of stressful conditions and family response to those conditions. However, it is important

Revised version of a paper presented at the annual meeting of the National Council on Family Relations, Washington, D.C., October, 1982. The suggestions of David M. Klein, Joan Aldous, Richard P. Shore, and Donna Dempster McClain are greatly appreciated. We wish to acknowledge as well the special contribution made by Glen H. Elder, Jr. to the conceptualization and development of this chapter.

to view temporality as more than a global concept, more than merely a sensitizing device. This chapter is concerned with time-related variables—duration of event, synchronization, scheduling, life-cycle stage, historical period, age, and cohort—that can be operationalized and, thereby, add a degree of specificity to temporality in studying families facing stress.

TIME AS AN EMERGENT VARIABLE

The family as an object of study and a unit of analysis is a recent, primarily 20th-century development (see reviews by Aldous, 1967; Elder, 1981, 1984; Hareven, 1984; Hill, 1980). Early studies were usually macroscopic and comparative, examining differences in norms and values across cultures, a focus that was gradually replaced by an emphasis on the family as a unit of interacting individuals. But studies of interpersonal relationships, of the family as a small group, or of the family as a structural/functional unit, usually involved only the consideration of these relationships at a single point in time; broad changes over the sweep of history might be hypothesized, but stability and change over the life cycle of individual families were generally disregarded.

However, one early scholar gave uncharacteristic attention to time as a variable. At the turn of the century, Rowntree (1901) undertook a study of York, England, in which he considered the effects of the family life cycle on poverty. Rowntree's pioneering work long stood as the exception, not the rule. Temporal considerations were not fully explored in the area of family studies until the emergence of the "family development" framework in the 1950s and the "life course" perspective in the 1970s.

The Family Development Approach

Family development has been defined as "the process of progressive structural differentiation and transformation over a family's history, the active acquisition and selective discarding of roles by incumbents of family positions to meet changing functional requisites for survival, and to adapt to recurring life stresses as a family system" (Hill & Mattessich, 1979). Since the 1950s, Reuben Hill and his colleagues have emphasized the importance of adaptation and change over the life cycle. A central theme of the developmental approach to the study of the family has been the significance of transitions over time (see, eg., Aldous, 1978; Hill, 1970; Rodgers, 1973). This perspective has sensitized those interested in families to the timing of events, the normative expectations concerning various individual and family transitions, and the implications of these transitions for the lives of individual family members.

Though often hampered by the limitations of cross-sectional data, studies of transitional events such as marriage (Rausch, Goodrich, & Campbell, 1963), parenthood (Jaccoby, 1969; Rossi, 1968), and the launching of the last child from the home (Lowenthal & Chiriboga, 1972) have underscored the predictable turning points in family life, and, hence, in the lives of individuals. Other research has documented stability and change in various facets of family life over time, such as the rise and fall of marital satisfaction and marital adjustment (Miller, 1976; Rollins & Cannon, 1974; Rollins & Feldman, 1970; Spanier, Lewis, & Cole, 1975), leisure (Rapoport & Rapoport, 1975) and women's labor force activity (Moen, 1985; Moen & Moorehouse, 1983; Waite & Stoltzenberg, 1976, 1980).

Important in this regard is the research documenting changes in both the need for and availability of resources over the life cycle (Aldous & Hill, 1969; Gove, Grimm, Motz, & Thompson, 1973; Moen, 1979, 1982; Oppenheimer, 1974; Schorr, 1966). This work is necessary for an understanding of families under stress, insofar as it points to the need to look beyond the family unit to other institutions in order to account for behavior and orientations found within the family. This attention to families in transaction with the rest of society is comparatively recent (Hill, 1980); however, it is crucial to understand fully the interplay between the lives of individual family members and the historical times in which they live, a central theme of the life-course perspective, discussed later in this chapter.

The descriptive value of the developmental approach for documenting changes in roles, resources, and orientations over time cannot be overemphasized (see Lansing & Kish, 1957). It highlights variations in needs and resources over the family career and charts the typical developmental path that many families follow over time. Yet despite the emphasis on temporality, the family development approach, as embodied in empirical work, has focused primarily on stability rather than on change. Much of the research using this framework has captured static snapshots at different stages of the family career. What exists in theory but is slighted in research is an emphasis on process and change. Most of the "transition" studies, such as the transition to parenthood, have focused on a discrete event as a rather short-lived phenomenon (not that parenthood is short-lived; rather, the transition itself is short-lived). Why have scholars of family development ignored process and change? Clearly, the family development *theoretical* perspective has been emphatic about the significance of change over time. What has been missing are the *methodological* tools required to chart these transitions over the life cycle. Missing as well has been sufficient attention to historical change. Though Hill and Mattessich (1979) suggest that a major challenge is to discover regularities that span cohorts and historical contexts, too often researchers treat life-cycle phenomena as invariant across time, without testing whether that is in fact the case. What is required is a strategy incorporating a dynamic focus on families in continuous transaction with other forces, engaging in a process of negotiation and renegotiation, adjustment and readjustment, over the course of the life cycle as well as across generations.

The Life-Course Perspective

Building on the developmental approach, the work of the Chicago school (especially W. I. Thomas; see Thomas & Znaneiki, 1918) and the sociology of age (Hagestad & Neugarten, 1984; Riley, 1987; Riley, Johnson, & Foner, 1972), the life-course perspective which emerged in the 1970s specifically addresses matters relating to time by incorporating such concepts as age, cohort, and historical context. The research and writings of Glen H. Elder, Jr. (1974, 1975, 1979, 1984, 1985; Elder, Liker, & Jaworski, 1984) as well as others (cf., Bengtson & Treas, 1980; Cherlin, 1983; Chudacoff, 1980; Featherman, 1982; Furstenberg, Brooks-Gunn, & Magan, 1987; Hareven, 1981, 1984; Hogan, 1978; Modell, Furstenberg, & Hershberg, 1976; Uhlenberg, 1980) have contributed to an elaboration of the meanings of age and time over the individual life span. Embodied within the life-course perspective are three traditions of inquiry:

1. *Lifetime.* Chronological age represents an approximate estimate of stage of position in the aging process. From a developmental standpoint, age alerts the investigator to subgroups that are differentially vulnerable to particular types of social change, such as the very young and old in economically hard times. In other words, social change has differential consequences for people of unequal age (see Ryder, 1965).

2. *Family or social time.* There are normatively accepted age-patterned or age-graded sequences of events (marriage, births, residential change, retirement) and social roles that occur in the life course of the individual. The notion of family time refers to the ordering of family events and social roles by age-linked expectations, sanctions, and options. The social meanings of age represent constructions that take the form of age norms and sanctions, social timetables for the occurrence and order of events, generalized age grades (childhood, adolescence), and age hierarchies in particular settings, such as work organizations and schools. A normative concept of family time specifies an appropriate time for leaving home, mating, and bearing children.

3. *Historical time.* Birth year (or other markers such as age at marriage or graduation) serves as an index of historical location, placing one within the context of social change. Birth year assigns family members to a birth cohort that is exposed to a particular dimension of historical experience in the process of aging. To understand the meaning and

implications of birth year and cohort membership, the analyst specifies the historical events, conditions, and trends of change at the time, as well as characteristics of the cohort (size, composition), which are themselves a product of historical times.

The interplay between an individual's life history, the life course of the family unit, and the larger macrostructure, such as the economy, at a particular point in history lies at the crux of life-course analysis. In addition, this perspective attends to the intersection of the multiple strands of the various careers that go to make up the life of the individual—the relationship, for example, between one's parenting or marital "career" and one's work career. As Elder (1978) points out:

> With the emergence of a cohort-historical approach in life-course analysis, we have become more aware of the complex meanings associated with age differentiation; in particular, that age locates individuals and family units in historical context by defining their cohort membership, and also places them in the social structure by indicating their career stage. To understand the impact of historical change on family life, we must know something of the process by which this effect occurred, a process that varies according to family stage and situation at the point of change. Such knowledge warrants priority on the agenda of family studies. (pp. 56–57).

Integration of the Developmental and Life-Course Approaches

The developmental and life-course perspectives share a number of theoretical and conceptual foci. Both strategies incorporate the themes of process, change, and career. The life-course perspective has elaborated on the notion of multiple interlocking careers, both across family members and within individual lives. For example, couples have increasingly to juggle the occupational careers of both husband and wife, and growing numbers of women must manage the often conflicting role obligations of family and job (see Moen, in press). The family development perspective has similarly attended to the interdependence of various careers over the life cycle of the family, an important area of convergence in the two perspectives (Aldous, 1978; Rodgers, 1973).

Both frameworks underscore the *timing* of events. The life-course perspective emphasizes the fact that there is a normatively sanctioned timetable, prescribing for a particular society or subgroup the optimal years for marriage, childbearing, and so on. Linking age with life-cycle stage enables the scholar to attend to the timing of these transitional activities. For example, a couple beginning childbearing in their 40s can be expected to have a different experience than one starting a family in their 20s. In addition to the socially prescribed timing and ordering of events, families construct their own timetables. For example, in his study of three generations, Hill (1970) found that some families perceived themselves as "on schedule" in the achievement of various transitions or goals, while other defined themselves as "ahead of" or "behind" schedule.

A key difference between the developmental and life-course perspectives lies in their respective units of analysis. Developmental theorists focus on *families* as they change over the years, while a life-course approach looks at the lives of *individual family members* as they progress and intersect with one another over time. Having distinctive units of analysis is not a trivial matter, meaning as it does that each perspective often studies different phenomena (family change vs. individual change). Yet, clearly, these are not independent processes; individual change and family change are closely related, and one can best be understood by attending to the other.

Another important distinction is the relative weight given by the two perspectives to micro (intrafamilial) change and macro (historical) change. The life-cycle stage concept (most often measured by the age of the oldest child) used in the family development framework locates individuals and families in terms of family structure and function; it also reveals changes in roles and resources over the years. However, it does not place individuals and families in historical time. In contrast, cohort analysis is typically used by life-course scholars to document historical effects. Locating an individual by birth year serves to identify the historical context in which various roles and events are played out (see, eg., Elder, 1975).

Research on families can benefit from the concepts of both perspectives. For example, cohort is a concept most often applied to individuals, not families. Yet it can be equally salient for both units. It is critical to provide a historical context for family change over the life cycle. Families beginning childbearing in the 1950s, for example, faced a world far different from that confronting couples starting their childbearing in the latter half of the 1980s, given the major transformation in gender role ideology (Moen, in press).

Just as age and cohort can be confounded in studies of the life course for individuals, so can life-cycle stage and generation be confused in studies of families. For example, are grandparents more conservative in their beliefs because of their locations in the social structure, because of their experience that comes with age, or because they reflect a particular cohort's values and orientations? Hill (1970) points out that in times of rapid change, each cohort "encounters at marriage a unique set of historical constraints and incentives which influence the timing of its crucial life decisions, making for marked generational dissimilarities in life-cycle patterns" (p. 322). The interplay between historical change and life-cycle change remains both unexplored and unexplained, but the persistence of particular behaviors or attitudes across stages of the life cycle provides one mechanism for identifying cohort effects on both individuals and families.

Family development and life-course perspectives have caused time, as a cluster of variables, to become of paramount importance in the study of families. A synthesis of both approaches unites two key components of time: age and kinship. Chronological age locates families in a historical setting through the family head's birth year and by age-related events over the life span. Age relates social structure and history in the family and individual life course (Elder, 1975). The conceptual language of kinship contributes two additional dimensions of time to the study of families: (1) the family cycle in which children are born, mature, and have offspring who eventually replace the parent generation; and (2) the lineal hierarchy of generational stations from child to parent, grandparent, and great-grandparent. Age and kinship are key elements of a dynamic perspective on family development and the life course. Both contribute to an approach to the family in which time, process, and context are important considerations.

The interplay between life-cycle stage, age, and historical period suggests an intriguing research agenda for the family scholar. The next two sections address the particular significance of time in understanding families under stress.

FAMILIES UNDER STRESS

The subject of families under stress can be dealt with in the larger context of studies of stress in general (see Cox, 1978; Kaplan, 1983). There has been no consensus achieved on the precise meaning of stress. In fact, one scholar suggests that it is a generic term of events, responses to the events, and the processes relating the two: "The arena that the stress area refers to consists of any event in which environmental demands, internal demands, or both, tax or exceed the adaptive resources of an individual, social system, or tissue system" (Lazarus, 1977, pp. 2–3). More specifically, families confronting such demands can be described as experiencing social (as contrasted to physiological or psychological) stress—that is, a disruption of a social unit or system (Monat & Lazarus, 1977), in this case, the family system (see discussions by Croog, 1970; Klein, 1983; McCubbin *et al.*, 1980).

A key element in the broader discussions of stress is an emphasis on events. This is exemplified by the work of Holmes and Rahe (1967) and others (cf., Dohrenwend & Dohrenwend, 1977), in which change itself is regarded as stressful, regardless of whether a change produces positive or negative consequences. For example, a stressful event is defined as one that is "either indicative of, or requires a change in, the ongoing life pattern of the individual. The emphasis is on change from the existing steady state and not on psychological meaning, emotional or social desirability" (Holmes & Masuda, 1974, p. 46). Missing from this perspective, however, is the role of personal resources and the subjective definition of the situation in conditioning the consequences of a stressor.

Scholars interested in families under stress also have typically defined stressors as disruptive events, in case studies of the effects of job loss on families during the Great Depression and the pioneering study by Hill (1949) of the crisis of war separation. Hill's (1949) definition of a family crisis, "any sharp or decisive change for which old patterns are inadequate" (p. 51) and Burr's (1973) definition, "the amount of disruptiveness, incapacitatedness or disorganization" (p. 200) emphasize the discontinuity embodied in stressful events, the fact that they produce a change in the family system.

Stress as it relates to families has never been viewed in purely objective terms. In fact, the contribution of family scholars to the study of stress lies in their early recognition of the interaction between a stressor and the family's response to that stressor in producing a state of disorganization. A major influence on both theory and research concerning family stress has been Hill's (1949) ABCX model, wherein a stressor event (A), a family's resources (B), and a family's definition of the situation (C) converge to produce a crisis (X). Subsequent elaborations of this model by Burr (1973); Burry, Leigh, Day, & Constantine, 1979), Hansen (1965; Hansen & Johnson, 1979; Hill & Hansen, 1964), and McCubbin *et al.* (1980) have distinguished between a family's vulnerability to stress (variation in ability to prevent a stressor event from creating a crisis in the family system; see Burr, 1973, pp. 201–202) and its regenerative power (the ability to recover from a crisis; see Hansen, 1965; Hansen and Hill, 1964). The work of Elder (1974) underscores the significance of subjective perspectives in his definition of a family crisis: "the problematic disparity between the claims of a family in a situation and its control of outcomes. Crisis may thus arise when claims are elevated well beyond control potential and realities, or when changes in the situation markedly diminish control of outcomes" (p. 10).

Whether seen as subjective or objective, stressors typically have been treated as occurring within a bounded period of time. What has been absent from most studies of families facing stress is attention to the disruptive effects of the ongoing strains, as opposed to discrete events, that are in fact endemnic to much of family life. For example, Koos (1946), in his study of low-income families in trouble, defined "trouble" as "situations outside the normal pattern of life" (p. 9), as opposed to day-to-day exigencies. Yet it can be argued that enduring life strains, what Goode (1960) described as the "felt difficulty in fulfilling role obligations" (p. 483) are equally if not more deleterious for families than are short-term, isolated events.

From a role-strain perspective, for example, it would be not only the transition to parenthood that is seen as potentially disruptive or stressful but the experience of parenthood itself. Conditions such as single-parent status, low-income, multiple earners, and the handicap or disability of a family member are best dealt with by a model of chronic role strain. The definition of a stressor has to be expanded to include the presence of continuous problems, which in turn can be subdivided into role conflicts (discrepant or inconsistent obligations) and role overloads (excessive demands).

An elaboration of the stress model that would include enduring life strains is particularly salient for emerging research issues such as living in blended families following remarriage or managing work–family role conflicts, which are neither of limited duration nor easily resolved. In fact, it is in the resolution of persistent adversity in the form of chronic strains that the concepts appropriate for an events model cease to apply. For example, families are realistically more likely to learn to accommodate to chronic life strains than to resolve them.

Important, from a temporal perspective, is the relationship between changes in life circumstances (stressor events) and enduring problematic experiences (ongoing strains), as well as the relative significance of each for family functioning, both short and long term. Such concerns point to the need for viewing the experience of and response to stress as a process, involving a series of events, strains, and adaptations. The work of Leonard Pearlin and his collaborators (1983; Pearlin & Lieberman, 1977; Pearlin, Lieberman, Menaghan, & Mullen, 1981) has done much to trace out this process of stress, unraveling the links between stressful life events, chronic role strains, and coping resources. In addition, Pearlin has made a major contribution to our understanding of the ways in which the resources of social support serve to mitigate the deleterious effects of adverse circumstances, underscoring the importance of the self-concept as a moderating factor.

Focusing on the stress process requires one to adopt a "branching tree" model of inquiry (see Aldous, 1978; Elder, 1974). Rather than starting with an outcome variable, one begins with a situation, such as a stressful event, and traces its several consequences for families. Similarly, Bronfenbrenner (1979) conceptualizes human development within an ecological framework. This approach invites the analysis of stress or events that occur at various levels. The implications of a particular event for various systems—the family or the workplace, for example, or society at large—can and should be appraised, as well as the impacts on the developing person. The branching tree model and the ecological framework sensitize the researcher both to multiple effects and to various sequences of events over time, for a particular family as well as for a given cohort of families.

TIME AND THE STRESS PROCESS

What is the significance of time in the conceptualization of families under stress? Hansen and Johnson (1979) have noted the general neglect of temporal issues in studies of family stress, while at the same time asserting the importance of such issues. We have suggested that looking at the temporal aspects of stress encourages a view of stress as a process rather than as a discrete experience. Major life changes in the form of stress-provoking events and conditions, can have pervasive effects, touching every aspect of family functioning. Moreover, the experience of a crisis event or prolonged life strains can have persistent and long-term consequences, not only for those experiencing them, but for their offspring as well. Adversity, such as economic misfortune and the ensuing adaptations to it, can become a legacy for members of the next generation, structuring, in turn, their options and resources for dealing with adversity, as well as altering the very shape of their lives.

We believe, therefore, that it is more productive analytically to deal with the *patterning* of stressors and family responses to them than with the occurrence of stress at any one point in time. Focusing on stress as a process highlights the significance of time and timing. When an event or life strain occurs, whether in terms of an individual's lifetime or a family's life cycle, can have important repercussions in the form and severity of its effects. The timing of stressful conditions colors virtually every aspect of the stress process.

To guide the discussion of the significance of time, we will use the process model presented in Figure 6-1. This model as it relates to economic loss has been discussed elsewhere (see Moen, Kain, & Elder, 1983). Here we concentrate on its temporal dimensions.

Stressful Circumstances

The likelihood and duration of individual family exposure to particular stressors are contingent on cohort, age, and life-cycle stage considerations. Cultural, political, and economic forces, in particular historical periods, render some aspects of family life more or less problematic. For example, during times of recession, the probability of unemployment and financial loss is greatly increased, resulting in intercohort differences in the economic situation of families. However, even within the same historical period, there are differences among families, depending on the ages of their members and stage of the family life cycle, as well as the educational background and work experience of those in the labor force. This is especially true for the character of the family economy, which fluctuates over time.

During the late 19th and early 20th centuries, a series of socioeconomic studies constructed a portrait of family dynamics in which economic level and need fulfillment varied in a systematic manner from marriage to old age according to household size and composition (Rubinow, 1916). The laboring man and his family were commonly lodged in a poverty cycle. Relative well-being occurred between marriage and the birth of the first child, a period during which the domestic unit had one or two earners. Hard times arrived with the birth of children as the loss of the wife's wages and the increased consumption needs pressed available income. Conditions improved as the children reached the age of employability and wives reentered the labor market. However, a sharp economic decline typically ensued after the children

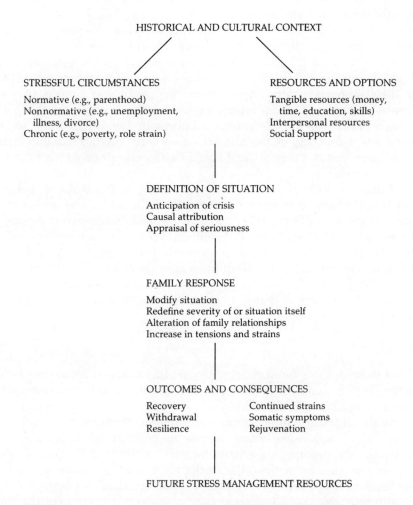

Figure 6-1. Dynamic model relating family adaptations to stress.

left home with their earnings, often plunging the couple back into poverty. Widowhood, of course, intensified this economic deprivation in old age.

An important, but generally disregarded, fact is that economic well-being fluctuates across the life cycle of working-class families and does so primarily in relation to change in family composition. This has significant implications regarding the movement of families into and out of poverty. The membership of the poverty class is not stable, but includes different family units from year to year. A recent nationwide panel study (Duncan, 1984) has illustrated convincingly the variations in economic hardship over time. In reviewing a 10-year period (1969–1978), the study found a surprisingly high proportion of families in poverty during at least one year. In fact, approximately 25% of the general population lived in families with incomes below the poverty line in one or more of the 10 years under study. However, less than 3% were poor for 5 years in a row. Family compositional change—divorce, death, launching a child from the home—were closely linked to changes in their economic status. Apart from the peaks and troughs of the national economy, families experience good times as well as hardship at various periods of the life course. Changes in family economic well-being are a function of the number of earners within a family, their wage rates and the number and ages of children, all of which tend to vary over time.

From the early studies of Rowntree (1901) to the work of Aldous and Hill (1969) to contemporary research on the life course during the Great Depression (Elder, 1974, 1981), it has been confirmed that families as well as individuals are differentially vulnerable to stressful conditions at different times. Adverse economic events tend to be concentrated in the first half of the adult life course (Moen, 1979, 1980; Pearlin et al., 1981), yet it is also clear that most families do not remain static, but move in and out of economic hardship as both external and internal circumstances change.

Resources

What individuals or families bring to stressful situations determines how these affect the family as a whole, as well as individual family members. Adverse conditions occur within a particular context and may have markedly different consequences for families differing in structure, composition, and career stage. A case in point is the importance of enduring relationships in the early stages of a child's development; the presence or absence of these ties in the early years can have enormous implications that extend well beyond childhood (Bronfenbrenner, 1979). Family resources, both economic and interpersonal, vary over the life cycle. Hence, the timing of adversity may be a major determinant of both its severity and the nature of the family's response to it, given the presence or absence of various options and resources. Consider, in this regard, that young parents have less ability to obtain credit and defer payments than do older couples (Elder, 1981) and are thus less equipped to cope with a spell of economic hardship. Similarly, faced with child-care responsibilities, young couples may find that having two earners results in chronic role overload, a situation less straining for those without children.

Cultural definitions and socially structured options, both historically grounded, are also important in establishing the implications of stress for families, since they affect the resources and hence the adaptive strategies available to them. For example, economic hardship in a period such as the 1930s when deprivation was commonplace is interpreted differently than loss in a period of relative prosperity. Notwithstanding the fact that in the 1980s there exist more supports than were available to families during the years of the Great Depression, family resources and options are constrained by a political climate that limits public support for families experiencing deprivation. Moreover, the stress of unemployment in the 1980s differs from that of the 1930s insofar as family labor reserves have changed. In the 1930s, a wife could often secure employment that enabled the family to weather financial hardship. In the 1980s, on the other hand, two salaries are increasingly necessary to maintain an adequate standard of living, making the wife's employment mandatory even under relatively stable economic conditions. Wives and mothers, therefore, are less likely to be a "reserve army of the unemployed" who can enter the labor force when their families face hard times.

Societal definitions of problems at different historical periods also affect the type of help families seek. For example, societal views about alcoholism and family violence have shifted markedly over the past several decades, such that these are topics that can now be discussed openly and for which formal social services are presently available. These problems are today generally defined as family-level rather than individual troubles.

The Definition of the Situation

Elder's (1974) specification of a crisis as the discrepancy between claims and control in a particular context emphasizes the subjective appraisal of the situation. Whether family members perceive an imbalance between the demands made of them and their ability to meet these demands depends both on the nature of the situation and the sources and options that are available to them. We have already shown that both the likelihood of stressful conditions and the availability of resources vary as a function of historical time as well as by age and life-cycle stage. It follows, therefore, that the subjective definition of the situation should also vary over time.

From a historical perspective, it is clear that the meaning of an event or condition is contingent on its context. For example, divorce in the early part of this century had a different connotation than does divorce in the 1980s, when it is a relatively commonplace event. Certainly the acceptability of maternal employment has been reassessed by both society and individual families with the increased labor-force participation over the last 30 years of mothers of young children.

The definition of the situation is also related to normative expectations. Some family transitions—getting married or having children, for example—carry no stigma and are not usually defined as problematic. In fact, Pearlin (1980) found that, with the exception of widowhood, key transitional events brought about little or no emotional distress. Again, however, the timing of the events is relevant to appraising them subjectively. Having a child out of wedlock, for example, changes the meaning of the transition to parenthood, and hence its consequences.

A significant consideration in defining adversity is the level of ambiguity experienced. Hansen and Johnson (1979) suggest that uncertainties accompanying a change are a major factor in the disruptive nature of the change, maintaining that the length of time a stressful event is anticipated is related negatively to the severity of its effects. However, this relationship may well depend on whether the period of anticipation serves to reduce or increase feelings of ambiguity.

For some, the very prospect of a change can create feelings of tension and strain. Rainwater (1974) underscores the importance of expectations in affecting the behavior and outlook of individuals, arguing that the amount of money one has at a particular moment is not nearly so critical as the "stream of resources that he has good reason to believe will be available to him in the future" (p. 36). Cobb and Kasl, in their study of plant closings (1977), found that one of the most distressing times was the period during which men *anticipated* eventual termination. Distress was exacerbated by the fact that employment assistance was made conditional on actual job loss; neither employment agencies nor federal retraining programs would provide support until the men had received their "pink slips."

Families possess both a history and, however ambiguous, an expectation regarding the future, both of which color perceptions of present conditions. Hansen and Johnson (1979) offer an interesting elaboration of Mead's (1932) concept of emergence, suggesting that present stressful situations can be related to both the past and the future, thereby providing a sense of continuity. However, when present circumstances are too disjunctive, a reinterpretation takes place, not only of the present but of the past and the future as well.

Both objective conditions and the resources and predispositions brought to these conditions influence perceptions of the situation. In line with Hill's (1949) ABCX model, all three sets of factors—the situation, the family's resources, and the definition of the situation—structure the family's adaptations to stress, and all three are contingent on historical period, cohort, age, and life-cycle stage.

Family Response

Families respond to stressful conditions by restructuring roles and resources, as well as by reappraising both the present situation and the prospects for the future. For example, families may respond to economic loss by altering the family economy, modifying family relationships, or by increasing the strains and tensions felt by individual family members. Some of these responses are adaptive coping strategies, while others, such as violence or drinking, may release pressure without ameliorating the situation. Pearlin and Schooler (1978) define coping as "any response to external lifestrains that serves to prevent, avoid, or control emotional distress" (p. 2). Coping behavior, they suggest, can take three forms: (1) eliminating or modifying problematic conditions, (2) reducing or controlling the meaning of those conditions, or (3) managing suffering or other emotional consequences. Changing the family economy can be viewed as an effort to eliminate or modify the problem of economic hardship. Altering family relationships can serve to control the effects of economic loss or manage their emotional consequences.

Family adaptations to stressful situations reflect a series of strategies, a process rather than a simple event. Different adaptations are used over time, as illustrated by Bakke's (1940) study of the responses of families during the Great Depression. The combination of adaptive strategies employed by families represents the process by which the family unit attempts to regain control over desired outcomes. The match between resources and claims is thrown out of balance by stressful events; it is through a series of adaptations that families recover a condition of equilibrium.

There are generally three forms of adaptation open to families under stress: alterations in family activities, changes in family relationships, and changes in the level of tensions and strains experienced by individual family members. The strategies adopted depend on the age of various family members, as well as on the stage of the family life cycle. For example, whether or not a wife moves into the labor force following the disablement of her husband depends upon her age as well as the number and ages of her children.

The kinds of adaptation employed by a family are patterned by historically structured options as well as by the family's stage and resources when the stressful circumstance arises. For example, in looking at responses to economic dislocation, one must situate the family in terms of historical time and consider how social trends and forces structure the options and choices available for family action (Elder, 1981; Sorokin & Merton, 1937). A case in point is the fact that today's child labor laws severely restrict employing children as a response to economic adversity.

In considering the family's adaptive response, Hill's (1949) "roller coaster" model posits a period of disorganization and reorganization. The fewer the family resources the longer the expected period of recovery. Basic to this conceptualization is a view of the family as returning to a state of normalcy, although it is equally applicable to families that move to a new state of organization, possibly involving changes in both family form and family functioning. This is in fact one means by which social change can been seen as operating through the changes in the lives of myriads of individuals. The Great Depression, the Second World War, Vietnam—each could serve to change the course of individual and family lives through time. As Elder (1978) points out, "The family represents a medium through which historical change leaves its imprint on the next generation" (p. 27). Hansen and Johnson (1979) acknowledge that vulnerability to stress and regeneration are separated primarily by time; both relate to disorganization, but at different periods in the stress process.

Outcomes

Adaptive strategies are the mechanisms that families use to regain control over desired outcomes in the face of either stressful life events or enduring life strains. It is important to remember that family response to a stress is a process, with different adaptations being played out over time as family circumstances themselves change. McCubbin and colleagues (1980) address this issue when they examine the "piling up" of adverse circumstances.

The decisions families make in the face of adversity can have both temporary and enduring repercussions. Strategies beneficial to the family as a whole may have far-ranging implications for particular family members. Responding to economic hardship, for example, with a more labor intensive household has enormous implications for the lives of women, as does the decision of a wife to enter the labor force (Bennett & Elder, 1979).

Strategies to regain control of a crisis situation or simply to manage a situation of prolonged role strain vary according to the timing of the experience in the lives of individual family members and in terms of the stage of the family life cycle. An example of this is the fact that families in the early years of household formation may have few existing financial resources to draw upon, while older families usually have established a savings reserve and also may more easily obtain loans and credit if needed.

The adaptive response (or responses) of families may be seen as mediating linkages between stressful conditions and their consequences for individual family members, as well as for the family as a whole. Some effects are direct and straightforward: For instance, a decline in family income and corresponding reductions in consumer expenditures can lead to a decline in the quality of life for all family members. Other repercussions of adversity are much less direct, a function of the household adaptations made in the face of the stressful circumstance. Elder (1974) has shown that families respond to economic distress in terms of immediate needs, with an eye toward specific and short-range consequences. Parental decisions concerning the family economy are made with a view to immediate economic survival, with little attention given to long-range implications for the children in the family. However, what seems beneficial in the short-run may have negative implications for the family's future way of life. For example, a range of financial strategies, from depleting savings to spiraling indebtedness, can, in effect, mortgage the family's financial future. Postponing the birth of a second child may effectively counteract some of the impact of economic loss, but also may prove to be the decisive act in forever remaining a one-child family (Elder, 1981).

It is important to recognize as well that the impact of particular stressors will be different depending upon the age of individuals within the family. The future fertility behavior of a daughter, for example, could be very different if the economic loss experienced by her family occurred when she was in her early teens rather than when she was at the eve of marriageable age. Elder's (1974) Oakland study of children in their early teens during the Great Depression found few adverse psychological impacts, but his study (Elder, 1979) of Berkeley children who were much younger during the 1930s revealed that those in families suffering economic loss evidenced a lack of self-esteem, assertiveness, and self-direction in adolescence. The long-range consequences of stressful circumstances for the lives of children cannot be estimated without taking into account subsequent events. For example, the impacts of the Great Depression on the adult lives of men and women who were children during the 1930s were contingent on their life patterns in early adulthood (Elder, 1979; Elder, Liker, & Jaworski, 1984).

The analytic framework utilized here argues for an interpretation of the relationship between stressful conditions and family and individual outcomes as a process. This process is governed by the expectations and options brought to the situation, the degree and type of stressful circumstance, and timing in the lives of both parents and children. To understand the impact of either discrete life changes or enduring strains also requires understanding the modes of adaptation played out over time.

EMERGING DIRECTIONS FOR RESEARCH

Sensitivity to the concepts of time as manifested in cohort, historical period, age, and life-cycle stage has obvious research implications. We shall here touch on some of the more promising areas for study.

Historical Change and Stress

History has been too long absent from studies of families under stress. Therefore, examining the links between historical change and family experience needs a prominent place on the research agenda of family scholars. For example, the historical period in which a family lives determines the likelihood of exposure to particular stressful events. Macro level stressors such as economic recession or war profoundly affect the family system; yet, too often these contextual circumstances have been ignored.

Historical time also enters into the definition of the situation by the family as well as the larger society. Public attitudes toward a number of social problems, such as mental illness, sexual assault, and alcoholism, have shifted markedly over time. There are three ways in which historically structured definitions bear on family adaptations to stress:

(1) *The definition by the family and by society of the magnitude or severity of a particular crisis.* Within limits, crises that society labels as severe can be expected to be met with counterpart increases in social support, yet these labels obviously alter over time. Witness the alterations in perceptions of sexual abuse in recent years, for example.

(2) *The options for response to stress.* If a family is limited to a few socially accepted responses, it is likely to experience still more stress. For example, in the case of marital discord, if support is not at hand, then the severity of any marital problem increases due to the lack of options to cope with it.

(3) *Attributing blame.* If an individual family member or family unit is faulted for experiencing a particular problem, the blame itself will be additionally stressful. Juvenile delinquency, sexual assault victimization, and alcoholism are examples of family crises for which blame is often assigned to the individual family member and the family as a whole, creating still another stressor with which to cope.

The relationship between the macro system (in terms of cultural values and definitions) and the family micro system is an arena well worth investigating (see Bronfenbrenner, 1979). Historically grounded contingencies reinforce the importance of examining cohort differences in how stressful circumstances are experienced, interpreted, and dealt with in families.

The Interplay between Life-Cycle Stage, Age, and Historical Period

There is an important intersection between historical contingencies and the family life cycle. Demographic data reveal striking differences in modal years for first marriage, first child, and the other stages of the cycle at various historical periods. Thus the ages at which family transitions occur have changed over time, sometimes cyclically, producing curves that look unique at different periods. Patterns of child spacing and the number of children similarly have varied, also affecting these curves. Thus, while the family life-cycle *concept* is useful at all historical periods, its variations and specifications at a given historical point in time need to be noted by researchers. The life-course perspective has recognized these variations for the individual; similar analyses can be accomplished for the family unit itself.

The Patterning of Stress over the Life Course of Families and Individuals

Normative crises are endemic to family development through the life cycle, as roles are dropped and added and power balances realigned. If a family is not "on time" in its passage through expected transitions, it may experience additional stress. For example, a couple that marries and has children considerably later than average begins the family life-cycle pattern at a different biological age than most of their cohort. As a consequence, they may have fewer informal or even formal social supports for their role transitions than do their age peers.

Nonnormative stress, or unanticipated crises, may conjoin with other more predictable stressors at various stages of the life cycle. A family with teenagers may anticipate some stressful events but cannot easily prepare for happenstance. Teenagers are statistically more vulnerable to auto accidents, suicide, and sexual assaults than other age groups, and these tragedies, linked to biological age, might arise in conjunction with other, normative stressors. Events outside the family, such as economic recessions and natural disasters, can similarly compound a family's problems. In short, the manner in which historical time and biological age interact to exacerbate life-cycle related stress deserves research attention, as does the interplay between events in the life course of families and individuals.

Ongoing Strains

Chronic stressors, such as the presence of a severely handicapped family member or one with a terminal illness, generally are harder to assess than the more striking disjunctive events such as divorce or unemployment. It is precisely for that reason that they should occupy a central position in research on families under stress in the 1980s. On the one hand, we could hypothesize that over time a family might make routine the stress and develop more family cohesiveness in the face of its constant difficulty. On the other hand, there is also the possibility that the pressure the family feels will manifest itself in various forms of dysfunction and disorganization. McCubbin (1979) incorporated coping skills and community support systems into the resources a family has available to mediate stress. Historical time may influence these tangible supports as decisions are made to bolster the social service system to better meet the needs of families. For example, government policies have begun to help families with members suffering terminal illness through home hospice care, and to consider the need for tax relief to help care for handicapped and aged relatives, but such ongoing strains have not been studied sufficiently, much less viewed from the perspective of life-cycle stage, age, period, or cohort.

Other chronic stressors emanate from the way institutions and societies are structured. For example, many of the difficulties families face in managing work roles and family roles reflect the way industrialized nations typically define expectations for workers and parents (Moen, in press). An important research issue is the ways that chronic role strains are "built in" to certain situations, periods of life, or family forms.

Time and Family Readiness for Crisis

Families are not merely helpless victims of stress. Hill and others (see Klein & Hill, 1979) have identified some of the factors related to families' problem-solving effectiveness and ability to recover or regenerate after experiencing a crisis. There are, however, at least three time-related issues that require additional research attention:

(1) Do families increase their resiliency to crisis as a result of successful coping experiences?

(2) Is there a generalized skill of coping? That is, can families transfer effective problem-solving skills from one type of problem to another?

(3) Is there a different impact for a single (or similar) chronic stressor versus a number of different stressors?

In sum, time, like space, provides a matrix for analyzing the process of family stress management. Historical time influences the likelihood of certain nonnormative crises occurring and the patterning of normative crises. Societal definitions of the crisis and acceptable responses are couched in historical time. Social or family time helps explain the normative crises associated with the family life cycle. If a family, for some reason, is not synchronized with the modal life-cycle patterns, its members might experience reduced social supports and consequently more stress. The view of the family as an ongoing system sensitizes us to the effects of a series of crises over time. Families develop both effective and destructive coping styles that form the basis for their future stress management resources.

CONCLUSIONS

Exposure to stress is intrinsic to family life, with responses to both crisis events and enduring strains offering evidence of the resources and durability of the family as an ongoing system. For over 3 decades, Reuben Hill enriched the body of knowledge about stress management by families. Among his contributions are the family development approach and his ABCX theory as a fundamental analytic framework for studying stress. Unfortunately, these two key aspects of Hill's contribution to the field often have been portrayed as belonging to separate domains.

The additional work of Elder and others using the life-course perspective have built on Hill's foundation and made his conceptualizations on temporality and stress all the more valuable by bringing these two interests together and locating them within the context of social change. We have argued here for the importance of variables related to time and timing in understanding the genesis of stress and the process of stress management in families. What is required is the use of time, not as a metaphor, but as a push to a more dynamic perspective.

Both long- and short-range repercussions of stressful circumstances across lives as well as across generations should also be the focus of scholars concerned with stress over the life cycle. Long-term implications of economic downturns as well as adolescent pregnancy are currently being documented (Elder, Caspi, & Downey, 1986; Elder, Liker, & Cross, 1984; Elder, Liker, & Jaworski, 1984; Furstenberg *et al.*, 1987) but similar studies examining other family crises would make an important contribution.

Certain concepts that recur in the work of family scholars—such as process, system, transition, and career—have hinted at the significance of temporality for family life in general and for families under stress in particular. Attention is required to the variables that make operational various facets of temporality. Such variables, we have suggested, include age, historical period, and cohort, in addition to life-cycle stage. They are not to be found in our model of the stress process; rather, they permeate every phase of the model. Incorporating these factors into the design of research can serve to illuminate the similarities and differences across and within families as they confront and cope with the stressors of their lives.

REFERENCES

Aldous, J. (1967). Introduction. In J. Aldous & R. Hill (Eds.), *International Bibliography of Research in Marriage and the Family, 1900-1964* (pp. 3-13). Minneapolis: University of Minnesota Press.
Aldous, J. (1978). *Family careers: Developmental change in families.* New York: Wiley.
Aldous, J., & Hill, R. (1969). Breaking the poverty cycle: Strategic points for intervention. *Social Work, 144,* 3-12.
Bakke, E. W. (1940). *Citizens without work.* New Haven, CT: Yale University Press.
Bengtson, V. L., & Treas, J. (1980). The changing family context of mental health and aging. In J. E. Birren & B. Sloane (Eds.), *Handbook of mental health and aging* (pp. 400-428). Englewood Cliffs, NJ: Prentice-Hall.
Bennett, S., & Elder, G. H., Jr. (1979). Women's work in the family economy: A study of depression hardship in women's lives. *Journal of Family History, 4*(2), 153-176.
Bronfenbrenner, U. (1979). *The ecology of human development.* Cambridge, MA: Harvard University Press.
Burr, W. R. (1973). *Theory construction and the sociology of the family.* New York: Wiley.
Burr, W. R., Leigh, G. K., Day, D. R., & Constantine, J. (1979). Symbolic interaction and the family. In W. R. Burr, R. Hill, F. I. Nye, & I. L. Reiss (Eds.), *Contemporary theories about the family* (Vol. 2, pp. 42-111). New York: Free Press.
Cherlin, A. (1983). A sense of history: Recent research on aging and the family. In M. W. Riley, B. B. Hess, & K. Bond (Eds.), *Aging in society: Selected reviews of recent research* (pp. 5-23). Hillsdale, NY: Erlbaum.
Chudacoff, H. P. (1980). The life course of women: Age and age consciousness: 1865-1915. *Journal of Family History, 5,* 274-292.
Cobb, S., & Kasl, S. (1977). *Termination: The consequences of job loss* (Publication No. 72-299). Washington, DC: Department of Health, Education, and Welfare (National Institute of Occupational Safety and Health).
Cox, T. (1978). *Stress.* Baltimore, MD: University Park Press.
Croog, S. H. (1970). The family as a source of stress. In S. Levine & N. A. Scotch (Eds.), *Social stress* (pp. 19-25). Chicago: Aldine.
Dohrenwend, B. P., & Dohrenwend, B. S. (Eds.). (1977). *Stressful life events: Their nature and effects.* New York: Wiley.
Duncan, G. J. (1984). *Years of poverty, years of plenty: The changing economic fortunes of American workers and families.* Ann Arbor, MI: Institute for Social Research.
Elder, G. H., Jr. (1974). *Children of the Great Depression: Social change in life experience.* Chicago: University of Chicago Press.
Elder, G. H., Jr. (1975). Age differentiation and the life course. In A. Inkeles, J. Coleman & N. Smelser (Eds.), *Annual review of sociology* (Vol. 1, pp. 165-190). Palo Alto, CA: Annual Reviews.

Elder, G. H., Jr. (1978). Family history and the life course. In T. Hareven (Ed.), *Transitions: The family and the life course in historical perspective* (pp. 17–64). New York: Academic Press.

Elder, G. H., Jr. (1979). Historical changes in life patterns and prsonality. In P. B. Baltes & O. Brim, Jr. (Eds.), *Life-span development and behavior* (Vol. 2, pp. 117–159). New York: Academic Press.

Elder, G. H., Jr. (1981). History and the family: The discovery of complexity. *Journal of Marriage and the Family, 43,* 489–519.

Elder, G. H., Jr. (1984). Families, kin and the life course: A sociological perspective. In R. D. Parke (Ed.), *Review of child development research. Vol. 7: The family* (pp. 80–136). Chicago: University of Chicago Press.

Elder, G. H., Jr. (Ed.). (1985). *Life course dynamics: Trajectories and trasitions, 1968–1980.* Ithaca, NY: Cornell University Press.

Elder, G. H., Jr., Caspi, A., & Downey, G. (1986). Problem behavior and family relationships: Life course and intergenerational themes. In A. Sorensen, F. Weinert, & L. Sherrod (Eds.), *Human development and the life course: Multidisciplinary perspectives* (pp. 293–340). Hillsdale, NJ: Erlbaum.

Elder, G. H., Jr., Liker, J. K., & Cross, C. E. (1984). Parent–child behavior in the Great Depression: Life course and intergenerational influences. In P. B. Baltes & O. G. Brim, Jr. (Eds.), *Life-span development and behavior* (Vol. 6, pp. 109–157). New York: Academic Press.

Elder, G. H., Jr., Liker, J. K., & Jaworski, B. J. (1984). Hardship and lives: Historical influences from the 1930's to old age in postwar America. In K. McCluskey & H. Reese (Eds.), *Life-span developmental psychology: Historical and cohort effects* (pp. 161–201). New York: Academic Press.

Featherman, D. (1982). The life-span perspective in social science research. In National Science Foundation, *Five-year outlook on science and technology, 1981 source materials* (Vol. 2, pp. 621–648). Washington, DC: Superintendent of Documents.

Furstenberg, F. F., Jr., Brooks-Gunn, J., & Morgan, S. P. (1987). *Adolescent mothers in later life.* Cambridge, England: Cambridge University Press.

Goode, W. I. (1960). A theory of role strain. *American Sociological Review, 35,* 483–496.

Gove, W., Grimm, J. W., Motz, S. C., & Thompson, J. P. (1973). The family life cycle: Internal dynamics and social consequences. *Sociology and Social Research, 57,* 182–195.

Hagestad, G. O., & Neugarten, B. L. (1984). Age and the life course. In R. Binstock & E. Shanas (Eds.), *Handbook of aging and the social sciences* (2nd ed., pp. 35–61). New York: Van Nostrand Reinhold.

Hansen, D. A. (1965). Personal and positional influence in formal groups: Propositions and theory for research on family vulnerability to stress. *Social Forces, 44,* 202–210.

Hansen, D. A., & Johnson, V. A. (1979). Rethinking family stress theory: Definitional aspects. In W. R. Burr (Ed.), *Contemporary theories about the family* (Vol. 1, pp. 582–603). New York: Free Press.

Hareven, T. (1981). *Industrial time and family time.* New York: Cambridge University Press.

Hareven, T. (1984). Themes in the historical development of the family. In R. D. Parke (Ed.), *Review of child development research. Vol. 7: The Family* (pp. 137–178). Chicago: University of Chicago Press.

Hill, R. (1949). *Families under stress.* New York: Harper and Row.

Hill, R. (1964). Methodological issues in family development research. *Family Process, 3,* 186–206.

Hill, R. (1970). *Family development in three generations.* Cambridge, MA: Schenkman.

Hill, R. (1980). Status of research on families. In U. S. Department of Health and Human Services, *The status of children, youth and families, 1979*. Washington, DC: Government Printing Office.

Hill, R., & Hansen, D. (1964). Families under stress. In A. Christensen (Ed.), *Handbook of marriage and the family* (pp. 782–822). Chicago: Rand McNally.

Hill, R., & Mattessich, P. (1979). Family development theory and life-span development. In P. Baltes & O. Brim, Jr. (Eds.), *Life-span development and behavior* (Vol. 2). New York: Academic Press.

Hill, R., & Rodgers, R. (1964). The developmental approach. In H. T. Christensen (Ed.), *Handbook of marriage and the family* (pp. 171–214). Chicago: Rand McNally.

Hogan, D. P. (1978). The variable order of events in the life course. *American Sociological Review, 43*, 573–586.

Holmes, T. H. & Masuda, M. (1974). Life change and illness susceptibility. In B. Dohrewend & B. Dohrenwend (Eds.), *Stressful life events: Their nature and effects*. New York: Wiley.

Holmes, T. H., & Rahe, R. H. (1967). The social readjustment rating scale. *Journal of Psychosomatic Research, 11*, 213–218.

Jaccoby, A. P. (1969). Transition to parenthood: A reassessment. *Journal of Marriage and the Family, 31*, 720–727.

Kaplan, H. B. (Ed.). (1983). *Psychosocial stress: Trends in theory and research*. New York: Academic Press.

Klein, D. M. (1983). Family problem solving and family stress. In H. I. McCubbin, M. Sussman, & J. Patterson (Eds.), *Social stress and the family: Advances and developments in family stress theory and research* (pp. 85–112). New York: Haworth Press.

Klein, D. M., & Hill, R. (1979). Determinants of family problem solving effectiveness. In W. R. Burr, R. Hill, F. I. Nye, & I. L. Reiss (Eds.), *Contemporary theories about the family* (Vol. 1, pp. 493–548). New York: Free Press.

Koos, E. L. (1946). *Families in trouble*. New York: King & Crown.

Lansing, J. B., & Kish, L. (1957). Family life cycle as an independent variable. *American Sociological Review, 22*, 512–519.

Lazarus, R. (1977). Stress and coping. In A. Monat & R. Lazarus (Eds.), *Stress and coping*. New York: Columbia University Press.

Lowenthal, M., & Chiriboga, D. (1972). Transition to the empty nest: Crisis, challenge or relief? *Archives of General Psychology, 26*, 8–14.

McCubbin, H. (1979). Integrating coping behavior in family stress theory. *Journal of Marriage and the Family, 41*, 237–244.

McCubbin, H., Joy, C., Cauble, A., Comeau, J., Patterson, J., & Needle, R. (1980). Family stress and coping: A decade review. *Journal of Marriage and the Family, 42*, 855–871.

Mead, G. H. (1932). *Philosophy of the present*. Chicago: University of Chicago Press.

Miller, B. C. (1976). A multivariate developmental model of marital satisfaction. *Journal of Marriage and the Family, 38*, 643–657.

Modell, J., Furstenberg, F. F., Jr., & Hershberg, T. (1976). Social change and transitions to adulthood in historical perspective. *Journal of Family History, 1*, 7–32.

Moen, P. (1979). Family impacts of the 1975 recession: Duration of unemployment. *Journal of Marriage and the Family, 4*, 561–572.

Moen, P. (1980). Developing family indicators: Financial hardship, a case in point. *Journal of Family Issues, 1(3)*, 5–30.

Moen, P. (1982). The two-provider family. In M. E. Lamb (Ed.), *Nontraditional families: Parenting and child development* (pp. 13–43). Hillsdale, NJ: Erlbaum.

Moen, P. (1985). Continuities and discontinuities in women's labor force activity. In G. H. Elder, Jr. (Ed.), *Life course dynamics: Trajectories and transitions, 1968–1980* (pp. 113–155). Ithaca, NY: Cornell University Press.

Moen, P. (in press). *Parallel roles: Working parents and well-being.* Madison, WI: University of Wisconsin Press.

Moen, P., Kain, E., & Elder, G. H., Jr. (1983). Economic conditions and family life: Contemporary and historical perspectives. In R. Nelson (Ed.), *The high costs of living: Economic and demographic conditions of American families* (pp. 213–259). Washington, DC: National Academy of Sciences.

Moen, P., & Moorehouse, M. (1983). Overtime over the life cycle: A test of the life cycle squeeze hypothesis. In J. H. Pleck & H. Z. Lopata (Eds.), *Research in the interweave of social roles: Volume 3. Families and jobs* (pp. 201–218). Greenwich, CT: JAI Press.

Monat, A., & Lazarus R. (Eds.). (1977). *Stress and coping.* New York: Columbia University Press.

Oppenheimer, V. K. (1974). The life-cycle squeeze: Interaction of men's occupational and family life cycles. *Demography, 11,* 227–245.

Pearlin, L. I. (1980). The life cycle and life strains. In H. M. Blalock (Ed.), *Sociological theory and research: A critical appraisal.* New York: Free Press.

Pearlin, L. I. (1983). Role strains and personal stress. In H. B. Kaplan (Ed.), *Psychosocial stress: Trends in theory and research* (pp. 3–32). New York: Academic Press.

Pearlin, L. I., & Lieberman, M. A. (1977). Social sources of emotional distress. In R. G. Simmons (Ed.), *Research in community and mental health* (pp. 217–248). Greenwich, CT: JAI Press.

Pearlin, L. I., Lieberman, M. A., Menaghan, E. G., & Mullen, J. T. (1981). The stress process. *Journal of Health and Social Behavior, 22,* 337–356.

Pearlin, L. I., & Schooler, C. (1978). The structure of coping. *Journal of Health and Social Behavior, 19,* 2–21.

Rainwater, L. (1974). Work, well-being and family life. In J. O'Toole (Ed.), *Work and the quality of life* (pp. 361–378). Cambridge, MA: MIT Press.

Rapoport, R., & Rapoport, R. (1975). The dual career family: A variant pattern and social change. *Human Relations, 22,* 3–13.

Rausch, R., Goodrich, W., & Campbell, J. D. (1963). Adaptation to the first years of marriage. *Psychiatry, 26,* 265–280.

Riley, M. W. (1987). On the significance of age in sociology. *American Sociological Review, 52,* 1–14.

Riley, M. W., Johnson, M. E., & Foner, A. (Eds.), (1972). *Aging and society: A sociology of age stratification* (Vol. 3). New York: Sage.

Rodgers, R. H. (1973). *The developmental approach.* Englewood Cliffs, NJ: Prentice-Hall.

Rollins, B. C., & Cannon, K. L. (1974). Marital satisfaction over the family life cycle: A re-evaluation. *Journal of Marriage and the Family, 36,* 271–282.

Rollins, B. C., & Feldman, H. (1970). Marital satisfaction over the family life cycle. *Journal of Marriage and the Family, 32,* 20–28.

Rossi, A. (1968). Transition to parenthood. *Journal of Marriage and the Family, 30,* 26–39.

Rowntree, B. S. (1901). *Poverty: A study of town life.* London: MacMillan.

Ryder, N. (1965). The cohort as a concept in thestudy of social change. *American Sociological Review, 30,* 843–861.

Schorr, A. L. (1966). The family cycle and income development. *Social Security Bulletin, 29,* 14–25.

Sorokin, P. A., & Merton, R. K. (1937). Social time: A methodological and functional analysis. *American Journal of Sociology, 5,* 615–629.

Spanier, G. B., Lewis, R. A., & Cole, C. C. (1975). Marital adjustment over the family live cycle: The issue of curvilinearity. *Journal of Marriage and the Family, 37,* 263–275.

Thomas, W. I., & Znanecki, F. (1918). *The Polish peasant in Europe and Amerca* (2 Vols). Chicago: University of Chicago Press.

Uhlenberg, P. (1980). Death and the family. *Journal of Family History*, 5, 313–320.

Waite, L. J., & Stoltzenberg, R. M. (1976). Intended childbearing and labor force participation of young women: Insights from nonrecursive models. *American Sociological Review, 41*, 235–52.

Waite, L. J., & Stoltzenberg, R. M. (1980). Working wives and the family life cycle. *American Journal of Sociology, 86*, 272–294.

7

The Timing of Military Service in Men's Lives

GLEN H. ELDER, JR.
SUSAN L. BAILEY
The University of North Carolina at Chapel Hill

Successive cohorts of American men have been marked by recurring periods of war mobilization in the 20th century. More than two thirds of all American men with birth dates in the 1920s served on active duty for at least 6 months, and an unknown number of these men saw their sons and daughters enter the armed forces during the Vietnam Era of the 1960s and 1970s. Considering the prominence of military times, it is surprising how little we know about the long-term influence of such transitions on the life course of individuals, families, or cohorts. This is especially true of the enduring personal consequences of military duty in World War II.

More is known about the short-term effects of such duty, as reported in *The American Soldier* (Stouffer *et al.*, 1949, Vols. I & II; see also Clausen, 1984) and in Reuben Hill's *Families Under Stress* (1949), a pioneering study of family adaptations to the departure of men for military duty in World War II and to their return several years later as veterans. Hill observed different adjustment processes in the two transitions, though both fit a general model of adaptation, called ABCX. Factor A refers to the event that, when combined with related hardships, interacts with family resources, Factor B. Family definitions of the situation (C) emerge from the interaction of Factors A and B, thereby producing a crisis (X). The basic theme of Hill's study is that families change through adaptation to the individual changes of members, in this case, the husband/father's transition into and out of the armed forces.

This chapter builds upon Hill's initial study by focusing on the way in which military transitions bear upon the life course and family

This study is based on a program of research on social change in the family and life course. Support from the National Institute of Mental Health (Grant MH-40556) is gratefully acknowledged (Glen H. Elder, Jr., principal investigator). The senior author was supported by a Guggenheim Fellowship during the completion of this research. We are indebted to the Institute of Human Development at the University of California, Berkeley, for permission to use the Oakland Growth data.

157

experience of men who served in World War II. The transitions refer to entry into the service and to the process of discharge. Judging from research to date, these transitions have implications for the paths men follow to adulthood, for their educational and occupational careers, and for their marital and parent–child relations. In the literature, military service represents a source of delayed career beginnings and nonnormative sequence (Hogan, 1981), a path to greater opportunities for the disadvantaged (Sharp, 1970), a potential destabilizing force in marriages (n.b., the rising divorce rate after wars), and a source of strain between the generations (Stolz, 1954). This strain has special relevance to veterans who experienced the popular success of World War II (Stouffer *et al.*, 1949, Vol. 1), and then confronted the antimilitary sentiments of their offspring and their offspring's age-mates in the 1960s. Overall the analysis reflects the life-course premise that historical events and transitions such as economic depressions and wars influence family patterns directly as well as indirectly through the personalities and lives of individuals such as the veterans of wars.

MILITARY EXPERIENCE IN THE OAKLAND COHORT

The men in this research are members of the longitudinal Oakland Growth Study which has been directed over the years by the Institute of Human Development at the University of California at Berkeley. Data collection began in the early 1930s and continues up to the present. The men grew up in the northeastern section of Oakland, California, and completed high school (circa 1939) just before the outbreak of war in Europe. Half came from middle-class families in the 1920s, and most were Protestant. Sixty-nine of the men were contacted, interviewed, and tested in adulthood by the age of 40, and thus represent the primary sample in our analysis. As described in *Children of the Great Depression* (Elder, 1974), a large number of the men encountered severe family hardships along with an ethos of social reform and pacifism by the end of the 1930s. Only one quarter of a million American men were on active military duty in 1935. This number rose to over 12 million by the end of World War II.

A sense of optimism concerning the future as well as a sentiment of pacifism were commonplace among the Oakland youth at the end of 1938. "Nearly three fourths of the boys felt that the Depression, as they had experienced it, was over" (Elder, 1974, p. 154). About 40% claimed that the country should "never go to war under any circumstance," though half acknowledged that "military preparedness is one of the best ways to prevent war" (p. 154). Within the short span of 5 additional years, nine out of ten of the Oakland boys found themselves in the armed forces. Equal numbers were in the army and navy (a total of

85%), with the remainder divided between the Marines, Air Force, and Coast Guard. The participation rate in the Oakland sample may seem high relative to the nationwide rate of 75%, but it is not an unusual rate for the Bay area, a region profoundly influenced by the war effort. This area was part of the Western military zone and functioned as a major point of embarkation for the Pacific theatre. Seven major shipyards dotted the shore of San Francisco Bay.

With military service a near universal event in the lives of the Oakland men, our attention focused on the *timing* of this experience in their life course. We begin with military service as a pathway out of the depressed 1930s, and then investigate the timing of education completion, first marriage, and first child in relation to the timing of military service and the factors affecting such timing. These events represent key markers of the transition to adulthood. If military service comes relatively early in the life course, such as before the age of 22 or so, it is less likely to scramble the usual order of life transitions? This usual order places full-time employment before marriage and first child. In the last section we trace the timing of military service to formal education and occupational achievement, and to marital stability and satisfactions.

FROM HARD TIMES TO WARTIME: PATHWAYS TO ADULTHOOD

The Oakland youth left high school just 3 months before the outbreak of war in Europe, September 1939. At the time, war mobilization was spurring economic recovery from the stagnation of the Depression era and generating new opportunities among the young. After years of privation, the change was dramatic, much "like watching blood drain back into the blanched face of a person who had fainted" (Mitchell, 1947, p. 371). The economic stimulus of mounting war pressures put an end to the Great Depression, but such could not erase the effects of the Depression on men who grew up in the hard-pressed families of the 1930s. Were these men more disadvantaged than other men through loss of educational opportunity and support, through an erratic work life, or through impaired health and personality? As noted in an earlier work (Elder, 1974), our answer to this question is both yes and no. More importantly, a satisfactory answer forces a long overdue consideration of World War II and military service in the lives of these men.

With birthdates in the early 1920s, the Oakland boys were members of a prime cohort for military duty during the early 1940s. Their induction became more probable when the "draft" became law on the 16th of September 1940. Nearly all of the Oakland men were in uniform by the time of the Normandy invasion in June 1944, and few were discharged before a completed term of 3 years. The pervasive experience of military duty during World War II was noted in a study of these men as "children of the Great Depression" (Elder, 1974), but little was said or developed about its full implications.

Three implications for pathways to adulthood bear directly on the life chances of men who became veterans of both severe hard times and a world war. First, military service removed the Oakland men from the immediate influence and setting of home and community. In this sense, the transition represented a passage from family dependence to independence and even personal autonomy. This family separation had noteworthy implications for men who came from mother-dominated or discordant families, as did a good many Oakland men. A veteran described the time he joined the army as the beginning of an ability to stand on his own two feet. The discipline of military life may have coupled this newfound autonomy, with personal responsibility and a more mature capacity to cooperate with others.

A second implication involves the benefits of a psychosocial moratorium, a time free of decision pressures. From one perspective, among others, military service represents a moratorium relative to the age-graded career, a legitimate time-out from the commitment pressures that Erikson (1968) once described in the concept of role confusion. This concept of service time appears in the recollections of a veteran who grew up in the Bay area of California: "I don't know what I wanted, though I probably wanted to get away from home and community. I didn't know what I wanted to take in college. I recall arguing with myself about maybe I'd grow up and settle down a bit if I got into the service." Separation from home and community, along with the legitimate time-out of military duty, established a conducive environment for fresh starts and turning points.

The third implication involves the educational and vocational benefits of military service, both during the period of active duty and after returning to civilian life. The postwar benefits are most tangibly linked to the benefits of the Servicemen's Readjustment Act of 1944, the GI Bill (Olson, 1974). The final provisions of the education bill offered the veteran 1 year of schooling if service time at least equaled 90 days and if he entered the service before the age of 25. The veteran was also offered a block of higher education beyond the first year that would match his overall time of active duty. Thus a term of 2 years in the army provided a man with college for a year under the first part of the bill, and another 2 years under the second part—a total of 3 years. The act included a maximum of $500 per school year for all fees, tuition costs, books, and supplies, as well as a monthly subsistence allowance ($50 for single, $75 for married veterans).

The GI Bill is remembered for the educational opportunities it provided veterans, though its enactment was primarily motivated by a fear of the social and political danger of possible widespread unemployment among returning veterans. The war economy pulled the country out of the Depression and kept unemployment low. What would happen in a peacetime economy burdened by millions of returning veterans? In April 1942 Eleanor Roosevelt expressed the warning that veterans might become "a dangerous pressure group in our midst" (Olson, 1974, p. 21). The GI Bill was indeed, as Olson points out, a "child of 1944; it symbolized the mood of a country immersed in war, recalling the depression, and worrying about the future" (p. 24).

In various ways, all three of these implications of military service are at least partially rooted in the hardships of the Depression decade. Conditions that made leaving home especially urgent and compelling (e.g., family turmoil, the dominance and martyr role of mother) were products of unemployment and prolonged deprivation. A legitimate time-out from decision pressures in military service had particular value to youth who grew up in the unpromising and unstable era of the 1930s. Lastly, the political pressure to establish educational and housing benefits through the GI Bill was fueled by worrisome Depression memories of mass unemployment and unrest, and their implications for postwar society upon the mass return of America's fighting men. Estimates suggest that nearly half a million veterans took advantage of a college education who might not have done so without the GI Bill. Some of these men were members of the Oakland cohort.

A decade of hard times for a large percentage of the population gave unusual significance to options created by the World War II. Equally important for our purposes, one can assume that wartime experiences and outcomes altered the Depression's legacy in men's lives. Some appreciation of this influence can be gained by comparing the hardship experience itself with Depression effects or outcomes. Family income at the end of the 1920s averaged slightly more than $3,000 among the Oakland families. Three years later this figure had dropped below $2,000.

The psychological handicap of family hardship was relatively small at midlife and was concentrated in the lives of men from working-class families. Men from the deprived middle class actually ranked higher than other subgroups on "their ability to surmount difficulties, to profit from experiences, and to use talents to their fullest advantage" (Elder, 1974, p. 248). The experiences and adult accomplishments of these men suggest that "a childhood which shelters the young from the hardships of life consequently fails to test adaptive capacities which are called upon in life crises. To engage and manage real-life (though not excessive) problems in childhood and adolescence is to participate in a sort of apprenticeship for adult life" (Elder, 1974, p. 250). The psychological well-being of the Oakland men at midlife may also reflect some developmental advantages stemming from their experience in the Armed Forces during World War II.

Over half of the men actually completed 4 years of college, a remarkably high figure for any generation, but especially for one that grew up in the Great Depression (Elder, 1974, p. 160). Men from the working class were less apt to reach this level of educational achievement, but even in this stratum family deprivation did not markedly lessen chances for higher education. The same conclusion applies to the occupational achievements of the Oakland men. Approximately half were employed in professional/managerial jobs at the ages of 38 to 40. Depression hardship, therefore, does not appear to have impaired such life chances to any noteworthy degree.

California's educational policy and the postwar opportunities of economic growth and the GI Bill help to make sense of these life outcomes. The state offered all youth with a high school diploma an opportunity for higher education, a tuition-free place in an institution of higher learning. A second counter-influence to the Depression was the state's booming, full-employment economy of the postwar era, a time when "any lad who could breathe was able to find a decent job" (Elder, 1974, p. 156). Such opportunity was enhanced by the educational and housing benefits of the GI Bill, a set of benefits open to most Oakland men via their military service. From the evidence at hand, a vast majority of the Oakland veterans took advantage of the educational provisions of the GI Bill. Presumably military service also broadened the perspectives and aspirations of some men, spurring them on to higher education through use of the GI Bill.

Considering that over 90% of the Oakland men were veterans of World War II, it is not possible to document precisely the contribution of military service and the GI Bill to their education or worklife. We can, however, examine the life-span influence of the *timing* of military service from the standpoint of entry and departure. If, as much evidence suggests, the service offered life opportunities as well as masculine pursuits and models, then one might expect a link between the experience of disadvantage and the decision to join up early. Were the disadvantaged the early joiners? By occurring right in the middle of the transition to adult status, military service may have delayed some events, accelerated others, and disorganized the overall pattern. In the next section, we take up both of these problem areas, the antecedents of early entry into the military and its consequences for the timing of employment, education exit, first marriage, and the birth of the first child.

MILITARY TIMING AND LIFE-SHAPING CHOICES

Between graduation from high school and their mid-20s, American men generally commit themselves to a number of life-shaping choices. These include the decision to leave or extend formal education, to obtain full-time employment, to establish an independent household, to get married, and to start a family. Pearl Harbor profoundly disrupted this flow of events. Whether by conscription or choice, military recruitment pulled some men out of jobs and marriages and others out of schools. Within the short span of 2 years after Pearl Harbor, four out of five Oakland men were in uniform. The concentration of this event relative to other events is vividly shown in Figure 7.1. The bar graph marks the point at which 20 and 80% of the cohort experienced each transition.

Though military induction is commonly viewed as a disruption of the normative life course, its controlled, uniform timing for the Oakland men could operate to actually reduce life variation, especially among early events. With most of the Oakland men in the armed forces at the same point in time, would this not increase the temporal compression of their early events? We do not have a comparison group by which to answer this question, but it is apparent that the compressed entry of the Oakland men brought no corresponding effect to other transitions in the life course.

The short range of entry years raises some doubt about whether there is any meaningful difference between the early and late entrants.

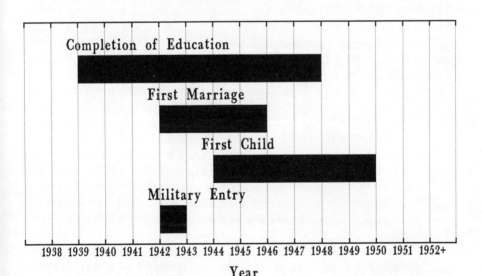

Figure 7-1. Spread of early life events for Oakland veterans (historical time between date at which 20 and 80% of men in cohort encountered event, rounded to year). (The standard of 20 and 80% cannot be determined for military timing because 78% of the Oakland males entered the service in 1942 and 1943.

Does time of entry actually matter for subsequent choices and outcomes in the life course? Moreover, are there life-history differences between men who entered early (with the first wave) and those who entered late, if they did so only a year later? From an opportunity standpoint, we have argued that early entrants are likely to include a disproportionate number of disadvantaged young men.

We considered four kinds of disadvantage. Depression hardship and misfortune is especially prominent for this generation, and we shall index it by a measure of relative income loss between 1929 and 1933. The economically deprived suffered a loss of income above 34%. The second form of disadvantage is socioeconomic standing, a social condition instead of a process. Family socioeconomic status in 1929 (Hollingshead's index) and the possible economic pressures of a large family serve as measures of this variable. The third dimension involves strained parent–child relations. This dimension is measured by the responses of Oakland men when asked about their closeness to and regard for parents in a follow-up carried out in the mid-1960s. Our treatment of disadvantage would be incomplete without school achievement and IQ, the fourth category or type. Were the less able boys with school difficulties more likely to join the Army or other services in World War II at the earliest moment, as compared to the more successful?

Apart from the attractions of military service among the disadvantaged, its appeal may also express personal values and experiences. The Oakland cohort was part of an age that valued pacifism, and a large number of the men expressed sentiments of this kind during the Depression years in high school. For example, two thirds of the cohort did not agree with the proposition that "all men above 18 should be required to take a certain amount of military training." The same proportion did not agree with support for military training in schools. More interesting and challenging than this view and its correspondence with ideologists at the time are the factors that account for military support. Were boys who expressed these views of support more apt to have fathers and relatives with some military training or experience? One of the Oakland men recalled that he was something of "a nut on World War I," owing partly to the military involvement of his father. "As a kid I drew a lot of war pictures and my dad took one to the VFW lodge. The picture was hanging there when I was 13."

The family influences that we have grouped under disadvantage are not related to the military attitudes of the Oakland men during their adolescence, and we have little more than anecdotal evidence concerning the military history of their families. Nevertheless it is clear that military support in the late 1930s was predictive of early entry into the armed forces among the Oakland men. Approximately 22 men were inducted before their 22nd birthday, and over half of them (53%)

voiced approval of the notion of universal military training in 1937–1938 (see Hollingshead, 1946). This compares to only a fourth of the men who entered later ($\chi^2 = 4.20$, $df = 1$, $p = .04$, $N = 55$). Support for military training in colleges and high schools produced a very similar result ($\chi^2 = 3.32$, $df = 1$, $p = .07$, $N = 55$). Both outcomes remain unchanged with adjustments for social class and high school grades.

Depression hardship was largely a memory when the Oakland cohort faced the imperative of service in the armed forces, and this background seems to have played no part at all in shaping the timing of their entry. Boys from privileged and deprived families were equally likely to be part of the first wave of servicemen. The significance of timing differences rests in large part on the assumption that choice is involved. However, we do not actually know whether the men were drafted, enlisted to avoid the draft, or simply volunteered. Nevertheless, the connection between military attitudes and time of entry suggest that the first wave includes a large number of enlistees.

This assumption also finds support in the link between family and personal disadvantage, on the one hand, and military entry, on the other. As predicted, early servicemen were more likely to come from large than from small families (44 vs. 31%). Family size was divided at the median in order to form the two groups. However, the disadvantage thesis does not hold up when we examine the results for social class as indexed by a 1929 Hollingshead measure. Men from the working class were actually *less* apt to enter early than were the sons of middle-class parents (21 vs. 44%); ($\chi^2 = 2.92$, $df = 1$, $p < .01$, $N = 60$). How can we explain this reversal?

One might expect middle-class boys to seek deferments in order to complete their college program before military duty, and yet they appear to have been more apt to enter the service at an early age. The picture begins to make greater sense when we examine the life circumstances of the two groups, middle and working class. Men from the working class were more likely to be employed than in college during the 1940s. Consequently, they were less available for the service at first, especially when working for war-related industries. By comparison, young men from the middle class were more apt to be in college than in the labor-force during the early 1940s.

The men who entered early were recruited disproportionately from the less able and less academically successful members of the cohort. For example, 46% of the men who ranked below average on high school grades were part of the first wave of servicemen, in comparison to only 32% of the more successful. The percentage differential was less pronounced on IQ scores, though in the same direction. The pattern of results on school achievement helps to bring some understanding to the class difference. The more accomplished males from the middle class tended to go on to higher education. As such, we find that they were much less likely to be early entrants than were men with less successful records in high school (33 vs. 62%). This interaction does not appear among men from working-class families, perhaps because higher education did not always represent a serious option for them.[1]

Does estrangement from parents or weak ties to family explain these results? Using midlife recollections of family relations in adolescence as well as contemporaneous reports, we find that men who entered the service in the first wave (before age 22) were more likely than late entrants to claim maternal dominance in their life, to describe parents as relatively uninterested in them, and to score high on rebelliousness. However, these differences are small and they are countered by substantial evidence that shows no difference on perceived family conflict, parent attractiveness, and parent reasonableness. All in all, it is clear that other modes of disadvantage are far more predictive of time of military entry among the Oakland men.

To sum up our results to this point, we find that the Oakland men who entered the armed forces before their 22nd birthday were distinguished from other veterans by their responsiveness to the opportunity they perceived in this service role. A small number of the early entrants joined up in response to a positive orientation toward the military, despite the pacifism of their generation. Other early entrants were distinguished by personal and family disadvantages that gave special value to the opportunities of military service. This group includes men from large families, the academically unsuccessful, and especially the low-achieving sons of middle-class families. Family patterns do not emerge as a powerful factor in shaping time of military induction.

With disadvantage (scholastic and a large family) as a distinctive feature of the life history of men who entered the service in the first wave, there is reason to expect differences in career beginnings between the two "entry" groups. Low achievement through high school suggests a relatively early termination of formal schooling, along with a corresponding pattern of early full-time employment, marriage, and childbearing. But in fact we observe no reliable difference between the timetables of early and late entrants on other events. Table 7-1 presents data on four event markers of the adult transition, in addition to the military transitions: work entry, education completion, marriage entry, and birth of first child. The later entrants generally had a full-time job, a wife, and a first child at a later age, on average, when compared to the men who joined the service before the age of 22, but these differences are too small to be reliable.[2]

In both groups, work entry generally occurred before military service. The early servicemen were less likely to have married and to have

Table 7-1. The Timing and Sequence of Early Life Events among the Oakland Men by Time of Military Entry in Averages and Percents

	Time of entry into the U.S. Armed Forces	
The timing and sequence of early life events	Early (before age 22)	Late (age 22 or later)
Average age at: ($\bar{X}$)	N = 20–22	N = 34–38
First full-time employment	22.1	23.2
First marriage	23.2	24.0
First child	27.2	26.7
Education completion	23.2	23.9
Activity sequences		
Military exit before: (%)	N = 18–19	N = 33–38
Work entry	21	18
Marriage entry	37[a]	12
First child	83[b]	48
Work entry before: (%)	N = 19–20	N = 33–34
Marriage	65	53
Birth of first child	84	76
Eduction exit before: (%)	N = 20–21	N = 33–38
Full-time employment	19	34
Marriage	67	50
Birth of first child	80	76

[a] $\chi^2 = 3.26$, $p < .10$.
[b] $\chi^2 = 4.56$, $p < .05$.

had a first child before returning to civilian life. By implication, the induction of these early men should have been less disruptive. The greater tendency toward a normative or customary sequence in the early group (as with school-leaving preceding marriage) is highly generalized or common. More early entrants got a full-time job and completed their schooling before committing themselves to marriage. However, the group differences are not strong enough to justify much interpretation.

Another perspective on military timing in the life course is to compare groups that typically follow different timetables, such as the working and middle class. Oakland men from the working class would ordinarily be expected to complete schooling earlier, much earlier than the sons of higher-status parents.[3] Family events and work entry should typically occur earlier in the former group. These differences do not hold when we compare men from the two strata who entered the service late—at age 22 or older. The working-class men entered full-time employment, were married for the first time, and had a first child before the middle-class men, but they also completed their formal education and military service at a later stage. Implied in these contrasts is the greater tendency of the working class to engage in multiple activities: to work before and during formal education, to have children during the education years, and to marry and have children while involved in military service. For example, approximately two thirds of the middle-class men postponed starting a family until they left the service, a percentage that was only 23 for the working class. Did this pattern of multiple activities entail stresses and strains that persisted in the life course, an influence of cross-pressures and overloads? The sequential arrangement in the middle class seems less stressful and taxing.

The incredibly rapid pace of military induction in World War II made time of entry far less a matter of consequence than it would have been in more ordinary circumstances. Yet even with the small variation in time of entry, early and late entrants were distinguished by different histories and experiences en route to adult careers. We turn now to the life course up to middle age, to education, work careers, marriage, and family.

INFLUENCES OF MILITARY TIMING TO MIDDLE AGE

Men who served in the armed forces may have followed life paths to the middle years that reflect their personal histories before the war as well as their military experience. War mobilization selected different men for the first and second waves, but are these differences expressed in their life course? The tendency for early entrants to have a poorer academic record at time of induction would increase the prospect of more deprivation along this line in the postwar years. At the same time the maturity and training offered by military service could revise a history of academic difficulty. To assess the effect of military service, apart from selection differences, we shall make statistical adjustments for the principal differences at entry into the service. These are class background, family size, and academic grades. In regression analyses, we also included time of entry (early vs. late).

A good many of the men who joined up early seemed destined by past academic difficulties for a limited educational future, though age at completion of formal education does not show evidence of this prediction. Most of the early and late entrants wrapped up their education before the age of 25. However, we do find evidence of continuing educational deprivation. The early entrants were less likely to complete a college degree than were the late entrants (a small difference of 16 percentage points), but this difference evaporates when adjustments are made for class origin, family size, and high school grades. The story of educational training in the service and of educational opportunities through the GI Bill must await the returns of a scheduled follow-up. But whatever the data, they are unlikely to change the picture reported here, except to provide a more complete understanding of the link between the military service and higher education. For example, the least able men would be least apt to take advantage of the education benefits of the GI Bill.

Time of military service had implications for men's work-life achievement in postwar America by determining when they entered the job market. Some veterans returned in late wartime, while others joined the flood of veterans following the war. From one angle, early entrants may have had a genuine advantage in time of service because they returned to a marketplace needing workers. Competition for jobs was undoubtedly more intense after the war, although a good many veterans had the option of returning to their old job. In both cases, returning veterans undoubtedly experienced a sense of lagging behind. Time in the service placed them behind workers who remained at the job throughout the war. Generally, however, this disadvantage was only temporary. Oakland veterans who reported this perceived lag in the 1960 interview typically added that they had caught up with non-veterans on the job.

Educational differences between early and late entrants are reflected in the veteran's occupational standing *after* completion of formal education. Approximately 33% of the early veterans occupied professional/managerial jobs, compared to 47% of the late entrants. Skilled, semiskilled, and unskilled jobs were nearly twice as common among the early entrants as among the late joiners. By the age of 40 or so, we still see this difference and in largely undiminished form. About three of five men in the late group held professional/managerial jobs, in contrast to less than half of the early entrants. The difference appears to be due to corresponding variations by education, and statistical analyses generally bear this out. Achievement differences are negligible with education controlled.

By far the most major change in work life up to middle age is the striking level of advancement. Literally the entire cohort shifted toward the upper middle class, owing partly to the postwar economic boom in the United States and especially in California. Sample attrition does not account for this shift (Elder, 1974, p. 321). Only 10% or less of the middle-aged men were still located within the working class. Over this postwar era, most of the Oakland veterans followed a stable course of advancement. Less than a third of the men had switched career lines between the end of the war and the 1960s, and this figure did not vary by time of military entry. From the end of the Korean War to the mid-1960s, the early entrants experienced more employers and jobs than the late entrants (avg. $\bar{X}$'s = 2.3 vs. 1.7), but the difference is not reliable. Overall, time of military service was not a prominent factor in the career lines and work achievements of the Oakland men. Perhaps the enduring influence is simply the experience itself without regard for matters of timing.

Time of entry also made little difference in family beginnings—age at marriage and children. Given this similarity, it is not surprising that the two groups of veterans, early and late entrants, are identical on number of children ever born ($\bar{X} = 3.01$). They are also very similar on the stability of their first marriages. All but two veterans had married, and 85% of these marriages were intact up to the middle years. Veterans who belonged to the group of early entrants were least likely to have experienced divorce (10 vs. 20% for the late entrants), but the impressive fact is the high stability of first marriages among veterans in both groups. By and large these results do not change with pre-military factors and education controlled.

This level of permanence up to the middle years may be due in part to the generalized effect of service time in delayed marital age and, consequently, in lowering the risk of divorce. For example, a younger cohort from the 1920s (Elder, 1986) shows that nonveterans married at a younger age than veterans who were similar to them in background ($\bar{X}$ ages = 22.0 vs. 23.7). These data were obtained from the Berkeley Guidance sample at the Institute of Human Development (birth years, 1928–1929). In the Oakland cohort, the slightly greater stability of veterans' marriages among early entrants tends to correspond with the advantages of service before marriage, such as the avoidance of long separations during the early years of relationship development. As an Oakland veteran put it, military service should occur right after high school and prior to marriage. "I worried about the long separation from my wife in World War II. It was too hard on her."

More life history detail is needed to link military service to marriage and family careers. Occasional records in the Oakland archive describe marriages that occurred after several dates during a single home leave. In one case, the marriage proposal was mailed from the South Pacific. Other cases document a process by which marital dates were changed to accommodate leaves, departures, and the uncertainty of tomorrow. One Oakland veteran from the Italian campaign acknowledged that "the war had quite an effect on getting married." By getting married before leaving the States, he reasoned that his "wife would have more to live on through the government allotment for dependents." But the decision was followed by the strain of long separations. As he recalled, "I was home only two weeks in the three years."

Considering all of the wartime pressures on young, seemingly fragile, and often hastily arranged marriages, one cannot avoid some amazement over their survival rate. How were so many marriages able to survive? Maturity at the time of marriage may be one factor along with, as one veteran put it, a conditioned willingness to work with others and to sacrifice for the welfare of the group. The demands of military life gave higher marks to cooperation than to preoccupation with self concerns. A Navy veteran recalled the "spirit of cooperation" among shipmates. This attitude may have enhanced the prospects of marital permanence.

CONCLUSION

Wars have influenced the lives and families of American men over the past century in ways that remain largely unknown. One of the most noteworthy birth cohorts from this standpoint of military influences includes men whose fathers served in World War I. These men grew up in the Great Depression and were called upon in great numbers to enter military service during World War II. This sequence of events reflects the cohort's historical timetable, its location on the historical record. The issue of timing also appears in the urgent demand for military manpower in World War II, and in the waves of recruits following Pearl Harbor.

This paper views the timing of military service during World War II from the vantage points of history and the life course. The men were born in 1920–1921 and became members of the Oakland Growth Study, a longitudinal project initiated during the early 1930s. The 69 men in the sample experienced childhood during the prosperous 1920s, entered high school during the 1930s, and were drawn into World War II shortly after Pearl Harbor. Well over half of the men experienced the harsh deprivations of Depression life, and 90% entered the armed forces. Most of the men joined up during a period of 24 months, from January 1942 to the end of 1943, and remained on active duty for 3 years.

Assuming that decisions on military entry could be made even with the pressure of a universal draft, we asked what factors distinguished between early and late servicemen, and whether this timing difference mattered for the life course—for the transition to adulthood, for education and occupational attainment, and for marital and parent–child relations. Historically, the Armed Services have appealed to men as a way of escaping hardship and disadvantage. Men have joined the service to escape from poverty, a domineering parent, the dislike of a parent, and the pain of failure in school. Men who grew up in hard-pressed Depression families were not more likely to enter the service early (before the age of 22), though a different background of disadvantage influenced this decision.

Early entrants were more likely to come from large families and to have a problematic academic record. The link between academic troubles and early entry was most pronounced in the middle class, a context in which educational achievement is favored over other routes of advancement. These men were less apt to be in school during the early phase of the war, when compared to more able men, and were less apt than working-class sons to be employed in critical war-related jobs at the time. Apart from the influence of disadvantage, some Oakland men responded to their own values on military service by joining up at an early age. In this era of pacificism, the men who as adolescents supported military training were more likely than other men to enter the service at an early date.

Time of military entry made no reliable difference in the timing of men's entry into adulthood. It did not markedly influence the timing of full-time employment, marriage, parenthood, or the completion of formal education. However, the early entrants were more apt to get into the service before marriage and parenthood, when compared to the late entrants.

The continuing influence of family background shows up when we examine the life course of late entrants from the middle and working classes. As one might expect, early entry into adulthood is especially common among the sons of working-class parents. They entered full-time employment, married, and had a child at an earlier age than did men from the middle class, but they also completed their formal education and military service at a later age. With the help of the GI Bill, a good many working-class offspring were able to start a family early and to complete their education at a much later time.

The social and economic disadvantages that favored early entry into the armed forces also restricted educational and occupational achievement. As a group, the late entrants were more likely to complete 4 years of college and to embark on careers in the managerial/professional field, when compared to the early joiners. These differences largely reflect the differences observed between these men before their active military duty, and consequently have little to do with the service experience itself. However, the service and its GI benefits may well have something to do with the unusually high level of education attained by the Oakland veterans. Military benefits, especially the GI Bill, presumably account in part for how nearly two thirds of the Oakland men were able to complete 4 years of college in a life shaped also by the limitations of the Depression and war.

Though late entry enabled some men to complete their higher education, it also invited particular strains in marriage and family relations. More of the late-entry men (vs. early-entry men) were married and had their first child before leaving the service. As such, the pressures of family separation were more common in their lives. Even with adjustments for pre-induction differences, we find that divorce was more common to the late entrants than to the early joiners. More important than this difference is the generally high level of marital permanence among the veterans as a group. By the middle years more than four out of five first marriages were still intact. The precise connection, if any, between military service and marital permanence cannot be identified with the information at hand, though qualities derived from service experience clearly warrant more attention as potential influences on family life.

This study underscores one process by which the life course is structured, the differential timing of historical and social events. The birth years of the Oakland men placed them in a cohort that experienced Depression hard times during adolescence, the manpower requirements of World War II in early adulthood, and the moral dilemmas of Vietnam in the experience of their older children. Along this cohort trajectory, some men came to military service at an earlier age than others following Pearl Harbor. The early joiners entered the service for reasons of military sentiment and to escape from a background of disadvantage, as distinguished by academic problems. This academic difference left an imprint on the educational attainment of the men and on their occupational careers and standing. The distinctive timing of lives has much to do with the variable course of life and its prospects.

NOTES

1. Efforts to model the interaction effect of social class and grades on service entry were generally unsuccessful. The small sample is one reason for this outcome. A middle-class background, relatively poor grades, and attitudinal support for military institutions made a difference in the time of entry of the Oakland males, but only class origins had a significant man effect ($p < .05$).

2. One might be struck by the relatively young age at completion of formal education among the Oakland veterans, especially in view of the large number who actually went on to college. In fact, we find that veterans from the Berkeley Guidance sample at the Institute (born in 1928–1929) were likely to complete their education at an older age, on average ($\bar{X} = 25.03$ vs. 23.67, Oakland). The age at which the Oakland veterans joined the service helps to make sense of the difference. They were far more likely to have completed their education *prior* to entry, when compared with the Berkeley veterans (56 vs. 41%). Most of the Oakland men were in their 22nd year when recruitment pressures became extreme, and this meant that a large percentage could graduate from college before donning a uniform.

3. Mean ages for the working class and middle class in the late entry group are: employment, 21.5 versus 24.4; first marriage, 23.0 versus 24.6; first child, 25.2 versus 27.6; education completion, 24.0 versus 23.9; military exit, 27.0 versus 26.2.

REFERENCES

Clausen, J. A. (1984). The American soldier and social psychology: Introduction. *Social Psychology Quarterly, 47,* 184–185.

Elder, G. H., Jr. (1974). *Children of the Great Depression.* Chicago: University of Chicago Press.

Elder, G. H., Jr. (1986). Military times and turning points in men's lives. *Developmental Psychology, 22,* 233–245.

Erikson, E. (1968). *Identity: Youth and crisis.* New York: Norton.

Hill, R. (1949). *Families under stress.* New York: Harper.

Hogan, D. P. (1981). *Transitions and social change.* New York: Academic Press.

Hollingshead, A. B. (1946). Adjustment to military life. *American Journal of Sociology, 51,* 439–447.

Mitchell, B. (1947). *Depression decade: From new era through the new deal, 1929–1941.* New York: Rinehart.

Olson, K. W. (1974). *The GI bill, the veterans and the colleges.* Lexington, KY: University Press of Kentucky.

Sharp, L. M. (1970). *Education and employment: The early careers of college graduates.* Baltimore, MD: Johns Hopkins University Press.

Stolz, L. (1954). *Father relations of war-born children.* Stanford, CA: Stanford University Press.

Stouffer, S. A., Suchman, E. A., DeVinney, L. C., Star, S. A., & Williams, R. M., Jr. (1949). *The American soldier: Adjustment during army life* (Vol. 1). Princeton, NJ: Princeton University Press.

Stouffer, S. A., Lumsdaine, A. A., Lumsdaine, M. H., Williams, R. M., Jr., Smith, M. B., Janis, I. L., Star, S. A., & Cottrell, L. S., Jr. (1949). *The American soldier: Combat and its aftermath* (Vol. 2). Princeton, NJ: Princeton University Press.

8

Institutional Consequences of Hard Times: Engagement in the 1930s

JOHN MODELL
Carnegie Mellon University

My discipline, history, is a late entrant to the multidisciplinary host converging upon the intimate institution. A large variety of reasons for this, internal to the profession, can be cited, and have been elsewhere (Gordon, 1978; Poster, 1978; Rapp, Ross, & Bridenthal, 1979; Rosenberg, 1975; Tilly & Cohen, 1982). One reason, not so commonly mentioned, deserves notice, since it has some bearing on the kind of family history my offering here constitutes, and suggests briefly some of my debt to Reuben Hill.

That reason is that unlike virtually all of the other participants in the multidisciplinary assault upon the delicate puzzle that is the family, history has no history of being thought useful as a guide to family policy, either micro or macro. Reuben Hill himself, proudly reflecting the origins of his specialty in providing good counsel to youth, has written exactly this kind of a guidebook (Duvall & Hill, 1949). And while one cannot imagine Gary Becker addressing kindly thoughts to young people—at least not of this sort and at least not in print—one often sees economists, demographers, and the like offering counsel to governments about family policy. But family historians speak mainly to one another, finding occasionally a patient social scientist who will listen in. (Reuben Hill was one.) And when they speak, historians most commonly complain of the abstractness of the treatments of family in the other disciplines that address family issues. I intend my treatment here to evoke time and place, and the view of it held by contemporaries.

The student of family history will recognize immediately one debt that we, and I, owe to Reuben Hill: the serious exploration of the family cycle as a device for describing family dynamics. This debt is thoroughly examined in a number of recent works (Elder, 1979; Hareven, 1978), and was crucial in my own case, in moving me toward my current project, of which the essay below is a small installment. In this larger work I am writing a history of the American family in the 20th century using the dynamic concept of the life course as a sensitizing mechanism. But in the piece below, I also owe a more immediate debt to Reuben Hill, one I understand precisely in terms of his concern for the well-being of actual families. I refer to this theme of family stress. Hill's *Families Under Stress* (1949) was one of the dozen or so important nonhistorical books on the family for me, for the odd reason that it looked at families embedded in a historical event and assessed the interaction of the family institution with specific strains produced by that event. As I have thought about the subject of change in the American family in the 20th century, I have increasingly concluded that we must seek ways of assessing the impact upon families—and upon the institution of the family— of major events. The Great Depression is one such event.

The dominant interpretation of the impact of the Depression upon the American family is one in which stress serves in effect to weed out the less resilient families, thereby reinstating the family institution with considerable vigor. Glen Elder's powerful work has especially had the effect of emphasizing this general conclusion. I not only am persuaded by it; I think he has uncovered in his account a most important general proposition about the family in the past (Elder, 1974; Modell, 1979). And yet there is another way we can turn the family-in-the-Depression question around to suggest a somewhat different conclusion. For if the institution of the family emerged from the Depression (and then from the war, as Hill's work suggests) strengthened—and I believe that it did—so also subtle changes at the level of the content of the institution were introduced by these events. My argument here looks at a single, quite narrow aspect of family building—engagement—and argues that the Depression subjected it to pressures that palpably modified its content. Thus modified, but still a common constituent of institutionalized family-building patterns, engagement contributed its bit to post-Depression and particularly postwar marriages that looked much the same as what had come before, but felt rather different. As is almost inevitable when one examines institutions historically, an emphasis on articulate and preserved ideas creates something of a class bias, at least in coverage. I hope the reader will recognize the pains I have taken to overcome this bias to the extent I am able.

In 1937, The Roper Organization posed to a representative sample of the American population a rather remarkable question: "Should the government give financial aid to young people to help them get married and establish homes?" Remote as this was from the nation's highly private conception of marriage, no fewer than 37.5% of all respondents answered "yes," and only 53.6% rejected it (Cantril, 1951). To be sure, the connection with legislative action is strictly speculative, the item highly hypothetical and out of context in the brief questionnaire. It is, for all the caveats it properly calls forth, however, suggestive of the terms in which not only the Roper Organization but large numbers of Americans were willing to contemplate the spectre of delayed marriage in this late Depression year. Roy Dickerson (1940), the marriage counselor, held that when "the natural hopes of [an engaged] couple are frustrated . . . they are likely to feel rebellious against a social system that they hold responsible for their disappointment" (p. 8). The latter, of course, did not happen. Perhaps instead, couples' "natural hopes" were redirected; the institutions channeling their hopes changed.

Highly responsible counsel like that of Carolyn Zachry, the respected expert on adolescence, reflected upon the marital-scheduling difficulties of the Depression as an opportunity to intermingle subsidy and socialization for marriage:

> To many an adolescent, a job is also the prime factor in determining whether or not he can get married. For those thousands of young people joblessness means frustration, not only of their ambitions in the business and professional world, but frustration of their psycho-sexual desires as well. Of course, in many boys and girls the desire for marriage is confused with their desire for status and prestige. . . . We—parents and educators and miscellaneous adults alike—[should] recognize that our task is much more than that of enabling young people to get married by helping them to become financially self-sufficient. We must also help them to achieve more mature attitudes toward marriage. (Zachry, 1942, pp. 224–225)

Addressing frustrated youth directly, pulp publisher Bernarr Macfadden (1942) spoke less of maturity, but trumpeted the same theme of the threat posed by frustration to the very institution of marriage:

> Young people are afraid to marry these days unless they can begin, materially, where their parents left off. They want all material comforts ready at hand, and an assurance that they will not have to give up one small thing for the added gift of love. . . . They get *things* but miss the fine edge of marriage. That fine edge belongs to youth. It is *youth*, the joy of struggling together, of building together. . . . Security is no gift from the outside. . . . Why not marry while young? (p. 4)

And marriage counselor and popular writer Paul Popenoe (1940) likewise urged direct action lest the road to marriage stretch so long that disastrous tensions develop: "In heaven's name, why wait? . . . If you are sincerely in love, old enough to know what you are doing, understand what marriage means and are free to enter into it, you have no right to let anything, least of all money, bar you from happiness. . . . I've never known of a home broken up by lack of money" (p. 22). The marriage counselor further noted that money worries were a special "ogre" of the engagement period, so much so that it is "so frightening that they wish they weren't engaged."

Who listened? The evidence suggests that at some level of attention, many did. A student poll at the University of Colorado in 1934 through

1938 reported that six in ten male and female students believed that financial aid from parents was acceptable to permit marriage; and almost this proportion said they would accept a "dowry" system. Family sociologists at Cornell University reported that as the Depression wore on, parental subsidy was offered more often than before and accepted (even expected) more often, although the students were still wary of the possible "strings" that might be attached to such support (Bernard, 1938; Rockwood & Ford, 1945). Their 1940–1941 survey at Cornell suggested that more than one third favored parental support for college marriages as well as for support while couples "get on their feet," and an additional fifth favored emergency aid (Rockwell & Ford, 1945, pp. 102–104). For these students, it would seem, parental aid was in the early stages of being institutionalized. No doubt, their perspective concurred with the newly conventional middle-class view expressed in *The Good Housekeeping Marriage Book* of 1938, that "an engaged couple who are sure of their hearts and minds should be helped to marry as soon as the plans for the marriage can be wisely worked out." And since "this usually involves financing . . . wise parents today cooperate so that the young couple do not have to wait too long" (McConaghy, 1938, p. 18). The Roper Organization thus really had some reason to ask about marriage subsidy.

Women were slightly more enthusiastic about the Roper proposition than were men, 41% of the former favoring the government subsidy to marriage as compared with 37% of the latter. In part, this was a product of fewer women than men having no opinion on this question (a reversal of the usual pattern on political questions that is quite understandable in view of the particular significance of marriage and, indeed, *prompt* marriage for women's "careers"). Surprisingly, the gender difference in favorability to the marital subsidy showed up not among the younger but among the older respondents. Older women were almost as favorable to the proposition as were younger women. Their vote was in a sense an assent to the critical importance of marriage to women generally, rather than to their own particular needs at the moment of the interview.

For men, however, age made a great deal of difference, attesting no doubt to their special responsibility for assuring the economic adequacy of the circumstances of marriage. Forty-three percent of both men and women under 24 supported the hypothetical proposition. This count was reduced to 37% among women 55 or older, but, by gradual steps, assent among the male respondents declined to 29% for this older group. Age does not seem simply to have been a proxy for economic well-being among men. In Table 8-1 below I present age-specific tabulations for proportions of all respondents (sexes combined) in favor of the hypothetical subsidy, for a set of economic statuses assigned by the

Roper interviews based on observation. (Those with no opinion did not vary systematically by the economic or age categories).

Occupational breakdowns confirm that it was poorer respondents, and younger respondents, the two factors operating independently and additively, that led so many Americans in the eighth year of the Great Depression to look if only hypothetically to the state to relieve what many evidently saw as a critical blockage in the marriage process.

Many people, in other words, and especially those who felt "frustrated" or could easily understand how others might, contemplated a change in some of the rules surrounding the marriage process, a reorganization of some elements to preserve the essence. An institution that was at the point in the life course of the maximum frustration was engagement. Too amorphous to be altered in any formal way, engagement was subtly modified in its meaning, particularly with regard to the constraint the institution placed upon sexual expression.

In the 1930s, probably not quite so much as now, engagement was an ambiguous institution, a stage in family formation of uncertain obligations. Neither an element of peer culture, like dating, nor a step of unquestioned legal significance, like marriage, engagement was nevertheless held by many (but not all) observers to be both a useful and an important aspect of contemporary courtship.[1] Even to the precipitous Paul Popenoe (1934, 1936) engagement was "a marked feature of every high type civilization." The Terman (1938) and Burgess (Burgess &

Table 8-1. Proportions Favoring Government Subsidy for Marriage, by Observer Economic Level Age

Age	Above average	Average	Rather poor	Poor	On relief
17–24	26.3 (19)	38.1 (226)	48.5 (103)	49.1 (108)	52.6 (19)
25–34	33.3 (63)	34.7 (236)	43.4 (143)	52.7 (131)	59.6 (57)
35–44	23.9 (67)	33.5 (230)	42.4 (151)	43.0 (114)	56.3 (80)
45–54	18.6 (118)	23.9 (197)	41.2 (114)	46.6 (131)	55.1 (78)
55+	17.7 (113)	29.5 (156)	34.6 (78)	35.6 (118)	44.2 (77)

Note. Tabulations from archival data at Roper Center, University of Connecticut, based on AIPO 99. A far-from-perfect correlation with a question asking whether "you think that government regulation of stock exchanges has helped investors" indicates that the marriage subsidy item did not simply tap a generalized favorability toward activist, interventionist government, or the New Deal.

Wallin, 1953) studies both included cross-tabulations of the duration of engagement by eventual marital happiness—both finding that long engagement periods enhanced marital success. According to Burgess and Wallin (who based their argument largely on data collected in the mid-1930s), engagement was an institution in transit, from a less to a more important function.

> In the past three decades (i.e., since about World War I) there has been a marked change in attitude toward engagement. It is now considered as the last stage in the selection process, . . . its pre-eminent function the final opportunity for the couple to find out if they are fitted for each other. (Burgess & Wallin, 1953, p. 272).

Etiquette books of the period, on the other hand, seem to reflect a substantial and recent trivialization of the betrothal, in that it no longer followed upon the suitor's having first gained permission from his prospective father-in-law, but was rather a private decision of the couple, announced with optional degree of ceremony to the prospective bride's parents. As the etiquette books observed, the bride's parents had already in fact passed whatever judgment they retained in permitting her earlier dating to get serious (Ames, 1935; Vogue's Book of Etiquette, 1936). In modern times, contemporary writers held, engagement had evolved from a rather formal, public, quasi-legal publication of marriage intentions, wherein community objections might be elicited. Now "even engagement has become a trial relationship during which love is assessed" (Burgess & Wallin, 1953, p. 184). Consequently, "The proportion of broken engagements is on the increase," a claim made without supporting evidence.

Engagement, in the view of those professionals to whom it mattered, served to help a couple navigate a safe course where tradition had largely ceased to guide expectations and behavior. By the 1930s, dating allowed couples to be formed and reformed without great social or emotional costs, and for young women and men to sense the range of personalities to be found among socially acceptable partners. However, dating depended upon the exchange between partners of the material and physical means of "a good time" to be an extent sufficient to give rise to more intense premarital relationships (Modell, 1983).

Paul Popenoe, concerned with eugenics, as were many other family counselors of this low-fertility period, saw modern engagement as a phase of mate-selection that might promote sexually compatible (and thus fertile) marriages, but might also promote immorality. Dating, clearly, served to locate partners who enjoyed one another's company, but sexual compatibility was something else again. The ideological problem was how to define this phase. "The social attitude toward betrothal should not be too rigid," wrote Popenoe, but should allow for a gradual, cautious loosening of the inhibitions that govern dating. "Where betrothal is regarded as equally sacred and binding with marriage," that is, governed by social controls rather than the situational application of internalized values regarding intimacy on the one hand and the double standard on the other, "this [exploratory] function is largely lost. Equal loss results from taking the betrothal too lightly—where it is merely regarded as a convenient cover for intimacies that would not otherwise be approved socially" (Popenoe, 1936, p. 4).

The critical distinction between the engagement period and dating lay in the way that the extent of physical intimacy was settled upon. In dating, boys proposed and girls disposed, this being one element of a culturally defined and peer-overseen negotiation. In engagement, the couple was now recognized as a unit, the constancy between the partners reinforced by the social recognition of the engagement.

> When courtship prospers it leads to the mutual fixing of affection and this in turn creates need of a public recognition of a special relationship. The betrothal expresses the wish of both the man and the woman for a sense of security and exclusiveness in their love. From the point of view of its function as related to marriage, the engagement, by removing uncertainty in their relationship provides favorable conditions for each person to become well acquainted with the other before making a commitment which is presumed to be a life union." (Groves, 1933, p. 145)

The assumption was that the period of bargaining ended at engagement, and that a period of "exploration and discovery of personalities, a period of adventuring in adjustments" ensued (Himes, 1940, p. 96). One no longer simply accepted what one was offered in the engagement period. Instead, one sought—and in theory this relationship was symmetrical by gender—to discern what suited one's partner, what changes one should and could make in order to enrich the unity of the couple.

> An engagement period of about six months is not too long . . . to be sure that upon the instinctive basis of sex attraction a truly personal love has been founded. For sex must be built upon to create love. . . . These ideals of sex relationships and love relationships should form part of that great bulk of questions that must be talked over between a betrothed couple. (Alsop & McBride, 1942, p. 96)

The suitable degree of physical intimacy for a couple short of coitus was thus exactly one of the things a couple was to discover in engagement. Coitus, so widely condemned, would in one way or another lead to "an anti-climax of relationship" (Groves, 1933, p. 146).

This deliberation was something of an exercise—a way of mutual education in affectional taste and style. Virtually all counselors saw the great variability in sex attitudes as a leading cause of marital discontent, when discovered too late by the couple. Or, as another expert wrote

from an explicit Christian perspective, the sexual tensions of engagement
were entirely congruent with the "frankness" appropriate to personality
exploration: "Frankness means that whenever either one becomes aware
of a rising surge of sexual desire, it will be possible to say, 'I think we
had better be doing something else'. . . . Engagement may be still
further enriched by the development of the spiritual resources of personality" (Dickerson, 1937). An author in the *Good Housekeeping Marriage Book* (McConaghy, 1938), reflecting the high level of ambiguity
engendered by an imperfectly defined institution in time of general
social stress and change, felt obliged to reassure his readers both that, on
the one hand, "if they have . . . decided to wait, they need have no fear
that this indicates a lack of sex feeling," and, on the other, if they find
waiting hard, "they would be glad that they do have 'sex hunger'" (pp.
22–23).

Entirely critical to the operation of engagement as practiced in the
1930s was the idea that, unlike marriage as valued and practiced, it
could be terminated without shame. All writers agreed with Groves
(1933) that "the engagement can have little value as a preliminary testing of the relationship before marriage unless with it goes the possibility
of breaking off the relationship" (p. 151). An etiquette for breaking off
the engagement was developed that was more completely elaborated
than that for establishing one. Burgess and Wallin (1953, pp. 273, 282–
295) found that 30% of their engaged respondents in the mid-1930s had
been previously engaged, and that 15% more would eventually break
up with their current fiancé(e)s. Correlates of engagements that foun-
dered included lack of agreement and commitment to harmonious relationship, and parental disapproval. The longer an engagement had
lasted, the more likely it was to end in marriage. Engagement was in
fact seen as an ongoing experiment.

A key word in many of these explorations of the functions of
engagement in the 1930s was "personality," a layer of personal reality
(highly variable, incorporating the results of different upbringings)
hardly touched in the more superficial dating period. Personality might
be reached through engagement over a substantial period of time—
conventionally given as at least half a year—and by the heightened emo-
tionalism said to color this period, "an opalescent mist of gossamer deli-
cacy," according to one authority (Richardson, 1925, p. 192), "a con-
tented feeling that the loved one has at last been discovered," according
to a usually sterner one (Himes, 1940, p. 98).

A contradiction lingered about this period of personality discovery,
just as it did with respect to premarital intercourse. The argument was
that a loving engaged couple would practice heightened sexual intimacy
in order to discover one another's sexual personalities but refrain from
coitus, so as not to expose the woman to the special risks imposed by the

double standard should their transgression become known. Couples were at once instructed to discover glowingly the most intimate nature of their fiancé(e)s, while at the same time asking not only of one another searching, important, and practical questions about economic outlooks and tastes. "If a young lover is to find out the significant features of his prospective spouse's personality" (Kuhn, 1942, p. 221), this was necessary.

Moreover, "no opportunity to visit with the affianced's parents should be missed." This was strictly a means of understanding one's fiancé(e)'s personality; the "feel" that comes from being in close quarters with someone's family enables "an unconscious or semiconscious sensing of similarity or strangeness in ways of behaving" thereby "to mitigate the blinding effects of romantic love." Yet at the same time, the author admitted that "the ordeal may seem somewhat painful at first," and this surely because one was in fact not just investigating one's intended on such visits. One was no less being looked at awfully closely oneself, and not just through the eyes of love (Kuhn, 1942, p. 221).

The ambiguity of engagement, even before the 1930s, thus pertained at once to sexuality and to the role of family in the publication and conduct of the state itself. So ambiguous was the institution that sometimes one mightn't know whether or not one was engaged: "About four months ago I met the man that I have chosen for my husband. He proposed about a month ago, but has not as yet given me an engagement ring. Should I consider myself engaged before I have the ring?" (N. K. to Martha Carr, St. Louis *Post-Dispatch*, May 4, 1931).

Despite the ambiguity of the content of engagement, the institution was very widespread. Students at the University of Southern California inquiring "at random" of married couples—skewing them thus toward the prosperous but including substantial numbers of blue-collar couples—found that only 5% said they had not been engaged before their marriages (Popenoe & Neptune, 1938). Data on Alfred Kinsey's respondents married during the Depression—similarly skewed—do not indicate quite this order of universality for engagement, but do suggest that between two thirds and three fourths were engaged prior to marriage, with engagement just slightly more common among the college-educated than among those who never went to college. We are dealing, then, with a pattern the legitimacy of which—for all its susceptibility to distinctive definition according to class and to whim—extended down into the working class. Kinsey's data also point to a slight and temporary decline of engagement during the Depression (Gebhard & Johnson, 1979, p. 342).

Some sense of the variability of engagement as an institution can be inferred from the great difference among instances of how long engagements lasted before marriage. Half a year to something over a year was generally held to be a fitting length for an engagement, but about one in three of Burgess' 1930s couples were engaged less than half a year before they married; Terman's findings were similar (Burgess & Wallin, 1953, p. 317; Terman, 1938, p. 199). A slightly greater proportion of the entire Kinsey sample, likewise, had short engagements. On the other hand, these same sources indicate that almost two in ten engagements might at their outset incorporate considerable certainty about a marriage date, or might imply nothing more than an intention to marry at some point either distant or simply to be determined by external happenings not yet even specified. Could one explore personality thoroughly enough in just a few months? In an engagement lasting indefinitely, could one sustain such a subtle interpenetration of egos without at the same time according one's partner other intimacies? The institution was a vulnerable one. Timing and content could not be separated: Both were ambiguous, and timing in many cases felt the impact of the Depression.

From a behavioral perspective, engagement timing seems not to have changed very much during the period we are considering. We have already noted a slight reduction during the Depression among Kinsey's married respondents in the proportions who had been engaged. The same cohort seems to have had on the average somewhat shorter engagements. The slight decline in the average length of engagement during the early Depression may be seen as an extension of a trend established during the previous decade. The data, however, do point to a considerably more rapid decline in the average length of engagements as World War II approached, a decline continuing through the war. (Over the period, it might be added, the period of acquaintance preceding engagement remained at approximately the same level.) Since, as we shall see, contemporaries who were concerned about the effect of the Depression on engagement spoke of *excessively long* engagements, the behavioral finding is rather surprising.

For an explanation, I think, we must recall a characteristic of American engagement in the 20th century: its ambiguity. Engagement was exactly that point in the family formation process in which young people were supposed to experience and weather their acute doubts about subsequent steps in that process. The "opalescent mist" was also almost of necessity a period of great if episodic tension. Longer engagements may or may not have promoted such doubts, but surely they were the occasion for them. It must be expected that the economic uncertainties of the period, given especially their powerful impact upon those in the family formation years, were commingled with the other anxieties felt by the engaged, and experienced as anxiety over delay.

Well before the Depression, etiquette writers for the well-to-do (e.g., Diescher, 1923) opposed long engagements because "engaged people are usually interesting only to themselves, their thoughts and

interests are centered on each other," and friends out of courtesy as well
as boredom give them a good deal of opportunity to "drift forgotten in a
backwater." Such separation implied a risk of scandal, but was challenged rather as poor preparation for marriage, since marriage was
viewed as a highly sociable state (Ames, 1935, pp. 104–105; Diescher,
1923, pp. 212–213; Post, 1922, pp. 308–309). Engagement had always
had but a weakly prescribed, and hardly described duration. The
Depression consequently induced a particularly focused eagerness to be
done with engagement. The war would soon provide an occasion for
this, as did the prosperity that followed. The family formation process
came to be modified through an eagerness to change its weakest, least
defined, least normatively satisfying element: engagement.

> I am 20 years old and am engaged to a fine boy who is 21. Unlike most
> boys, he realizes that it is not right to monopolize me and keep me from
> going with other boys, because he is not working seriously and cannot
> afford to take me everywhere or to marry just now (Little Girl to Martha
> Carr, *St. Louis Post-Dispatch*, October 16, 1931).

What was to be the content of engagement that was thrown off
schedule, where mutual exploration would lead perilously close to for-
bidden sexuality, where even day-to-day pleasures were either riskily
domestic or prohibitively costly? The eighth of "Ten Modern Commandments" (1935) of love was that "thou shalt make use of thy emotion
energy through sublimation," and the third, the "right to a full, free,
happy and complete love life." Engagement if anything rendered sublimation the harder. It followed that "society's job just now is to make it
economically possible for young folks of marriageable age, who are in
love, to find fulfillment within marriage" ("Ten Modern Commandments," 1935, p. 64). Love, then, in conjunction with a firm commitment to the ideal of chastity before marriage, could conquer all. But the
Depression tested it with fire.

The terms of the test were laid out in high relief by a 1935 *True
Confessions* story, "Love Hazards." The story purports to be parallel
interviews with an engaged pair, Dorothy, 20, and Bill, 22, who have
realized, after two years of waiting in the engaged state, that another
two years' wait will be required. The editorial presence asks: "What is
Society [capitalized; academic sociologists are not alone in reifying this
concept] going to do about them—all these young people who want to
get married and can't?" (p. 22). The editor says that the Depression is
immediately to blame for this tension, but that really it is built into the
mores and the economy more generally. The whole is a mythic explanation for, and, thereby, justification of, institutional change.

"But Gosh," exclaims Bill in his text. "Nature never meant the prel-
iminaries to last two years! Nature never intended the courtship to be

dragged out forever. . . . I can't think that it's anything but natural for a chap who's in love to want his girl. I can't think he'd be much of a lover or much of a man if he didn't." Bill worries, on the one hand, that if unsatisfied, his "urgent physical need of her" would so structure their engagement that all her other attentions would hardly please him. "Our engagement and my disposition are being ruined." Bill contemplates having recourse to Jenny, "an easy girl, a good-natured, cheap little girl," to slake his immediate cravings, but tentatively rejects this solution, out of respect for Dorothy (not Jenny). He also looks forward to heightened sublimation through his studies. Yet he cannot believe that the institution of engagement is binding enough to prevent jealousy from creeping in, given a long delay. "Can I expect a gay, pretty girl to stay home and hold her hands evening after evening for me?"

Bill proposes, as a solution to this dilemma, immediate sexual consummation with his fiancée, this an emotionally appropriate if morally mediocre expression of intimacy in engagement dragged out too long. "Suppose I knew she was all mine—really mine. Do you suppose I'd be jealous of any chap then? Not I. And do you suppose I'd ever look at another girl?" He quiets his moral qualms in classic fashion: "It's not us that's wrong, but Society."

Dorothy says no, and the matter is in limbo as of the narrative present. Dorothy protests that her physical needs are every bit as urgent as Bill's, although her lover can't believe this. "Girls aren't different. I do want you." (She nominally educates a man here, but of course the text in fact addresses an almost entirely female readership.) "But don't you see, don't you see, you're so worth waiting for." Where Bill evokes nature, Dorothy evokes "a sentimental little picture in my mind of our wedding night—mine and Bill's, myself in white satin and lace, shy and yet eager, Bill ardent and glowing." Under proper restraint, Bill's fancied animality suits Dorothy's conception of things, but much of the time, now, it seems all too much like Bill is lusting after cheap, easy Jenny. Dorothy is convinced that sex drives, despite the strength of her own, are not a sufficient basis for lasting marriage. And she is "frightened, badly frightened" for the future of her match. Dorothy protests that "much as I want to belong to Bill, I can be happy just being engaged to him." But Bill puts it thus: "She'll someday be my wife, legally as well as actually."

Mapped on the somewhat shaky double standard of the day, the idea that sexuality is the touchstone of possession together with the enlightened, volitional definition of engagement as a period of growing mutual commitment had made the institution itself a murky battleground between the genders. In my interpretation, just such quiet ideological conflicts have been close to much of the change in aspects of the American family in the past century.

We are offered an unresolved mythic struggle between nature and culture, following the then polite convention of man as natural, woman as cultural. The context, however, is distinctly historical. On the one hand, in their different ways, both Bill and Dorothy deny the operating assumptions of the double standard of sexual conduct. Bill cannot simply slake his desires on Jenny because he feels this would be unfair to Dorothy; Dorothy denies that her sexual urges are any less than Bill's, it is only that her faith in social institutions is greater. Each, thus, is drawn into the orbit of the other by their convictions, and, yet, under the circumstances, the operation of a symmetrically structured family formation process cannot be fully worked out. Even if the sexual and moral natures of male and female were no longer assumed to be at opposite poles, nevertheless Dorothy's sense of the strength of their love is only enhanced by the challenge the economic pinch poses to their shared timetable.[2] For Bill, "Society" proved bankrupt when it failed to provide the couple in timely fashion with the socially sanctioned marriage they had been led to expect. For Dorothy, her investment is in the symbolic halo of proper marriage, and in one sense this may even be enhanced by the struggle that shakes Bill.

Contemporary students of mores recognized the difficulties of the situation. McGill and Matthews, in their superb *The Youth of New York City* (1940), based on a 1935 survey, spoke at some length and with feeling of the special hardships faced by those of marriageable age. Even dating was hard for them to accomplish, partly because so many had to work long hours to support their families, and partly because so few had their accustomed pocket money. But even worse was a decline in the quality of friendships between boys and girls, because of "what happens to friendship between the sexes when this important possibility [marriage] is ruled out" (p. 318). McGill and Matthews were explicitly concerned both about the possibility of distance and wariness, and about premarital intercourse. Cavan and Ranck (1938) note that employed girls had the advantage that income brought to their dating lives, citing such forlorn expressions among girls of marriageable age but not employed as "has boyfriends but no clothes to wear when she goes out" and "the boys do not have jobs" (p. 168). The boys similarly were much influenced by their employment status, although the authors speculate that an age difference may also have its effect here: "The unemployed group are in general less interested in girls and marriage than the employed group. . . . Either they expressed no attitude at all on the subject, or they stated that they were not interested in girls or did not go with girls" (p. 172).

Moral leaders, even quite conventional moral leaders, were concerned, and were prepared to jettison some conventional patterns to retain others. Roy E. Dickerson (1937), prolific love-and-marriage authority of the YMCA, for instance, urged couples who knew they were in love to marry now, rather than to prolong engagement overmuch in hope of attaining the proper economic circumstances for marriage. Wives might have to work, or parents provide some support for the newlyweds. "An honest effort should be made to reach a decision without being over-influenced by purely traditional attitudes. . . . How reasonable is that position under present conditions?" Rockwood and Ford's (1945) college survey, conducted in 1940, strongly confirmed that these views had spread.

Our second imperfect document suggests that in many instances not Dickerson (nor Dorothy) but rather Bill prevailed. His lusty insistence, and Dorothy's presumptively demure acceptance of it, changed engagement, not initially destroying the institution but building into it greater sexual commitment, and thereby removing its unique quality. Hints can be found by retabulating the sex-history data made available by the Institute of Sex Research, Indiana University. The results will be seen in Table 8-2, based for the sake of simplicity upon ever-married whites who had attended college.

The data show that those who had not been engaged before they married had long been those whose sexuality had evidently been the less constrained by social conventions. This relationship held true in the Depression, and remarkably—if parameter estimates from this unrepresentative sample can be believed—engagement may even have become more prevalent at the time. But we find Bill and Dorothy there. Long engagements in the Depression led, to an extent they had not led previously, to premarital coitus. Premarital coitus, indeed, was especially common among this marriage cohort in general, but it was also especially prominently associated with long engagements. Coitus for the war-marriage cohort was more common than before the Depression, less common than during the Depression. But what also seems to have been lessened was both the association between long engagements and premarital coitus, and in fact long engagement itself.

This evidence if far from conclusive, suffering as it does from sample truncation at the more recent end. I think, however, that its suggestive finding is plausible. The change in the institution of engagement was not particularly alarming, nor necessarily particularly apparent. Nevertheless, we see appropriate modifications in the kinds of sources that instruct by purporting to describe—here an influential text in family sociology, that edited by Becker and Hill. The first edition appeared in 1942; the second 6 years later, after the influences of the Depression and the war were fairly well sorted out. In the later edition, the author on engagement, Manfred Hinshaw Kuhn of the University of Iowa, added a new section titled "The Engagement in Our Society: Sacred or Secular," following a largely unchanged section on the functions of

Table 8-2. Proportions of Subsequently Married Partners Who Had Had Premarital Coitus with Their Eventual Husband or Wife, by Sex, Length of Engagement, and Marriage Cohort

Marriage cohort and sex		Length of engagement			
	Not engaged	¼ yr or less	¼–¾ yr	¾–1½ yr	1½ yr +
Pre-1919					
Men	23.5	7.7	13.0	19.4	15.6
	(51)	(26)	(46)	(31)	(32)
Women	41.4	16.7	11.5	12.8	22.7
	(25)	(6)	(26)	(39)	(22)
1919–1928					
Men	45.9	31.9	20.0	17.9	33.3
	(172)	(72)	(110)	(84)	(39)
Women	55.4	32.3	29.6	30.4	28.1
	(65)	(31)	(54)	(69)	(57)
1929–1940					
Men	64.6	47.2	45.6	45.9	55.8
	(444)	(193)	(204)	(133)	(77)
Women	62.3	57.3	36.2	35.2	69.6
	(138)	(89)	(127)	(105)	(46)
1941–1945					
Men	62.0	40.3	43.1	36.3	34.1
	(266)	(196)	(153)	(80)	(44)
Women	66.3	41.2	44.1	36.4	45.0
	(83)	(85)	(121)	(55)	(20)

Note. Whites with at least some college only; cell *N*'s shown in parentheses. Data type provided the author by Dr. Paul H. Gebhard, Director, Institute for Sex Research, Bloomington, Indiana. For description of data, see Gebhard and Johnson (1979). College-educated whites only here included in tabulations.

engagement (Kuhn, 1942, 1948). In the added section, Kuhn expatiates on this timeworn dichotomy, distinguishing the growing emphasis on "Alternatives" in American society from the stolidly sacred character of "primitive and Oriental societies." Herewith, he notes that there are nevertheless degrees of difference to be found within American society.

> It is obvious that marriage and family have by no means lost all their sacred, sanctioned, traditional forms. It is, however, probably true that the engagement as such in our society has gone much further over into the realm of Alternatives than have marriage and the family. (1948, p. 281).

Kuhn is not wringing his hands, however:

> The purpose of this discussion has been to point out the potentially adaptive character of the secularization of the engagement. To the degree that we have cultural Alternatives in this area of behavior, to that degree it is possi-

ble for us to be instrumental, rational, and adjusted to the changing functions of marriage and the family. (p. 281)

Someone more attuned that Kuhn to a life-course perspective might well be tempted to remark that such an instrumental, rational, and adjusted engagement institution could conduce to different kinds of marriages. One also might wonder whether such an institution, no longer containing but rather expressing a highly sexualized intimacy, shorter, and associated with younger marriage age might not over time lose the special, tentative, exploratory quality that Kuhn, and others, applauded. Perhaps some of this quality was passed onto the marriage itself. I think, also, that a less functionalist account of the history of engagement might well argue that the change in the institution was not so much the result of evolution as of the capture of the institution by the cohort most directly affected by it.

NOTES

1. In law, engagement was equivalent to a contract to marry, but a contract quite open to discrepant construction:

> The offer must be made to the other party, . . . [but no] formal language [is] necessary. The acceptance of the offer of marriage . . . need not be in express words, but may be inferred from the promisee's conduct and behavior. . . . While a promise to marry must be based on a consideration, the promise of one party is the usual and a sufficient condition for the promise of the other.

The engagement ring was legally interpreted as such a consideration (and hence was returnable in case of fairly abrogated engagement), but both legal texts and advice texts indicate that many couples saw the ring rather as a gift, as they no doubt viewed engagement as less than a contract. Thus, in 1953, a Gallup Poll would ask whether "when an engaged couple break off their engagement," the ring should be returned to the man or kept by the woman. Eight percent had no opinion, suggesting general familiarity with the institution and the ritual item, but only 65% agreed with legal doctrine, and called for the ring's return (58% of men, 69% of women). Eleven percent considered it an outright gift, while 17% felt it was the woman's to keep unless it was she who broke the engagement (Mach & Kiser, 1938, XX, pp. 776-81; "The Law of Engagement Rings" (1934); Gallup (1972), II, pp. 1145).

2. Another *True Confessions* heroine put it nicely. "Seems like to me—maybe I don't know what I'm talking about—but I think hard times demand unusual courage, don't you? . . . Hard times and troubles and problems can't really hurt you, or damage your love, unless you're weak and *let them*, can they?" (Winn, 1933, p. 55).

REFERENCES

Alsop, G. F., & McBride, M. F. (1942). *She's off to marriage*. New York: Vanguard Press.

Ames, E. (1935). *Book of modern etiquette.* New York: Walter J. Black.

Bernard, W. S. (1938). Student attitudes on marriage and the family. *American Sociological Review, 3,* 354–361.

Burgess, E. W., & Wallin, P. (1953). *Engagement and marriage.* Philadelphia: Lippincott.

Cantril, H. (1951). *Public opinion, 1935–1946.* Princeton, NJ: Princeton University Press.

Cavan, R. S., & Ranck, K. H. (1938). *The family and the Depression.* Chicago: University of Chicago Press.

Dickerson, R. E. (1937). *Getting started in marriage.* International Association of YMCAs.

Diescher, V. H. (1923). *The book of good manners.* New York: Social Culture Publications.

Duvall, E. M., & Hill, R. (1949). *When you marry.* New York: Association Press.

Elder, G. H., Jr. (1974). *Children of the Great Depression.* Chicago: University of Chicago Press.

Elder, G. H., Jr. (1979). Approaches to social change and the family. In J. Demos & S. S. Boocock (Eds.), *Turning points: Historical and sociological essays on the family.* Supplement to *American Journal of Sociology* (Vol. 84).

Gallup, G. (1972). *The Gallup Poll* (Vol. 2, p. 1145). New York: Random House.

Gebhard, P. H., & Johnson, A. B. (1979). *The Kinsey data: Marginal tabulations of the 1938–1963 interviews.* Philadelphia: Saunders.

Gordon, M. (Ed.). (1978). *The American family in social-historical perspective* (2nd ed.). New York: St. Martin's Press.

Groves, E. R. (1933). *Marriage.* New York: Henry Holt & Company.

Hareven, T. K. (Ed.). (1978). *Transitions: The family and the life course in historical perspective.* New York: Academic Press.

Hill, R. (1949). *Families under stress.* New York: Harper.

Himes, N. E. (1940). *Your marriage.* New York: Farrar & Reinhart.

Kuhn, M. H. (1942). The engagement. In H. Becker & R. Hill (Eds.), *Marriage and the family.* Boston: D.C. Heath.

Kuhn, M. H. (1948). The engagement: Thinking about marriage. In. H. Becker & R. Hill (Eds.), *Family, marriage, and parenthood.* Boston: D. C. Heath.

The Law of Engagement Rings. (1934). *United States Law Review, 68:* 342–351.

Love Hazards. (1935, April). *True Confessions, 26,* p. 22.

MacFadden, B. (1942, March). Why not marry? *True Romances,* p. 4.

Mach, W., & Kiser, D. J. (Eds.). (1938). *Corpus juris secundum.* Brooklyn, NY: American Law Book Company.

McConaghy, J. L. (1938). Now that you are engaged. In W. F. Bigelow (Ed.), *The Good Housekeeping marriage book.* New York: Prentice-Hall.

McGill, N. P., & Matthews, E. N. (1940). *The youth of New York City.* New York: Macmillan.

Modell, J. (1979). Changing risks, changing adaptations: American families in the nineteenth and twentieth centuries. In A. J. Litchtman & J. Challinor (Eds.), *Kin and communities.* Washington, DC: Smithsonian Institute Press.

Modell, J. (1983). Dating becomes the way of American youth. In L. P. Moch & G. Stark (Eds.), *Essays on the family and historical change.* College Station, TX: Texas A & M Press.

Popenoe, P. (1934). Betrothal. *American Journal of Social Hygiene, 20,* pp. 444–448.

Popenoe, P. (1936). *Betrothal.* New York: American Social Hygiene Association.

Popenoe, P. (1940, June). Two million lovers are desperately asking: When can we marry? *The American Magazine, 129,* p. 22.

Popenoe, P., & Neptune, D. W. (1938). Acquaintance and betrothal. *Social Forces, 16,* 552–555.

Post, E. (1922). *Etiquette.* New York: Funk and Wagnalls.

Poster, M. (1978). *Critical theory of the family.* New York: Seabury Press.

Rapp, R., Ross, E., & Bridenthal, R. (1979). Examining family history. *Feminist Studies,* 5, 174–200.

Rockwood, L. D., & Ford, M. E. N. (1945). *Youth, marriage, and parenthood.* New York: Wiley.

Richardson, A. S. (1925). *Standard etiquette.* New York: Harper.

Rosenberg, C. E. (Ed.). (1975). *The family in history.* Philadelphia: University of Pennsylvania Press.

Ten modern commandments. (1935, February). *True Confessions, 26,* p. 62.

Terman, L. M. (1938). *Psychological factors in marital happiness.* New York: McGraw-Hill.

Tilly, L., & Cohen, M. (1982). Does the family have a history? *Social Science History, 6,* 131–179.

Vogue's book of etiquette. (1936). Garden City, NY: Doubleday, Doran.

Winn, M. (1933, August). Depression lovers. *True Confessions, 23,* p. 55.

Zachry, C. (1942). The adolescent and his problems today. In S. M. Gruenberg (Ed.), *The family in a world at war.* New York: Harper.

PART THREE

FAMILY DEVELOPMENT AND POLICY ISSUES

9

Family Dynamics and Family Planning

KURT W. BACK
Duke University

FAMILIES AND GROUPS

Procreation is a natural process, depending on intermittent action of individual organisms. Family planning is a concerted, long-range activity by a social unit or group of two or more people. The first is a necessary biological event; the second a human activity, social and personal. It would seem reasonable that efforts to control human population could stress the purely human effort and emphasize joint action, without neglecting, to be sure, the general biological necessities.

The facts have been different, however. The study of population control has been motivated on the one hand by large considerations of the society—macroeconomics and macrosiology—and on the other hand, by studying the individual use of birth-control techniques, the decision-making of starting or ending contraception. The intermediate level, the planning with the family, has been almost pointedly neglected. Reuben Hill's contribution shines as an exception and as an example of the importance of this aspect. As background to his contribution, we must place his work in the context of research on the individual and groups.

Reuben Hill has consistently treated the family as a dynamic unit, applying different approaches from sociological theory to discuss the several functions of the family. Behind these facets there was a general model that looked at the family as a small group and analyzed internal as well as external functions in concrete detail, but conformed to a general theory of group behavior. Fertility and contraception can then be treated as genuine family planning (Hill, 1967).

The essence of this approach is to see the family as a group. The group is the extension of the individual in space and time. Groups provide primary networks for interaction with other people, extending the person into a social sphere. Groups also provide continuity in time—throughout and even beyond the individual life. In this context, the family is a prime example. It is one of the oldest and most persistent

Work on this chapter was supported in part by a grant from the Duke University Research Council.

forms of association, and it keeps strong emotional bonds and exerts influence throughout the member's life (Back, 1981).

One would think it natural to be a consequence for families to be studied with the group framework, but small group theory has inherent obstacles to this kind of application. Groups are not given immediately to cognition as is an individual, and they are less pervasive or visible in their products than large social units. In studying them we can only immediately see aggregates of people, with all the difficulties of dealing with the multiplicity of traits of individuals while we are looking for group variables such as cohesion, group goals, power, and communication structure.

The history of small group research has exposed this difficult position; in many regards high hopes and energetic advances have been followed by disappointment at the results (Back, 1979), especially if applied to particular group interactions. This then led to renewed emphasis on individual and large-scale factors that are more easily comprehensible, have a larger history of theory and research, and are more plausible in producing immediate changes. Group dynamics has developed as a general branch of social psychology, but it is rarely effective as basis for a particular area of social life. Thus family planning is seldom seen in group terms. On the one hand programs are directed at individual persuasion, on the other hand the hope is expressed that general economic development will lead automatically to rational population control. The group perspective, namely that family planning is a function of a family over its own life course, is given little consideration.

Like any group, the family can be a perceptual unit (Tamney, 1967). We can mark a beginning of family formation, even in an extended family system where the individual couple is just one unit in a larger, multigenerational whole. The family can be seen by others as well as by the participants as a unit that progresses over time and that has norms of this progress. Fertility, the function of this group that changes it size and transforms it, in addition to being one of its important functions, can be seen in the same time frame. This means that an incisive approach to fertility in the family framework should look at the family both as a group network and as a unit extending or changing in time. The changes in the family that occur as a result of fertility—and even the lack of such changes as in problems of sterility—are potential sources of gratification and irritation. This effect can be cushioned by the physical and social situation, especially by personal and family resources and by prevailing norms.

Biological, interpersonal, social, ideological, and historical conditions influence the smooth course of this plan. Failures, imposed limitations, and changes in plan can put stress on the functioning of the family while it pursues what its members think of as its normal destiny. In this framework we can place the work on family planning in its proper setting and can inquire under which conditions the importance of the family as a focus of concern can be recognized.

THE BACKGROUND OF FAMILY PLANNING

Demographic Need

Concern with overpopulation is one source of family planning. For a long time the basic theory of the stabilization of population size has been the theory of demographic transition (Thompson, 1929). Essentially, the theory says that given economic, social, and medical development the death rate will drop first and later the birth rate will drop as well. Therefore we can distinguish three stages: (1) the traditional society with high death rates and high birth rates balancing each other; (2) the transitional stage where the drop in death rates will lead to a rapidly expanding population; (3) and modern society where the low death rate is balanced by a low birth rate. This theory seemed to describe the Western experience of the 19th and 20th centuries, causing demographers to generalize this experience as a universal rule in human history.

Clearly the main immediate interest in the application of the theory is the change from the second to third stage, the demographic transition in the narrow sense. A more detailed look at change from a rapid population expansion to decline in the birth is indicated.

Malthus (1798/1970) was the first to express this concern in an organized fashion. In opposition to contemporary welfare theorists such as (and in particular) William Godwin, he tried to prove that population increase would vitiate any improvement in public welfare; that population would always expand to the extreme limit of food supply. In the present context it is remarkable that Malthus considered that fertility only occurred within the family, but that once a family was formed it would occur automatically. Thus the only remedies for overpopulation were the negative ones via such causes for an increase of mortality as war and epidemic, and the only positive one was via the decrease in fertility due to delay of marriage. Other fertility decreases he condemned as vice. In fact the decline in fertility during this period—up to the middle of the 19th century—was really related to changes in family formation, and hence is called by Ansley Coale (1973) the "Malthusian Decline of Fertility." However, there had previously been times when fertility changed with economic conditions, a sign that people could control fertility within the family when it seemed to be necessary.

A second stage consists of the decline of fertility within marriage. This Coale has called the "Neo-Malthusian stage." The reasons for the beginning of the second stage are still controversial. The traditional theory (Himes, 1963) has held that the desire to control fertility is universal but that the improved birth control methods enabled people to act accordingly; Ariès (1960) claims, on the other hand, that there are wide variations in sexual activity and desire. At the critical time, there was a switch from acceptance of birth as a fact of nature to a desire of control fertility; the available means were adapted, and new techniques found ready markets. Supportive evidence for both theories points to an interaction of availability and desire: If the need for contraception is high, then techniques will be developed, but techniques can create needs by themselves.

Demographic Theory

In its classical form as well as in its elaborations, transition theory assumed large-scale influences within the society to which individuals as well as families would conform. Any desired changes such as acceleration of the decline in fertility would then have to be induced by changes in the large-scale factors, such as education, industrialization, or women's employment outside the home. Influence on the individual or the family would not have to be attempted. Extreme application of the theory would imply an almost automatic adjustment to the decline in mortality.

Transition theory has not lived up to this ideal in this simple form. Even more sophisticated analyses of the transition such as the one by Coale describe only the facts, but do not analyze the process. Later analysis has also shown that the theory is deficient even as a description of the Western experience. The decline in European fertility started before the decline of mortality (McKeown, 1976). Furthermore, the current conditions in less developed countries are sufficiently different from the European experience that extrapolation becomes extremely questionable.

The stability of modern society that is implied by the theory also failed to occur. Demographic transition theory also has its difficulties in explaining the current fluctuation in industrialized countries (Höhn & Mackensen, 1980). The different phases of post-1945 fertility changes— the baby boom, baby bust, and relative increases after 1975—and the questions of teenage pregnancy do not conform to the long-range trends of the demographic transition theory and thus need new, particularized, explanations. The difficulties with the original theory in representing the Western fertility changes and its doubtful pertinence to other countries have less reliance on the social forces, and more acceptance on an individual orientation.

Contraception

The impetus for promoting contraception came not from any concern with national economic problems but with individual well-being. The need for safe and effective contraceptives arose as a medical problem for women whose health suffered by almost continuous pregnancies, especially those in poverty conditions. Other motives include help for women's economic independence and social status, and even radical changes in society. All groups and individuals concerned with these issues—physicians, social workers, nurses, feminists, anarchists—saw the problems of the individual and saw in birth control a way to aid individuals to manage their personal deprivations and their status in society (Kennedy, 1970; Reed, 1978).

The medical channeling of contraceptive practice emphasized the individual orientation. The interest of physicians and the legitimation of the emerging specialty of gynecology helped to make birth control respectable, and even the new medical clinics tried to gain acceptance by following the medical model. This model also followed the individual treatment procedure, treating women as persons rather than members of families.

Family Sociology

Concern for the family as a unit was quite independent from developments in family planning (Howard, 1981). Family sociology dealt first with such topics as comparative studies of different forms of family types, the family and the legal system, family formation and dissolution—that is, looking at the family from the outside, or from a macroscopic perspective. Only in the 1940s and later were internal events added to the discussion. These included authority relations and the areas of different authority and decision making, intensity of the relationship of the nuclear and extended family, stages of family relations in different ages, and the family as a consumption unit. An interactional framework accordingly developed (Hill, 1958). The study of the family as also related to different theories in sociology, and the place of the family in different schemes, such as Parsons' Adaptation-Gratification-Integration-Latent Pattern Maintenance system (AGIL), was treated in detail (Parsons & Bales, 1955).

The two principal approaches from family sociology have been the institutional and interactional. The first looks at the family from the outside, as part of society; the second from the inside, as the actions of the family members toward each other. The institutional approach would look at fertility in a way similar to that of the demographer, viewing them in the context of different family arrangements. The interactional approach would go much more into the processes of sex and birth—the decisions, rituals, and activities that would lead to different fertility patterns.

Neither of these approaches was very effective in dealing with population control. It can be said that this was connected to a reluctance to deal with sex and fear that dealing with it would bring family sociology into disrepute. Institutional family sociologists thus dealt with fertility by itself, without considering the sexual basis to any great degree, while interactionists shied away from the whole topic, preferring to deal with the child after he or she was born.

This reluctance of family researchers is shown in early empirical research in contraception (Back, 1980). Some early demographic studies documented large-scale trends in fertility, if not in contraceptive behavior. At the time—in the 1930s—the trend of the studies was to explain the decline of the birth rate and, if any action was called for, to counteract it. Similarly in the first survey, research studies in fertility such as the Indianapolis study (Whelpton & Kiser, 1946–1958), the concern motivating the study was population decline and general questions on contraception and the desired number of children. When in the decades following World War II concern about overpopulation arose, especially in East Asia and the Caribbean, the same model was followed.

This emphasis has meant that the two aspects of population control, the national needs and individual acts, had been kept separate. Micro studies were directed toward individual action, and work on the family was neglected in family planning.

THE PUERTO RICAN STUDY

Reuben Hill's contribution in this situation was to combine these strands in one research project. The Puerto Rican study was motivated by the need for population control, conducted in the framework of contraception and concentrated within the family setting. In a first pilot study, Stycos (1955) had drawn attention to the different perceptions of men and women regarding issues connected with contraceptive use. Reuben Hill then helped lead the study in the direction of integrating family sociology with demographic concerns.

One can see the significance and, for better or worse, the uniqueness of Hill's contribution in the design of the Puerto Rican Study. It gave equal place to family structure, motivation, and information, in the design of the study as well as in theory and analysis. The family was studied not as an abstract pattern or simple cohabitation of two people, but as a dynamic unit. It can be studied through its interrelations of power, communication, and perception. These internal conditions of the family were studied through direct indicators such as questions about power relations and topics of communication, as well as through indirect conditions such as agreement, empathy, and type of marital arrangement (Hill, Stycos, & Back, 1959).

The study also included an action research program where family conditions were included. Family variables (communication, wife's activity and dominance) were used to select respondents who could profit by the program; attempts at changing these variables, especially communication, also figured as a content of the program itself. Sketchy as it was, it was an attempt to integrate family education into family planning programs.

The design represented an interactional point of view of the family, with the balance toward individual contributions to the interaction process. This emphasis is in part a reaction to the prevailing institutional explanation of fertility, such as economic value of children, religious proscription of family planning, or desire for continuity of the family. The rapid social change in Puerto Rico should have undermined all these obstacles to family planning. In fact, governmental policy was, for its time, one of the most antinativist in the world. But this encouragement, through government clinics and support of private groups, did not translate itself into fertility decline, that is, the ultimate action of individuals. Thus, the source of the difficulty rested in the action of the individual, singly or jointly in the family.

The results of the study showed the role of the internal family conditions. They were not effective in starting contraceptive behavior or in setting fertility goals; any specific organization of the family can lead either to large or to small families. However, once a decision has been made—or putting it less strongly, once a favorable tendency in any direction exists—family structure will determine whether efficient action will be taken, especially over a longer period of time. Thus, the influence of family dynamics or of change in it will not be apparent immediately, but will be important in the long run. Families, like groups in general, provide inertia to action systems; they provide the resistance to rapid change but give massive support of a continuation once it has started. The discrepancy between a decision and the possibility of its execution is one aspect of the effectiveness of a particular family. Family education that reduces stress will also aid in achieving family size goals.

Reuben Hill also identified social characteristics of a family along a folk–modern continuum that were related to family functioning as well as to fertility control. Here a family could be measured as a whole group characterized by urban residence, legal marriage, and high education. This typology showed the influence of structural conditions on family dynamics and indicated how large-scale social changes could eventually lead to modern family types, which are efficient in pursuing new goals, including fertility plans. This analysis can lead to suggestions of general policy and programs directed expressly toward family planning, by providing families with conditions for necessary change.

It would be gratifying to report that these ideas have been taken up in population research and are now an essential part of family planning programs. However, this has not been the case. In fact, follow-up on the family variables in family planning has been so sparse that the findings of the study are generally accepted, uncontroverted because not restudied.

The reasons for this paradoxical situation—the facts accepted but not implemented—are complex. Some of them are cognitive and technical, such as the fact that it is difficult to handle groups as units. Others are political and ideological. *Family* is a value-laden term, and family policies follow the vagaries of social change and social fashion. The next sections discuss these two sets of conditions.

TECHNICAL OBSTACLES

Defects in Theory

A crucial characteristic of the family as a small group is its time perspective. The progress of time from family formation or entry of a person into a family remains salient in the perception of the state of the group. There is a naturally and culturally determined norm of progression that is implicitly accepted and used as a standard of comparison of one's own desires and performance. All groups have a temporal dimension of this kind. Some are relatively stable, or the time dimension does not imply any definite progression. The family, however, is defined as much by its temporal as by its spatial dimensions.

Theorizing about individual decision making is relatively simple. Complexities are introduced by considering more than one person or by studying the process over time. Studying both together confounds the problem; if considering the family in fertility research makes a time dimension imperative, then many scholars may prefer to stay away from the family for the time being. The classification of groups is exceedingly difficult even if done only on a cross-sectional basis. It is remarkable that group dynamics has studied the common features of groups but has made little effort toward a taxonomy. Such would distinguish groups according to their site, function, or important characteristics. This may be difficult in static models. The theory used in the Puerto Rican study was based on Hill's classification of six theories that included essentially static models (Hill, 1951). It is likely that later revisions of this list, which included the developmental model, were influenced by the Puerto Rican experience (Hill & Mattessich, 1979). The developmental approach is now considered one of the main theoretical models, principally through Hill's own work. It is, however, difficult to apply the theory in its present stage to specific problems such as family planning. Main expositions of this theory, such as Aldous' *Family Careers* (1978) do not reach the detailed questions of family planning or decision making about first and additional children at different stages of the developing family. Clearly much additional conceptual work is needed on this topic.

In retrospect, it is unfortunate that no questions were asked that derived directly from a time perspective, such as comparisons with an implied schedule or even the nuclear family's fit into a larger family, lineage, or generation. This would be an agenda for future research growing out of this work. In a place of rapid social change and industrialization such as Puerto Rico was, social mobility across generations is a meaningful idea for most people. But if one wants to help one's children to have a better life, then one has to think as well about who those children are going to be. Short-range changes within a family must be balanced against long-range social change, with all the stress that the contrast between the two frameworks implies. In this way fertility and social mobility and social change could be united in one family theory (Lindahl & Back, 1987).

Measurement

Theoretical as well as applied work on groups has been handicapped by the difficulty of measurement, especially because much data are obtained from individuals rather than from groups. Some measures are natural to groups, such as fertility of a family or stability of membership. But in those cases when the group data are combinations of individual responses, the step to measures of the family is problematic. This becomes important because such a high proportion of data are collected through survey research, which is an individual-oriented method.

Transformation of individual measures into those of social conditions demands both conceptual and methodological skills. Conceptually, one wants to decide whether data collected from individuals are to be used at the individual or the social level. If it is to be the latter, there has to be a decision as to how the individual measures should be processed for their use as measures of social units. Even in the smallest unit, the dyad or the marital couple, several strategies are possible, such as the average of the two members, the higher score, or the difference between the two. For such a situation, Klein (in press) has distinguished five different strategies that have been used and has suggested their appropriate use for specific conditions. The most common use, the average of the individual measures, disregards the peculiar structure of a family and the relations within it. It thus looks simple to substitute purely individual measures as representing the unit, and to take, for instance, the wife's attitude toward contraception as the determining factor. This procedure represents a return to the individual level under a new disguise.

Action

The immediate goal of most family planning programs is the adoption of contraception, as measured by distribution or by other indicators. As we have seen, family conditions are mainly effective in maintaining already initiated use, and an effect of a program in this direction would only be noticed through long-term elevated consumption rates and declining fertility. Justification of action programs comes through rapid success. In addition, extreme opposition to and failures of population control programs is frequently related to family conditions and can be attacked most easily at this place. But, again, these problem cases only appear after initially favorable population groups have been reached; such residual problems will not be important in the first flush of population control programs.

Immediate success became even more important when action programs were taken over from private organizations (especially planned parenthood organizations) by government agencies. These agencies were under an obligation to show rapid results and to use spectacular, easily explainable changes. In places where such a program was new—and the rapid spread of the population control movement, stimulated by foreign aid, always found new places—one could always find borderline individuals. They were ready to use contraception but needed a slight push from the delivery of products, some additional information, or even an increased saliency of the issue to become users. This group had been shown to be of considerable size in many developing countries, and their existence guaranteed the initial success of any program that could be instituted. With mass information or interest-raising programs being so successful there was little reason to design the more cumbersome programs of family education that would lead to results in the future. Without them, however, the programs would have to be repeated or continued. This may be a drawback but could sometimes be an advantage for the bureaucratic mind.

In 1977, Cuca and Pierce reviewed 96 experiments in contraception; only the Puerto Rican Study—called, significantly, "communication/content"—included intervention of family functioning. In one other study, in Narangwal, India, family planning was an intervention on family planning education, which might have included some content about general family condition. This treatment had initially the highest success rate, but the whole study was not completed for political reasons. With this one possible exception, family matters have not been part of experimental content and are therefore unlikely to become parts of programs that were related to these initial interventions.

Of course, one can hardly expect the experimental treatment in the study, which concentrated on family functioning and omitted any information on birth control, to be used as a model for an action program. Most programs have been concerned with the mechanics of delivery of contraceptives and the best use of personnel; in fact, Cuca and Pierce list the Puerto Rican Study under personnel. A larger scale view, trying to fit a place for family planning into the general life of the society, is of little concern to direct action agencies. The Puerto Rican Study is therefore more appreciated by the social scientists for its design, than by workers in the field for its leads on family functioning (Back, 1980; Namboodiri, Carter, & Blalock, 1975; Hilton & Lumsdaine, 1975).

The control of population programs by governments had additional consequences. Few political leaders are willing to interfere with traditional patterns of personal life unless it is absolutely necessary. Even administrations committed to large-scale change are usually fully occupied by economic planning and new power arrangements, so that they would not tend to engage government agents in changing family dynamics. Thus, with few exceptions, the government apparatus is little suited to family programs as compared to other points of leverage. In the organization of family planning programs we find the parallel of the difficulty of small group action: Family planning is either put under a ministry of planning with its tradition of large-scale social intervention, or under a department of health, with the medical tradition of one-on-one work. Even Reuben Hill himself, while working as a consultant for the Ford Foundation, did not include family dynamics in programs discussed with government officials.

IDEOLOGY

Besides the many practical reasons for neglecting family factors in work on population control, other conditions made the connection of family and population pattern difficult in the industrialized nations, especially the United States. The family is a special kind of small group, so much so that some theorists have excluded it from consideration in small group research. Application of general principles of family conditions has been difficult. Of all kinds of groups, its importance seems to have been changing most in recent years. Although the decline of the Western family has been more a rhetorical than a statement of fact, belief in a decline has certainly hampered work on the family as a source of power and influence in the current scene. Thus, ideological orientation has militated here against the consideration of the family.

Two main reasons have inhibited concern of action programs of the family. They may seem contradictory and are in fact supported by different groups, but they work together in opposing concern with family functioning. These are the feeling of the sanctity of the family and the belief in the decline of the family, especially as part of feminist ideology.

Traditionally, the family has been the sanctuary from public control, the "haven in a heartless world" (Lasch, 1977). The mentality articulated by the phrase of "My home is my castle" has been undermined by the state's concern for welfare of the individual and by society's assumption of control over education, health, and discipline (Dozelot, 1979). This has left very little space for private life within the home; the residue consists of the emotional personal actions. These are important in contraception decision making on eventual family size and spacing, plans for the future, and management of sex life. Any overt policy on these matters, such as laws, agency rules, or even publicly sponsored education and propaganda can easily arouse emotional resistance. This resistance can lead to organized political resistance that in turn can jeopardize other government programs.

Demographic trends have given some support to the assumptions of declining family influence. Surging divorce rates would seem to make long-range family planning less realistic; however, the number of broken homes has not necessarily risen. Divorce has replaced bereavement as a cause. Sexual activity outside marriage—especially among teenagers—has increased, and pregnancy and childbearing outside of marriage have become more important. Even here, attention to the spectacular rise has obscured the fact that we are talking about a minority of the population, based on a cross-sectional slice of life. Most fertility and fertility planning occurs within relatively stable families. Over the life course, people still spend a long time in families. For the same reason—attention to changes in a minority—some writers may ignore the still considerable influence of the family in fertility-relevant actions. Even where problems such as the rise in teenage fertility occur, the possible importance of family influence has been relatively neglected (Back, 1983).

The demise of the family has been assumed and sometimes applauded. The emphasis on women's rights as well as homoesexual rights has been directed against the family. Feminists, especially at the early phases of the current feminist movements, have seen the family more as a locus for power struggle than as a forum for decision making (Leghorn & Parker, 1981). As the Hunter College Women's Collective

(1983) noted with approval: "Feminist utopian literature seems generally to argue against the institution of marriage" (p. 275). From this point of view too, individual attention on contraception instead of family planning is preferred.

Both of these trends are influential among "progressive" social scientists and combine in opposition to policies and action programs that are based primarily on the family and address the family as a unit. Attempts to throw responsibility for teenage pregnancy on the family are not only controversial but are immediately ridiculed. A bill to support research into adolescent pregnancy, to initiate programs to control teenage sexual behavior, and to encourage adoption is called the "chastity bill." Regulations to inform parents of the use of contraceptives by dependent children is called the "squeal rule." This opposition is summarized in a discussion on "The Futility of Family Policy" (Steiner, 1981).

NEW NEEDS FOR FAMILY ORIENTATION

In the world-wide concern about the population explosion and domestic concerns about social issues, the importance of the family has been relatively neglected. The place of the family in maintaining the appropriate action that Reuben Hill had demonstrated in theory and research has not been doubted in principle, but the array of circumstances that we sketched have led to their temporary eclipse in the amount of attention given to it. In an overview of the development of population control, we can see that this might have been a reasonable development. Input into organizations or groups must consist of a body of knowledge and a set of goals. Only then can the group organize itself to achieve these aims. Thus, an emphasis on popularizing small families and acceptability of birth control methods was a necessary first step in population control. Concomitant social changes diverted attention to the stresses within the family instead of its strength. Once the possible success of family planning is demonstrated, interest can return to the mechanisms that can maintain it. Here the influence of efficient family structure may be paramount.

The easy initial successes of population control, reaching the population groups that were ready and eager for it, have been achieved. The beginnings of family developmental theory have helped in improving the theoretical foundations, and improved methodology has made new research techniques possible. The persistence of the family in economic and social change is becoming more and more evident (Inkeles, 1984). Even feminist leaders are appreciating the family as a necessary and valuable social unit (Friedan, 1982; Greer, 1984). In general, the link between personal family size goals and appropriate behavior that a family action program was to provide is assuming more importance. Such does much to vindicate Reuben Hill's work as a pioneering effort, raising the hope that this valuable work might mark the way for future study. We may now have reached the time to fill in the pieces of his grand design.

REFERENCES

Aldous, J. (1978). *Family careers.* New York: Wiley.
Ariès, P. (1960). Interpretation pour une histoire des mentalités. In H. Berques (Ed.), *La prevention des naissances dans la famille: Les origines dans les temps modernes.* Paris: INED, Presses Universitaires de France.
Back, K. W. (1979). The small group—tightrope between sociology and personality. *Journal of Applied Behavioral Sciences, 15*(3), 283–294.
Back, K. W. (1980). The role of social psychology in population control. In L. Festinger (Ed.), *Retrospections in social psychology.* New York: Oxford University Press.
Back, K. W. (1981). Small groups. In M. Rosenberg & R. H. Turner (Eds.), *Social psychology.* New York: Basic Books.
Back, K. W. (1983). Teenage pregnancy: Science and ideology in applied social psychology. In R. F. Kidd & M. J. Saks (Eds.), *Advances in applied social psychology* (Vol. 2). Hillsdale, NJ: Erlbaum.
Coale, A. J. (1973). The demographic transition reconsidered. In *International population conference* (Vol. 1). Liege, Belgium: Council of the International Union for the Scientific Study of Population.
Cuca, R., & Pierce, C. S. (1977). *Experiments in family planning.* Baltimore, MD: Johns Hopkins University Press.
Donzelot, J. (1979). *The policing of families.* New York: Pantheon.
Friedan, B. (1982). *The second stage.* New York: Summit Books.
Greer, G. (1984). *Sex and destiny: The politics of human fertility.* New York: Harper & Row.
Hill, R. (1951). Review of current research on marriage and the family. *American Sociological Review, 16,* 694–701.
Hill, R. (1958). Sociology of marriage and family behavior 1945–56: A trend report and bibliography. *Current Sociology, 7*(1), 1–98.
Hill, R. (1967). The significance of the family in population research. In W. T. Liu (Ed.), *Family and fertility.* Notre Dame, IN: University of Notre Dame Press.
Hill, R., & Mattessich, O. (1979). Family development theory and life span development. In P. B. Baltes & O. G. Brim, Jr. (Eds.), *Life-span development and behavior* (pp. 162–204). New York: Academic Press.
Hill, R., Stycos, J. M., & Back, K. W. (1959). *The family and population control.* Chapel Hill, NC: University of North Carolina Press.
Hilton, E. T., & Lumsdaine, A. A. (1975). Field trial designs in gauging the impact of fertility planning programs. In C. A. Bennett & A. A. Lumsdaine (Eds.), *Evaluation and experiments.* New York: Academic Press.
Himes, N. (1963). *The medical history of contraception.* New York: Gamut.
Höhn, C., & Mackensen, R. (1980). *Determinants of fertility trends: Theories reexamined.* Liege, Belgium: Ordina.
Howard, R. L. (1981). *A social history of American family sociology 1865–1940.* Westport, CT: Greenwood.
Hunter College Women's Study Collective. (1983). *Women's realities, women's choices.* New York: Oxford University Press.

Inkeles, A. (1984). The responsiveness of family patterns to economic change in the United States. *The Tocqueville Review, 6,* 5–50.

Kennedy, D. M. (1970). *Birth control in America: The career of Margaret Sanger.* New Haven, CT: Yale University Press.

Klein, D. (in press). The problem of multiple perception family research. In L. Larson & J. White (Eds.), *Interpersonal perceptions in families.*

Lasch, C. (1977). *Haven in a heartless world.* New York: Basic Books.

Leghorn, L., & Parker, K. (1981). *Woman's worth.* Boston: Routledge and Kegan Paul.

Lindahl, M. L., & Back, K. W. (1987). Lineage identity and generational continuity: Family history and family reunions. *Comprehensive Gerontology, 1*(8), 30–34.

Malthus, T. (1798/1970). *An essay on the principles of population.* Hammondsworth, England: Penguin.

McKeown, T. (1976). *The modern rise of population.* London: E. Arnold.

Namboodiri, N. K., Carter, L. F., & Blalock, H. M., Jr. (1975). *Applied multivariate analysis and experimental design.* New York: McGraw-Hill.

Parsons, T., & Bales, R. F. (1955). *Family, socialization and interaction process.* Glencoe, IL: Free Press.

Reed, J. (1978). *From private vice to public virtue.* New York: Basic Books.

Steiner, G. Y. (1981). *The futility of family policy.* Washington, DC: Brookings.

Stycos, J. M. (1955). *Family and fertility in Puerto Rico.* New York: Columbia University Press.

Tamney, J. B. (1967). Family solidarity and fertility. In W. T. Liu (Eds.), *Family and fertility.* Notre Dame, IN: University of Notre Dame Press.

Thompson, W. C. (1929). Population. *American Journal of Sociology, 34,* 961–962.

Whelpton, P. K., & Kiser, C. V. (1946–1958). *Social and psychological factors affecting fertility* (Vols. 1–5). New York: Milbank Memorial Fund.

10

Adolescent Fertility-Related Behavior and Its Family Linkages

BRENT C. MILLER
Utah State University
STEPHEN R. JORGENSEN
Texas Tech University

INTRODUCTION

There is a well-established research tradition about fertility related behavior,[1] but the specific focus on adolescents is relatively recent. Attention to adolescent fertility was probably stimulated by the recognition that negative health consequences are associated with early childbearing, and by increasing rates of nonmarital adolescent childbearing (National Center for Health Statistics (NCHS), 1984). Epidemiological data show higher obsterical complications among teen mothers and higher health risks for their infants (Menken, 1980). It is now well documented, however, that most negative maternal and infant health outcomes are not the direct result of the mother's age or biological immaturity, but rather the result of less adequate prenatal care and the social and economic disadvantages of early parenthood (Makinson, 1985; Mednick, Baker, & Sutton-Smith, 1979; Nortman, 1974). In addition to health and medical risks, however, there are many psychological, social, and economic reasons to be concerned about adolescent fertility-related behaviors (Alan Guttmacher Institute, 1981; Baldwin & Cain, 1980; Bolton, 1980; Card & Wise, 1978; Hayes, 1987; McAnarney, 1982; Nye & Lamberts, 1980).

Interest in specifying the family linkages to adolescent fertility-related behavior seems to have come about for several reasons. One impetus for increasing our knowledge in this area stems directly from federal legislation. Passage of the Adolescent Family Life Act of 1981 mandated that family-centered demonstration programs be provided to promote parental involvement in reducing the problems of adolescent pregnancy (Mecklenburg & Thompson, 1983). Adolescent fertility-related issues are extremely controversial, of course, including as they do such topics as sex education, sexual behavior, contraception, abortion, childbearing, and the rights of children vis-à-vis their parents. Social and educational programs targeted at teens have sometimes by-passed parents (Ooms, 1981), and some have expressed concern that parental rights and roles have been ignored. As a result, program planners and policy makers often seek to understand better how the family fits into the picture of adolescent fertility-related behavior. Another reason for clarifying the linkages between family and fertility is the impetus common to all basic theory and research: to understand better the antecedents and consequences of an important realm of life.

This chapter addresses the relationships between adolescent fertility-related behaviors and family structures and processes. We first place family-oriented fertility research in the broader context of fertility studies in general. We then provide an overview of contemporary fertility-related behavior among adolescents and summarize what is known about the association of family variables with teen fertility-related behavior. In the final section we summarize our findings and make recommendations for further research in understanding family–fertility linkages among adolescents.

FERTILITY RESEARCH AND THE FAMILY

The most prominent approaches to fertility research emphasize demographic rates and trends in large population categories, or relate societal level economic variables to fertility-related outcomes. A psychological and social-psychological approach, which emphasizes individual decision making, motivations, and values of children, has emerged relatively recently (Fawcett, 1972, 1973; Hoffman & Manis, 1979; Pohlman, 1969).

Marriage and family variables are not often recognized as being important to the understanding of fertility behavior (Cogswell & Sussman, 1979), except as regulating variables such as the age of marriage. A well-known way of conceptualizing how marital and familial events affect childbearing was first formalized by Davis and Blake (1956) as a set of "intermediate variables" that intervene between macro level social norms on the one hand, and fertility levels on the other. For example, the age at marriage, the proportion of those who marry versus those who remain single, the proportion of those who divorce, and the amount of time before remarriage are all related to fertility because of their bearing on exposure to sexual intercourse in marital contexts that are socially approved for childbearing (Westoff, 1978a, 1978b). Relationships between fertility and some family characteristics such as divorce, extendedness, and polygamy are very complex and are still not clearly understood (Levin & O'Hara, 1978; Miller, 1987; Okaka, Yaukey, & Chevan, 1977; Ryder, 1976; Thornton, 1978).

Another way of linking family to fertility is to examine lineage patterns in childbearing. Many studies have found a positive relationship, for example, between the number of siblings and the number of children (see Thornton, 1980, for a review). It can be argued that macro level social, economic, and other cultural influences on fertility are partly transmitted intergenerationally through socialization experiences in the family. Thornton's (1980) critical assessment of mechanisms that could produce relationships between family of origin characteristics and fertility included: (1) socialization toward similar standards of living and economic consumption that appear to be related to childbearing; (2) socialization toward similar aspirations, preferences, and desires about family size; (3) the transmission of parental knowledge or ignorance about contraception and its utilization; (4) children's attempts to recreate role relationships that existed in their own families of orientation; and (5) the biological transmission of varying fecundity through heredity.

Although the "intermediate" family variables have long been recognized as being important in understanding fertility, the internal workings of families had been virtually ignored until the Puerto Rican studies of Hill, Stycos, and Back (1959). The unusual feature of their research was the degree to which internal family relationships and marital dynamics were incorporated into the study of fertility planning and behavior. Focusing on marital communication patterns and power relationships, Hill *et al.* (1959) found strong relationships between fertility behavior and the ways that families operate internally. Fertility was highest among families in which the wife remained at home under the rule of a strongly dominating husband who placed many restrictions on her activities and in which marital communication about sexual aspects of the marital relationship and family planning was most limited. Fertility was lowest among families in which the wife worked outside the home, where her husband was less dominant and restrictive, and where communication channels were open and two-way in the sexual and family planning domains of the relationship. In sum, marital communication patterns and power relations were found to be strongly related to competence in fertility planning and success in fertility control.

After the Hill *et al.* (1959) work, few fertility studies have included, much less emphasized, family dynamics or internal processes. One exception is Rainwater's (1965) research. The most effective contraceptive use and family size limitation patterns in Rainwater's sample of low income and working-class couples were those in which: (1) marital role organization was shared between spouses (division of labor and decision making) and (2) sexual mutuality existed in the form of each partner being concerned for the sexual gratification and fulfillment of the other. Another example is Scanzoni's (1975, 1976) studies of gender roles in society and within marriage in relation to fertility outcomes. Linking together his studies of women's sex role orientations, work, and fertility,

Scanzoni (1979) suggested that "sex role modern" women negotiate more explicitly and effectively with their husbands for innovative work and fertility control sequences early in their marriages, thus achieving lower fertility.

ISSUES IN UNDERSTANDING ADOLESCENT FERTILITY-RELATED BEHAVIOR

Before considering family linkages to adolescent fertility-related behavior, it is critically important to understand the nature and scope of this adolescent problem. By first defining key terms and presenting rates and trends, the reader should be better prepared to comprehend how family variables are associated with adolescent fertility-related behavior.

At the outset, it is important to distinguish between adolescent *pregnancy* and *childbearing* (Chilman, 1980a). In the past adolescent childbearing was sometimes used as an approximation of adolescent pregnancy, but since the legalization of abortion in 1973, this practice is increasingly misleading (Miller, 1985). Fewer than one half of all adolescents who experience a pregnancy actually carry it to term and deliver the baby, due to pregnancy losses through miscarriage, stillbirths, and induced abortion (Baldwin, 1983; Hayes, 1987). Nonetheless, there often are adverse effects of a pregnancy for the adolescent female or male regardless of whether or not the pregnancy is carried to term. We will therefore focus on adolescent pregnancy, a concept that includes pregnancies that result in live births and those which do not.

It is also important to define age parameters because researchers vary in their operational definitions of "adolescent," often confusing the term with "teenager." Many major studies include only 15- to 19-year olds without adequate recognition of the fact that fertility-related behavior is also salient for some younger adolescents—from 10 or 11 to 14. Failing to differentiate older adolescents (ages 18 or 19) from younger ones (ages 15 or 16) within the 15- to 19-year-old category is also misleading in that older adolescents have far better expected medical outcomes following pregnancy and are more likely to have completed a high school education (Baldwin, 1982). For our purposes here, we will be concerned with the population age 19 and under where fertility control is a salient issue (usually down to 10 or 11 years of age), differentiating by age category where age-specific data are available.

Both the numbers and rates of births among adolescents have gone through gradual up-and-down fluctuations in the 1960s and 1970s (Baldwin 1982; National Center for Health Statistics, 1984). In general, the following conclusions can be drawn from the national fertility statistics on 14- to 19-year-old adolescent females (Baldwin, 1985):

1. The number of births increased between 1960 (609,141) and 1970 (656,460), but declined between 1970 and 1982 (523,531).

2. The number and rate of nonmarital (illegitimate) births increased between 1960 (91,700 and 15.3 per 1,000) and 1970 (199,900 and 22.4 per 1,000), and between 1970 and 1982 (269,346 and 28.9 per 1,000) as a growing percentage of adolescent mothers remained single.

3. The decline in the total number and rate of births to adolescents since 1970 has been concentrated among older adolescents (18–19 years of age), while not until the late 1970s did birth rates among younger adolescents (ages 17 and under) begin to decline.

4. Adolescent childbearing rates are substantially higher for blacks than whites, with the black–white adolescent birth rate ratio greater for younger (4.8:1 for 14-year-olds) than older adolescents (1.8:1 for 19-year-olds).

5. The percentage of 15- to 19-year-old adolescent mothers who kept their babies rather than giving them up for adoption rose from 86% in 1971 to 93% in 1979, and appears to have changed very little since then (Bachrach, 1985).

Although the childbearing data presented above are important, adolescent pregnancy, not childbearing, is an even more meaningful indicator of adolescent fertility-related behavior. Unfortunately, the national statistics on pregnancies to females under age 20 are less accurate than those on childbearing because of reporting differences across states and reporting errors and omissions. In regard to the *number* of pregnancies, we can say that in every year from 1980 to 1984 more than 1 million pregnancies—perhaps as many as 1.2 to 1.3 million—occurred to adolescent females under age 20 in the United States (Hayes, 1987). Most of these occurred outside of marriage, and most were unintended. This statistic appears to have leveled off during the early 1980s.

In regard to adolescent pregnancy rates, the most reliable estimates are provided by the national survey data of Zelnik and Kantner (1980), who found that the rate of premarital pregnancies among all 15- to 19-year-old females grew significantly from 9% (1 in 11) in 1971 to 13% (1 in 8) in 1976, and then to 16% (1 in 6) in 1979. Among all sexually active 15- to 19-year-old adolescents in 1979, approximately 36% experienced a pregnancy (Koenig & Zelnik, 1982). This percentage is up from 32% found in the 1976 survey. Since the Zelnik & Kantner data do not include information about pregnacies for adolescents under 15 years of age, we do not have a precise estimate of the pregnancy rate for all adolescents. However, data provided by Baldwin (1982) show that in 1979 there were 10,699 births and 15,110 abortions to adolescents 14 years of age and younger. These figures yield a crude estimate of at least 26,000 pregnancies to adolescents younger than 15 in 1979, and this is an underestimate because miscarriage and stillbirths were not included.

REVIEW OF LITERATURE LINKING THE FAMILY TO
ADOLESCENT FERTILITY-RELATED BEHAVIOR

Our approach in this section will be to review studies that have related
a family variable or characteristic to adolescent fertility-related
behavior, emphasizing sexual intercourse and contraceptive use patterns
as the two major components of adolescent pregnancy risk. We first provide an overview of these two major pregnancy risk factors, after which
the family connections are made explicit under the broad headings of
family structure, family processes, and dyadic relationships.

Adolescent Pregnancy Risk

Zelnik and Kantner (1980) found increases in the percentage of 15- to
19-year-old adolescent females reporting sexual activity (have had intercourse, more frequent intercourse, greater number of sex partners) in
their national probability samples drawn in 1971, 1976, and 1979.
Sixty-nine percent of the females in the 1979 sample reported having
had premarital intercourse by age 19, up from 59% in 1976 and 47% in
1971. Although older adolescents are more likely to experience sexual
intercourse, Kantner and Zelnik found that 48.5% of the 17-year-olds,
37.8% of the 16-year-olds, and 22.5% of the 15-year-olds in their 1979
never-married sample had experienced intercourse, representing greater
proportional increases from 1971 than for the older (ages 18–19) adolescents. Males were not included in the 1971 or 1976 surveys, but almost
70% of the never-married adolescent males (ages 17–21) in the 1979
sample reported having had sexual intercourse, over half (55%) by age
17, and two thirds (66%) by age 18 (Zelnik & Kantner, 1980).

Despite these increases in sexual activity, contraceptive use by sexually active adolescents continues to be sporadic, ineffective, or absent
among a large number. Although adolescent contraceptive use increased
between the 1971 and 1976 surveys, Zelnik and Kantner (1980) found a
decline in use of more effective methods (e.g., the oral contraceptive
pill) and an increase in the use of less effective methods (e.g., rhythm
and withdrawal). Adolescents typically delay seeking and obtaining an
effective birth control method, often for 12 months or longer following
first intercourse (Zabin, Kantner, & Zelnik, 1979). Only half of sexually
active adolescents in 1979 used any type of contraceptive method at first
intercourse, most of which were of the nonprescription and less effective
variety (Koenig & Zelnik, 1982). More than one in four (27%) reported
using no method at all in 1979, regardless of the frequency of intercourse. Younger adolescents are less likely than older adolescents to use
contraception at first or subsequent sexual encounters, a major concern
given the greater proportionate increase in sexual activity found among

younger adolescents over the past decade. Younger adolescents were thereby at greater risk of a pregnancy in 1979 than in earlier years due to increased sexual activity combined with comparatively low rates of contraceptive use, especially of the more effective methods.

The results of these trends in adolescent sexual and contraceptive behavior are evident in the preceding discussion of the continuing high rate and numbers of adolescent pregnancies in the 1980s. Nearly one half of all adolescent pregnancies occur within 6 months after first intercourse, while 22% occur within 1 month following the initial sexual experience (Zabin et al., 1979). Unless significant changes occur in the proportion of adolescents who place themselves in a pregnancy-risk situation by engaging in unprotected sexual intercourse, we can expect little or no decrease in the number and rate of adolescent pregnancies. What role do families play in this situation?

Family Structure

The term "family structure" refers to family configuration or composition. Single-parent family structure has been the target of greatest interest in understanding structural family linkages to adolescent fertility-related behavior. Concerns have focused on understanding family of orientation structure as a partial explanation or cause of adolescent sexual activity, contraception, abortion, and childbearing.

In the case of sexual activity, Chilman's (1980b) summary of factors empirically associated with adolescent nonmarital intercourse included single-parent family status. Adolescents from single-parent families are, apparently, more likely to engage in nonmarital sexual intercourse than those from two-parent families. Perhaps because of this, mothers in female-headed households are more likely to talk with their daughters about sex and birth control than are mothers in two-parent families (Fox, 1981). Recent analyses (Miller & Bingham, in press) suggest that social class and religiosity are important mechanisms through which parents' marital status affects children's sexual behavior. Thornton and Camburn (1987) recently reported that adolescents had more sexually permissive attitudes and behavior if their parents had been divorced and remarried than if they had been divorced but not remarried or if they had never been divorced. In a longitudinal analysis, Newcomer and Udry (1987) found that the initial state of being in a mother-only household predicted the later sexual activity of daughters but not sons; sons' initiation of sexual activity was related to disruption of the parents' marriage between interviews in the study. In large national data sets, Rindfuss and St. John (1983) found no direct relationship between living with only one parent and age at first birth, although a small indirect effect was observed: Family structure was related to age at first birth through the intervening variable of education.

Rodgers (1983) reported associations between the sexual behavior of 11- to 16-year-olds and various aspects of their family configuration. Although the number of parents showed a weak relationship to adolescent sexual behavior, with those from single-parent families being most permissive, the strongest result was found for sibling structure: "Controlling for many possible confounding influences, there was a significant positive relationship between number of brothers and intercourse behavior" (Rodgers, 1983, p. 80). This intriguing finding appears not to have been replicated yet by additional studies (Miller & Bingham, in press; Miller, Higginson, & McCoy, 1987).

While single-parent family structure has been linked empirically to adolescent sexual activity and might be linked to other fertility-related behaviors, family structure also can be viewed as an outcome or consequence of adolescent fertility-related behavior. Adolescent pregnancy, for example, raises the question about whether or not marriage should or will occur. Marriage was once the most common resolution to adolescent pregnancy, but trends in nonmarital fertility and abortion have made early family formation a less likely outcome of adolescent pregnancy and childbearing than it once was. In 1980, 44% of all births to adolescents under age 20 were out of wedlock, rendering the illegitimacy rate among adolescents close to the highest ever known in the United States (Baldwin, 1985). The continuing high rate of nonmarital adolescent childbearing and small rates of relinquishing for adoption means that there is a rather sizeable new group of young, single-parent mothers each year. Single parenthood—even among adults—is known for its stresses and strains, and these situations are bound to be exacerbated for adolescents.

Regardless of whether or not adolescent parents marry, the birth of their child often influences their extended family. Studies have shown that nearly three fourths of adolescent mothers live with one or both parents at the time of the baby's birth, with nearly one in three still living in the parental home 5 years after childbirth (Baldwin, 1983). Research on adolescent mothers who continue to reside in the parental home, compared to those who are on their own as single parents or in adolescent marriages, has found that the former group are more likely to have finished high school, be employed, earn more income, and be free of welfare dependency (Baldwin, 1983; Furstenberg & Crawford, 1978). In addition, living at home with parents seems for many to generate the family support necessary for the adolescent to cope with the complex transition to the parenthood period (Miller & Sollie, 1980). This includes assistance with child care, room, food, and normal types of parenting responsibilities (e.g., discipline and socialization). Nonetheless, once the "honeymoon" period associated with having a new baby in the home is over, the family is likely to experience some degree of disillusionment and stress (Baldwin, 1983). Some adolescent mothers come to see their own mothers as less affectionate and more controlling and become dissatisfied with the mother–daughter relationship as a result. The arrival of a grandchild who moves into the parental home also has the potential for causing stress in the marital relationship of the adolescent's parents, as well as in sibling relationships in the family.

For adolescents who bear a child there is the option of adoption. As mentioned earlier, over 90% of all adolescents who deliver a baby decide to raise the child, either as a single parent or as a young married couple. As recent reports of the U.S. Office of Adolescent Pregnancy Programs (OAPP) have shown, however, there is little empirical evidence by which to understand the adoption decision (OAPP, 1982). We do not know, for example, the variables that distinguish those who decide in favor of adoption versus those who do not; what role parents and other family members play in the decision process, as well as the role of the child's father; or how children raised by an adolescent parent differ from those raised by adoptive parents. Research in this area is clearly needed and is currently being conducted.

Marital structure is influenced by adolescent childbearing in yet another way. When young people do marry, their marriages are less stable than the marriages of older mothers. Combined with parenthood, the younger the age at marriage, the higher the probability of divorce (Teachman, 1983) and subsequent single-parent family structure (Kellman, Adams, Brown, & Ensminger, 1982). Kellam *et al.* (1982, p. 552) concluded a recent report by stating that "the teenage mother is more likely to begin as the only adult at home and remain so, or to become an only adult member." So, family structure in the family of procreation appears to be influenced by adolescent childbearing.

Another way that family structure is important in understanding adolescent fertility-related behavior is as an antecedent of infant and child outcomes in the families of adolescent parents. In general, research about the effects of "father absence" is a confusing morass (Blechman, 1982), but in the case of adolescent parents detrimental effects of single parenthood may be more clear-cut. One study of disadvantaged black adolescent mothers who were the only adults in their families reported that they did in fact have less help in childbearing (Kellam *et al.*, 1982), and their childrens' early school performance and psychological well-being appeared to be adversely affected (Kellam, Ensminger, & Brown, 1979; Kellam, Ensminger, & Turner, 1977).

Family Processes and Dynamics

Like the family structure variables discussed in the previous section, family processes and dynamics can be helpful in explaining adolescent pregnancy risk and fertility. Just as Hill *et al.* (1959) found in their

Puerto Rico fertility control study, and later Rainwater (1960, 1965) reported in his studies of family planning and sexuality in American working-class marriages, family process variables are key links between sociodemographic background variables (e.g., race, income, ethnicity, education, and religion) and fertility-related behavior of adolescents.

Theorists and researchers have begun, for example, to focus on interaction processes within adolescents' parental families to predict pregnancy risk-taking behavior. Specifically, the focus has been on communication, power, and affection structures in the parent–adolescent relationship as they influence sexual behavior and contraceptive use. First among the major studies to do so was Furstenberg's (1971, 1976) analysis of unmarried pregnant black females. Adolescents who had been contraceptive users prior to pregnancy were more likely than nonusers to have mothers who communicated information about how and where to obtain contraceptives and who held a realistic understanding of sexuality and the sexual feelings of their daughters. A recent analysis by Furstenberg, Herceg-Baron, Shea, and Webb (1984) has not supported the relationship between mother–daughter communication and contraceptive use, but most other studies have supported and extended Furstenberg's earlier results. They show that daughters who have talked to their mothers about sexual and contraceptive matters are more likely than others to forestall or postpone sexual activity, and to employ more effective contraceptive methods if they do become sexually active (Fox, 1980; Fox & Inazu, 1980; Inazu & Fox, 1980; Lewis, 1973; Lindemann, 1974; Miller, Jenson, Krueger, Peterson, & Weiner, 1981; Walters & Walters, 1983).

However, researchers have also found a lack of parent–child communication about sexuality and contraception (Aldous, 1983) in the general population. Many researchers have reported that the initial source of sex information among young adolescents is peers (Gebhard, 1977; Jorgensen, 1981; Spanier, 1977; Thornburg, 1978, 1981). Although the mother–adolescent daughter relationship has tremendous potential for sexual socialization, according to Fox (1980) it is typically underutilized to a significant degree. Primary among the reasons for this appears to be an underlying discomfort with the topic of sexuality among mothers and daughters, perhaps because mothers have not fully come to grips with their own sexuality.

There also exist intrinsic strains in the typical mother–daughter relationship. These strains result from a mismatch in the major developmental tasks confronting mothers and daughters in their respective stages of personal development, as well as internal inconsistencies in the demands of the mother's role set. Adolescent daughters, on the one hand, are striving for autonomy and separation from the family; for consolidation and crystalization of the self-concept and identity; for establishing age-appropriate relationships with persons outside the family; and for self-mastery in the form of controlling impulses and accurately projecting consequences of present behavior. Mothers of adolescents, on the other hand, assume the dual tasks of protecting the "daughter-as-child" and guiding the "daughter-as-woman." As Fox (1980) points out, these tasks require a delicate balancing act for mothers:

> There are few clear guidelines for managing the conflict between these two aspects of the mother role, that is, as protector and guide. Discerning when to let go and when not to yield, when to share information and when not to, when to allow one's child to find her own way and to live out the consequences of her own decisions and when instead to take charge and make decisions on her behalf—discerning these things is hard work. (p. 26)

In addition, mothers of adolescents have their own agenda of midlife developmental tasks (or crises), which includes finding meaning in life beyond or as an extension of motherhood; making important decisions relating to careers, work changes, or educational advancement; and coping with the physical and emotional changes brought on by aging. These conflicts between mothers' tasks as parents and as developing individuals, coupled with the different foci of their tasks compared to their daughters, can greatly circumscribe the mother's ability to effectively play the role of sexual/family planning socialization agent for her adolescent daughter.

A different way of conceptualizing the mother's influence on the sexual behavior of children has recently been introduced by Newcomer and Udry (1984). Their research suggests a strong relationship between the mother's own sexual experience as an adolescent and the sexual behavior of her teenage children. They interpret their data as showing that little of this lineage effect on sexual behavior is transmitted through differential attitudes or communication patterns. Instead, they interpret their data to suggest that an inherited tendency for early sexual maturation provides the best explanation for the similarity in adolescent sexual experience between mothers and their daughters.

Building on another line of research and theory (Reiss & Miller, 1979) about the relative effects of parents and peers on adolescent sexual attitudes, Shah and Zelnik (1981) have extended earlier findings that both sources of influence are important in adolescent sexual behavior, contraceptive use, and pregnancy experience. In their national probability sample of 15- to 19-year-olds, young women's attitudes about having premarital sex are reported to be much more like the attitudes of their friends than their parents. However, adolescents whose views about sex before marriage are more like those of parents are much less likely to be sexually experienced than women whose attitudes are more like those of their peers. White adolescents influenced more by parents than peers are less likely to use contraception; however, if young women influenced more by parents do use contraceptives, they use them much more consistently. Because of these differing levels of sexual experience and contraceptive use, the premarital pregnancy rates for young women influenced more by friends is about four times as high as for those influenced more by parents.

Dyadic Relationships and Adolescent Pregnancy Risk

Another major development in research on adolescent pregnancy-risk is an extension of the Hill *et al.* (1959), Rainwater (1960, 1965), and Scanzoni (1975, 1976, 1979) findings regarding the influence of the male–female relationship on fertility-related behavior. In those studies, spousal relationships and interaction were found to be related to effective family planning behavior and fertility control. Studies of adolescent pregnancy risk are also beginning to show the influence of dyadic relationship properties on adolescent sexual behavior and contraception. For example, Thompson and Spanier's (1978) study of 434 sexually active, never-married college-age (17- to 24-year-old) males and females found that qualities of the relationship with the sexual partner were more influential in predicting contraceptive use than were relationship qualities with parents and peers. The more committed the individual was to continuing the sexual relationship into the future, and the more that the sexual partner exerted influence on the individual by expecting or demanding contraceptive protection, the greater the likelihood that effective contraception was being used.

In a parallel study using a significantly younger adolescent female sample (ages 12–18), Jorgensen, King, and Torrey (1980) also found that dyadic properties of the adolescent couple were often more predictive of fertility-related behavior than were relationships with peers and family. Specifically, sexual intercourse was more likely to occur, and to occur more frequently, among adolescent couples in love and where traditional gender role patterns of male dominance prevailed in the couple's relationship. Contraceptive use, on the other hand, was more prevalent in couples where mutual communication about sexual and contraceptive matters took place and in which the female had more decision-making power relative to the male (egalitarian gender roles). These findings are generally consistent with other reports (Miller, McCoy, & Olson, 1986) that early dating, especially early steady dating, is related to sexual activity, and that sexually experienced adolescent females hold more traditional sex role attitudes than virgins who had not ruled out sexual intercourse (Cvetkovich, Grote, Lieberman, & Miller, 1978).

SUMMARY AND IMPLICATIONS

The study of fertility-related behavior has generally omitted or only superficially included marriage and family variables. The structures and processes within marriages and families are, however, clearly linked with reproductive behavior. Recently, adolescent sexual activity, contraception, abortion, childbearing, and parenthood have become national concerns. Scientists and policymakers alike have become increasingly interested in understanding family–fertility linkages, and federal legislation in 1981 mandated the involvement of parents in programs to reduce the negative consequences of adolescent fertility-related behavior.

Family variables have been linked to adolescent fertility-related behavior in several ways. Family structure, especially single parenthood, has been found to be both an antecedent and consequence of adolescent fertility-related behavior. Adolescents from single-parent families of orientation appear more likely to be sexually active and become pregnant. Adolescent parents disproportionately form single-parent families of their own, either by remaining single following parenthood, or because of their higher rates of divorce.

The evidence is overwhelming that parents are not the initial source of sexual information for adolescents. This offers a significant possibility for intervention, because parent–child communication (especially between mothers and daughters) appears to be related to remaining sexually abstinent, postponing sexual activity, and using contraception.

Implications for Research

The linkages between mother–son, father–son, and father–daughter communication and pregnancy risk-taking behavior of adolescents need to be better understood. Presumably, communication about sexual and contraceptive matters in these relationships would be of no higher quantity or quality than the low levels found in the mother–daughter relationship. Indeed, it may well be less.

In addition to measuring and comparing communication in these other dyads, future research is warranted to determine the relative impact that such communication has on the sexual and contraceptive behavior of female and male adolescents. In one recent study (Moore, Paterson, & Furstenberg, 1986), it was reported that parental communication effects on teenagers' sexual experience depended on both parental values and the teens' gender; that is, daughters, not sons, of communicative parents were more likely to be sexually abstinent only if parents held traditional or conservative values. These findings raise other questions: To what extent is an adolescent daughter's sexual and contraceptive behavior influenced by communication with both her mother and her father? Likewise, is an adolescent son's fertility-related behavior shaped more by communication with his father or with his mother? Are there additive effects of having two communicative parents, is the content or quality of the communication most important, and how important are parental values or beliefs?

While evidence is beginning to accumulate regarding the effects of parent–child communication, less is known about the linkages between the parent–adolescent power structure and adolescents' sexual and contraceptive behavior. Theoretical models of premarital sexual permissiveness lead to the prediction that autonomy of adolescents from parental controls in the dating system is positively related to sexually permissive attitudes and behavior (Reiss & Miller, 1979). That is, sexual intercourse is more likely to occur among adolescents who are given freedom to date whom they want, to date at an early age, and to control their own activities (where to go on dates, when to come home, etc.). The data from several studies (Hogan & Kitagawa, 1985; Miller, McCoy, Olson, & Wallace, 1986) are strongly consistent with this reasoning, but other studies (Inazu & Fox, 1980; Newcomer & Udry, 1984) have found no relationship between parental supervision and adolescent sexual behavior. These discrepant findings might be partly explained if parental strictness and rules about dating are related in a curvilinear fashion to sexual intercourse experience of teenagers. In one recent study, adolescents who reported that their parents were not strict at all and had no rules were most likely to have had coitus, those whose parents were moderately strict and had a moderate number of rules were least likely to have had coitus, and teenagers who reported their parents to be very strict and rule-oriented were the next most likely to have had sexual intercourse (Miller, McCoy, Olson, & Wallace, 1986). We need to know more about how adolescent sexual behavior varies according to authoritarian, egalitarian, democratic, or laissez-faire (Elder, 1962) power structures. How is the likelihood of sexual activity, or of seeking and utilizing effective contraceptive methods by sexually active adolescents influenced by the type of power structure in the home? Do the effects of different power structures vary by sex of child or by sex of child/sex of parent combinations? What is the relative impact of authoritarian versus more egalitarian parent–adolescent power structures on the sexually active adolescent's seeking and using an effective contraceptive method? How do parent–adolescent power structures influence contraceptive continuation patterns among sexually active adolescent males and females, knowing that "fear of discovery" is often a reason invoked by adolescents for not attending a clinic and using an effective contraceptive method (Zabin & Clark, 1981)?

Even less is known about the influences of affection giving and receiving patterns among adolescents and their parents and the adolescents' fertility-related behavior. To what extent do adolescents who perceive themselves as affectionally close to their parents manifest different patterns of sexual and contraceptive behavior than adolescents and parents who are more distant? In a particularly complex and convincing recent study (Weinstein & Thornton, 1987), it was reported that the influence of maternal attitudes and values on children's sexual behavior depends on the quality of the parent-child relationship; children having close affectionate relationships with their mothers held attitudes and acted in ways that were consistent with the mothers' values and beliefs. These findings raise further questions such as whether the effects of various structures of adolescent/parent affection giving are different for adolescent males and females, and whether some sex-by-generation combinations are more influential than others? Knowing that an important developmental task of adolescence is establishing autonomy from the parental home over time, especially in terms of becoming more peer-oriented in regard to affiliation preferences and normative value stance (Bowerman & Kinch, 1959; McArthur, 1962), what impact does the timing of this task have on adolescent fertility-related behavior? It is reasonable to predict, for example, that those shifting orientation toward peers and away from parents earlier, especially in terms of feelings of affection and closeness, will be more likely to engage in sexual activity and to do so on a more frequent basis.

Considering the above research questions together, it seems logical for future research to study the effects of various combinations of family affection, communication, and power structures on adolescent sexual or contraceptive behavior. The study by Weinstein and Thornton (1987) is outstanding in this regard. In another complex recent analysis (Hanson, Myers, & Ginsburg, 1987), it was found that parental concerns and values for their teens reduced adolescent childbearing indirectly by increasing teens' educational expectations and by reducing patterns of steady dating. As Aldous (1978) points out, often there are discernible clusters of interaction structures that emerge in families. For example, authoritarian power structures are frequently found with one-way and restricted (parent-to-child) communication structures and restrained patterns of affection exchange. Conversely, more egalitarian family power structures foster two-way and open channels of communication and affection exchange between parents and children.

Finally, we know very little about the effects of siblings on adolescent fertility-related behavior. What impact does an older sibling's attitudes and behavior regarding sex and contraception have on a younger sibling? Are adolescents more or less prone to experience a premarital pregnancy when a male or female sibling has been involved in one? What are the differential effects of various age-by-sex combinations? Based on Brim's (1958) findings concerning sibling effects on sex role socialization, we might speculate that the attitudes, behavior, and experiences of older adolescents will be more influential on the fertility-related behavior of younger siblings than vice versa. We might also expect to find a stronger effect in same-sex sibling groups than in cross-sex ones. This expectation, however, has recently been called into question by Rodgers' (1983) finding that number of brothers is positively related to intercourse experience more strongly for adolescent females than males. Do siblings exert more or less influence on fertility-related behavior than do the adolescent's peers? Under what conditions might the influences of siblings be greater or lesser than that of peers?

In sum, although parental, sibling, and peer influences on adolescent fertility-related behavior continue to be documented, it now appears that a comprehensive understanding of this complex phenomenon will require a more detailed examination of relationships in the family and in the adolescent male–female dyad. Clearly, theoretical models that incorporate family variables, along with adolescent dyadic relationship variables, could lead to research that will complement and extend existing knowledge about the influence of sociodemographic and psychological determinants of adolescent sexual behavior, contraceptive use, and pregnancy.

Implications for Practitioners

Although, as has been documented above, a number of deficits remain in our knowledge about adolescent fertility-related behavior, the research does have implications for practitioners concerned with the prevention of adolescent pregnancy and with serving the needs of pregnant adolescents. These implications reflect the central role that family relations of adolescents have both in pregnancy prevention and in postpregnancy intervention.

In regard to postpregnancy outcomes for the adolescent, research findings support the idea that the adolescent mother's family can be very helpful in negotiating the adolescent's transition to parenthood. For example, Furstenberg and Crawford (1978) found that adolescent mothers living with parents or kin demonstrated significantly more positive outcomes than did those who were on their own as single parents or with a spouse. Those living in a supportive family atmosphere were more likely to have completed their educations and to have received useful advice, material assistance, and child-care help. The support of the families of adolescent parents has also has positive outcomes for their infants' development—physically, socially, and cognitively (Kellam *et al.*, 1982).

The arrival of a baby propels the adolescent male or female toward adulthood and interrupts their normal pace of working though developmental tasks of this stage, and some tasks may be left unresolved as the responsibilities and burdens of parenthood—economic, physical, and psychological—complicate one's life. In essence, demands normally associated with adulthood in our society compete with the adolescent's personal developmental needs, creating role conflict and stress. It is no wonder that the assistance of a family support network at this time promotes favorable developmental outcomes for adolescent parent and child alike.

In regard to adolescent pregnancy prevention, researchers and practitioners usually identify the need to develop sex and family life education programs in schools and in other settings (Jorgensen & Alexander, 1981, 1983). Education is typically viewed as a major element in the solution of the adolescent pregnancy problem. Education is a vehicle by which adolescents can learn responsible sexual decision making. However, it is well known that the provision of information through educational programs alone is not enough to effect desired behavioral changes. While such programs can provide accurate and essential information, it is an entirely different matter as to whether the information is used by the adolescent. As Brim and Wheeler (1966) pointed out, in order to play any social role effectively one must possess the necessary motivation and ability to assume the role, in addition to knowledge of the expectations and behaviors constituting it. Thus, while educational programs can be invaluable in providing the information adolescents need to be responsible in their sexual roles, they still might lack the motivation or ability to translate that information into practice.

In addition, a national survey of large city school districts in 1982 found that sex education programs in elementary, junior, and senior high schools vary dramatically in terms of hours offered, curriculum, content, program goals, and instructional format (Sonenstein & Pittman, 1984). In fact, rather than offering a separate course or program in sex education, most districts include their sex education material with other subjects (e.g., health, home economics, biology, or physical education). Unfortunately, given this diversity of program structure and the variability of its content, we lack properly controlled evaluation studies of the long-term effectiveness of school-based educational programs necessary to determine which if any are effective in pregnancy prevention. Neither do we know which specific program components are most effective.

Family linkages are important when considering preventive program development by means of educational efforts. Parents and other family members, having little or no sex or family life education themselves, are often limited in the support that they can give to adolescents enrolled in such programs. Parents' naiveté can often lead them to oppose or at least fail to support actively, the implementation of preventive educational programs in schools, churches, community agencies, or other locations. Hence, not only are parents unlikely to serve as major sources of sexual information and socialization, as discussed earlier in this chapter, but they are sometimes not in a position to be a major source of support for their children's learning in an educational program striving to reduce adolescent pregnancy risk. Without this family support for educational programs that focus on sexually responsible behavior and pregnancy prevention, the prospects of realizing success are severely reduced.

Despite the uncertain status and effectiveness of school-based educational programs for reducing the risk of unwanted adolescent fertility, major strides have been made in the past few years in developing more comprehensive preventive programs in areas where adolescent pregnancy rates have been historically high. For example, school-based comprehensive health clinics have been designed to meet the health care needs of adolescents in family planning as well as other areas. Reports of the establishment and effectiveness of such programs have been increasing; Dryfoos (1985) found that at least 14 American cities have such programs underway, while several other cities are developing a program. The first school-based health clinic was the St. Paul (Minnesota) Maternal and Infant Care Project, established in 1973 (Edwards, Steinman, Arnold, & Hakanson, 1980). Located on the campus of an inner-city junior/senior high school with a history of high pregnancy rates among its students, the St. Paul program received local school board approval to provide prenatal, postpartum, and general reproductive health care services to students. Contraceptive education, counseling, and referrals were a part of this school-based program. Contraceptive examinations and prescriptions were made on school premises, so that availability and convenience of birth control services were not issues. Students could obtain contraceptives at a nearby clinic. Later the services were expanded to include weight control, drug education and counseling, immunizations, well-child physicals, and physical examinations for athletics, college entry, and job applications. The effectiveness of the program was evident by the sharp declines in pregnancy rates—more than a 50% drop during the first three years of operation—and the dramatic increase in continuous contraceptive use among the students participating.

The developers of the St. Paul program have attributed its success to a number of factors. First is the comprehensive range of service providers available to work with the adolescent clientele. Included on the staff were a physician, nurse practitioner, nutritionist, social worker, and dental hygienist. Hence, a wide range of health care needs, not just family planning, could be addressed in the program. Second, the confidentiality of medical appointments and records, combined with the staff's ability to establish trusting "friendship" types of relationships with the adolescent participants, promoted the adolescents' motivation to continue in the program. To have someone to talk to as a confidant, a caring person willing to listen to personal problems and to give sound advice, was critical to the adolescents' program continuation. Staff became "surrogate parents" because of their availability and accessibility (Brann *et al.*, 1978). Finally, the program had the strong support of the local school board and community. An advisory board was established, comprised of school administrators, teachers, students, and perhaps most importantly, parents. All were involved in the design of the program and in its implementation. Parents and families supported the program, constituting an important family linkage in the development of this successful effort. The St. Paul program has since expanded to include four participating schools, each showing a continuing decline in adolescent pregnancy rates through 1984 (Dryfoos, 1985).

Dryfoos notes that several other comprehensive school-based programs have been modeled after the highly successful St. Paul project, but that considerable variability exists in the structure and operation from one to the next. Among the few that have conducted evaluation research, the results are similar to those from the St. Paul project: lower rates of first and repeat adolescent pregnancy, increased regular use of contraception, and increased use of general health care services by the adolescent student population as a whole. It is anticipated that future research on other programs will yield similar encouraging results. The important point is that progress *is* being made in some sectors of our society in reducing the risk and rate of adolescent pregnancy. But it is taking a more radical approach than has been tried in the past, when we have relied either on families or schools alone to solve the problem by the limited amount of "education" that each could provide.

It is clear that practitioners designing preventive educational programs face major obstacles in reducing the risk of adolescent pregnancy, and that at least some of the obstacles are linked to the families of adolescents. Program developers must consider the needs of parents for information and involvement in program design and, as much as possible, the need to involve all family members in the sex and family life education process. This is no small task, as it requires the cooperation of schools, community service agencies, and families if it is to be accomplished. Research has shown that adolescent fertility-related behavior involves a complex interweaving of physical, psychological, and social variables, many of which are linked to the adolescent's family. There will, as a result, be no simple solutions or panaceas for the adolescent pregnancy problem. But regardless of what prevention or intervention approach is taken, programs are likely to be more effective if they intentionally take account of and include the critical role of the family.

NOTE

1. We use the term "adolescent fertility-related behavior" to encompass a number of behaviors that are associated with the fertility of adolescents. These include sexual intercourse and other types of sexual activity, contraceptive use (or non-use), pregnancy, and pregnancy outcomes (childbearing, abortion, miscarriage, and adoption). We review theory and research that pertain to the family linkages of one or more of these behaviors that are related to adolescent fertility.

REFERENCES

Alan Guttmacher Institute. (1981). *Teenage pregnancy: The problem that hasn't gone away.* New York: Private printing.

Aldous, J. (1978). *Family careers: Developmental change in families.* New York: Wiley.

Aldous, J. (1983). Birth control socialization: How to avoid discussing the subject. Population and Environment: Behavioral and Social Issues, 6, 27–38.

Bachrach, C. A. (1985). *Adoption plans, adopted children and adoptive mothers: United States, 1982.* Working Paper No. 22, Family Growth Survey Branch, Division of Vital Statistics, National Center for Health Statistics, Washington, DC.

Baldwin, W. (1982). Trends in adolescent contraception, pregnancy, and childbearing. In E. R. McAnarney (Ed.), *Premature adolescent pregnancy and parenthood.* New York: Grune and Stratton.

Baldwin, W. (1983, July). *Statement on trends and consequences of adolescent childbearing in the United States.* Select Committee on Children, Youth, and Families, U.S. Congress, Washington, DC.

Baldwin, W. (1985, April). *Adolescent pregnancy and childbearing—rates, trends and research findings from the CPR, NICHD.* Unpublished Report, Center for Population Research, National Institute of Child Health and Human Development, Washington, DC.

Baldwin, W. H., & Cain, V. S. (1980). The children of teenage parents. *Family Planning Perspectives, 12,* 34–43.

Blechman, E. A. (1982). Are children with one parent at psychological risk? A methodological review. *Journal of Marriage and the Family, 44,* 179–195.

Bolton, F. G., Jr. (1980). *The pregnant adolescent: Problems of premature parenthood.* Beverly Hills, CA: Sage.

Bowerman, C. E., & Kinch, J. W. (1959). Changes in family and peer orientation of children between the fourth and tenth grades. *Social Forces, 37,* 206–211.

Brann, E. A., Edwards, L., Callicott, T., Story, E. S., Berg, P. A., Mahoney, J. E., Stine, J. L., & Hixson, A. (1978, October). *Strategies for the prevention of pregnancy in adolescents.* Paper presented at the annual meeting of the National Council on Family Relations, Philadelphia, PA.

Brim, O. G., Jr. (1958). Family Structure and sex-role learning by children. *Sociometry, 21,* 1–16.

Brim, O. G., Jr., & N. Wheeler, S. (1966). *Socialization after childhood: Two essays.* New York: Wiley.

Card, J. J., & Wise, L. L. (1978). Teenage mothers and teenage fathers: The impact of early childbearing on their personal and professional lives. *Family Planning Perspectives, 10,* 199–205.

Chilman, C. S. (Ed.) (1980a). *Adolescent pregnancy and childbearing: Findings from research.* Washington, DC: U.S. Government Printing Office.

Chilman, C. S. (1980b). Social and psychological research concerning adolescent child-bearing: 1970–1980. *Journal of Marriage and the Family, 42,* 793–805.

Cogswell, B. E., & Sussman, M. B. (1979). Family and fertility. In W. R. Burr, R. Hill, F. I. Nye, & I. L. Reiss (Eds.), *Contemporary theories about the family* (Vol. 1). New York: Free Press.

Cvetkovich, G., Grote, B., Lieberman, E. J., & Miller, W. (1978). Sex role development and teenage fertility-related behavior. *Adolescence, 13,* 231–236.

Davis, K., & Blake, J. (1956). Social structure and fertility: An analytical framework. Economic Development and Cultural Change, 4, 211–235.

Dryfoos, J. (1985). School-based health clinics: A new approach to preventing Adolescent Pregnancy? *Family Planning Perspectives, 17,* 70–75.

Edwards, L., Steinman, M., Arnold, K., & Hahanson, E. (1980). Adolescent pregnancy prevention services in high school clinics. *Family Planning Perspectives, 12,* 6–14.

Elder, G. H., Jr. (1962). Structural variations in the child rearing relationship. *Sociometry, 25,* 241–262.

Fawcett, J. T. (Ed.). (1972). *The satisfactions and costs of children: Theories, concepts, methods.* Honolulu, HI: East–West Population Institute, East–West Center.

Fawcett, J. T. (Ed.). (1973). *Psychological perspectives on population.* New York: Basic Books.

Fox, G. L. (1980). The mother–adolescent daughter relationship as a sexual socialization structure: A research review. *Family Relations, 29,* 21–28.

Fox, G. L. (1981). The family's role in adolescent sexual behavior. In K. T. Ooms (Ed.), *Teenage pregnancy in a family context: Implications for policy.* Philadelphia: Temple University Press.

Fox, G. L., & Inazu, J. K. (1980). Patterns and outcomes of mother–daughter communication about sexuality. *Journal of Social Issues, 36,* 7–29.

Furstenberg, F. F., Jr. (1971). Birth control experience among pregnant adolescents: The process of unplanned parenthood. *Social Problems, 19,* 192–203.

Furstenberg, F. F., Jr. (1976). The social consequences of teenage parenthood. *Family Planning Perspectives, 8,* 148–164.

Furstenberg, F. F., Jr., & Crawford, A. G. (1978). Family support: Helping teenage mothers to cope. *Family Planning Perspective, 10,* 322–333.

Furstenberg, F. F., Jr., Herceg-Baron, R., Shea, J., & Webb, D. (1984). Family communication and teenagers contraceptive use. *Family Planning Perspectives, 16,* 163–170.

Gebhard, P. H. (1977). The acquisition of basic sex information. *Journal of Sex Research, 13,* 148–169.

Hanson, S. L., Myers, D. E., & Ginsburg, A. L. (1987). The role of responsibility and knowledge in reducing teenage out-of-wedlock childbearing. *Journal of Marriage and the Family, 49,* 241–256.

Hayes, C. D. (ed.). (1987). *Risking the future: Adolescent sexuality, pregnancy, and childbearing* (Vol. I). Washington, DC: National Academy Press.

Hill, R. J., Stycos, M., & Back, K. W. (1959). *The family and population control.* Chapel Hill: University of North Carolina Press.

Hoffman, L. W., & Manis, J. D. (1979). The value of children in the United States: A new approach to the study of fertility. *Journal of Marriage and the Family, 41,* 583–596.

Hogan, D. P., & Kitagawa, E. M. (1985). The impact of social status, family structure, and neighborhood on the fertility of black adolescents. *American Journal of Sociology, 90,* 825–855.

Inazu, J. K., & Fox, G. L. (1980). Maternal influence on the sexual behavior of teenage daughters: Direct and indirect sources. *Journal of Family Issues, 1,* 81–102.

Jorgensen, S. R. (1981). Sex education and the reduction of adolescent pregnancies: Prospects for the 1980s. *Journal of Early Adolescence, 1,* 38–52.

Jorgensen, S. R., & Alexander, S. (1981). Reducing the risk of adolescent pregnancy: Toward certification of family life educators. *The High School Journal, 64,* 257–268.

Jorgensen, S. R., & Alexander, S. J. (1983). Research on adolescent pregnancy-risk: Implications for sex education programs. *Theory Into Practice, 22,* 125–133.

Jorgensen, S. R., King, S. L., & Torrey, B. A. (1980). Dyadic and social network influences on adolescent exposure to pregnancy-risk. *Journal of Marriage and the Family, 42,* 141–155.

Kellam, S. G., Adams, R. G., Brown, C. H., & Ensminger, M. E. (1982). The long-term evolution of the family structure of teenage and older mothers. *Journal of Marriage and the Family, 44,* 539–554.

Kellam, S. G., Ensminger, M. E., & Brown, C. H. (1979, Winter). Epimediological research into the antecedents in early childhood of psychiatric symptoms and drug use in mid-adolescence. *Newsletter, Society for Research in Child Development,* 6–7.

Kellam, S. G., Ensminger, M. E., & Turner, R. J. (1977). Family structure and the mental health of children: Concurrent and longitudinal community-wide studies. *Archives of General Psychiatry, 34,* 1012–1022.

Koenig, M. A., & Zelnik, M. (1982). The risk of premarital first pregnancy among metropolitan-area teenagers: 1976 and 1979. *Family Planning Perspectives, 14,* 239–247.

Levin, M. L., & O'Hara, C. J. (1978). The impact of marital history of current husband on fertility of remarried white women in the United States. *Journal of Marriage and the Family, 40,* 95–102.

Lewis, R. A. (1973). Parents and peers: Socialization agents in the coital behavior of young adults. *Journal of Sex Research, 9,* 156–170.

Lindemann, C. (1974). *Birth Control and Unmarried Young Women.* New York: Springer.

Makinson, C. (1985). The health consequences of teenage fertility. *Family Planning Perspectives, 17,* 132–139.

McAnarney, E. R. (Ed.). (1982). *Premature adolescent pregnancy and parenthood.* New York: Grune and Stratton.

McArthur, A. (1962). Developmental tasks and parent–adolescent conflict. *Marriage and Family Living, 24,* 189–191.

Mecklenburg, M., & Thompson, P. G. (1983). The adolescent family life program as a preventive measure. *Public Health Reports, 98,* 21.

Mednick, B. R., Baker, R. L., & Sutton-Smith, B. (1979). Teenage pregnancy and perinatal mortality. *Journal of Youth and Adolescence, 8,* 343–357.

Menken, J. (1980). The health and demographic consequences of adolescent pregnancy and childbearing. In C. S. Chilman (Ed.), *Adolescent pregnancy and childbearing: Findings from research.* Washington, DC: U.S. Government Printing Office.

Miller, B. C. (1985). Adolescent pregnancy and childbearing in Utah and the U.S. *Utah Science, 46,* 32–35.

Miller, B. C. (1987). Marriage, family, and fertility. In M. Sussman & S. Steinmetz (Eds.), *Handbook of Marriage and the Family.* New York: Plenum.

Miller, B. C., & Bingham, C. R. (in press). *Family configuration in relation to the sexual behavior of female adolescents. Journal of Marriage and the Family.*

Miller, B. C., Jenson, G. O., Kreuger, M. N., Peterson, T. C., & Weiner, A. M. (1981). *Teenage pregnancy: A comparison of certain characteristics among Utah youth.* Salt Lake City: Utah State Office of Education.

Miller, B. C., Higginson, R., & McCoy, J. K. (1987). Family configuration and adolescent sexual attitudes and behavior. *Population and Environment, 9,* 111–123.

Miller, B. C., McCoy, J. K., Olson, T. D., & Wallace, C. M. (1986). Parental discipline and control attempts in relation to adolescent sexual attitudes and behavior. *Journal of Marriage and the Family, 48,* 503–512.

Miller, B. C., McCoy, J. K., & Olson, T. D. (1986). Dating age and stage as correlates of adolescent sexual attitudes and behavior. *Journal of Adolescent Research, 1,* 361–371.

Miller, B. C., & Sollie, D. L. (1980). Normal stresses during the transition to parenthood. *Family Relations, 29,* 459–465.

Moore, K. A., Peterson, J. L., & Furstenberg, F. F., Jr. (1986). Parental attitudes and the occurrence of early sexual activity. *Journal of Marriage and the Family, 48,* 777–782.

National Center for Health Statistics (1984). Ventura: trends in teenage childbearing, United States, 1970–81. *Vital and Health Statistics, Series 21, No. 41* (DHHS Publishing No. PHS 84-1919). Washington, DC: Government Printing Office.

Newcomer, S. F., & Udry, J. R. (1984). Mothers' influence on the sexual behavior of their teenage children. *Journal of Marriage and the Family, 46,* 477–485.

Newcomer, S., & Udry, J. R. (1987). Parental marital status effects on adolescent sexual behavior. *Journal of Marriage and the Family, 49,* 235–240.

Nortman, D. (1974). *Parental age as a factor in pregnancy outcome.* New York: The Population Council.

Nye, I. F., & Lamberts, M. B. (1980). *School-age parenthood: Consequences for babies, mothers, fathers, grandparents, and others.* Extention Bulletin 66, Cooperative Extension Services. Pullman, WA: Washington State University.

Office of Adolescent Pregnancy Programs. (1982). Request for Research Grant Applications (RFA): Adolescent Family Life. *Federal Register,* (March 1), *47,* 40.

Onaka, A. T., Yaukey, D., & Chevan, A. (1977). Reproductive time lost through marital dissolution in metropolitan Latin America. *Social Biology, 24,* 100–115.

Ooms, T. (1981). *Teenage pregnancy in a family context: Implications for policy.* Philadelphia: Temple University Press.

Polhman, E. W. (1969). *The psychology of birth planning.* Cambridge, MA: Schenkman.

Rainwater, L. (1960). *And the poor get children.* Chicago: Quadrangle.

Rainwater, L. (1965). *Family Design.* Chicago: Aldine.

Reiss, I. L., & Miller, B. C. (1979). Heterosexual permissiveness: A theoretical analysis. In W. Burr, R. Hill, F. I. Nye, & I. L. Reiss (Eds.), *Contemporary theories about the family* (Vol. 1). New York: Free Press.

Rindfuss, R. R., & St. John, C. (1983). Social determinants of age at first birth. *Journal of Marriage and the Family, 45,* 553–565.

Rodgers, J. L. (1983). Family configuration and adolescent sexual behavior. *Population and Environment, 6,* 73–83.

Ryder, J. W. (1976). Interrelations between family structure and fertility in Yucatan. *Human Biology, 48,* 93–100.

Scanzoni, J. (1975). *Sex roles, life styles, and childbearing: Changing patterns in marriage and the family.* New York: Free Press.

Scanzoni, J. (1976). Gender roles and the process of fertility control. *Journal of Marriage and the Family, 38,* 678–691.

Scanzoni, J. (1979). Work and fertility control sequences among younger married women. *Journal of Marriage and the Family, 41,* 739–748.

Shah, F., & Zelnik, M. (1981). Parent and peer influence on sexual behavior, contraceptive use and pregnancy experience of young women. *Journal of Marriage and the Family, 42,* 339–348.

Sonenstein, F. L., & Pittman, K. J. (1984). The availability of sex education in large city school districts. *Family Planning Perspectives, 16,* 19–25.

Spanier, G. B. (1977). Sources of sex information and premarital sexual behavior. *Journal of Sex Research, 13,* 73–88.

Teachman, J. D. (1983). Early marriage, premarital fertility, and marital dissolution. *Journal of Family Issues, 4,* 105–126.

Thompson, L., & Spanier, G. B. (1978). Influence of parents, peers, and partners on the contraceptive use of college men and women. *Journal of Marriage and the Family, 40,* 481–492.

Thornburg, H. (1978). Adolescent sources of initial sex information. *Sex Psychiatric Annals, 8,* 419–423.

Thornburg, H. (1981). The amount of sex information learning obtained during early adolescence. *Journal of Early Adolescence, 1,* 171–183.

Thornton, A. (1980). The influence of first generation fertility and economic status on second generation fertility. *Population and Environment, 3,* 51–52.

Thonton, A., & Camburn, D. (1987). The influence of the family on premarital sexual attitudes and behaviors. *Demography, 24,* 323–340.

Walters, J., & Walters, L. H. (1983). The role of the family in sex education. *Journal of Research and Development in Education, 16,* 8–15.

Weinstein, M., & Thornton, A. (1987, May 1). *Mother–child relations and adolescent sexual attitudes and behavior.* Paper presented at the annual meeting of the Population Association of America, Chicago.

Westoff, C. F. (1978a). Marriage and fertility in the developed countries. *Scientific American, 239,* 51–57.

Westoff, C. F. (1978b). Some speculations on the future of marriage and fertility. *Family Planning Perspectives, 10,* 79–83.

Zabin, L. S., & Clark, S. D. (1981). Why they delay: A study of teenage family planning clinic patients. *Family Planning Perspectives, 13,* 205–217.

Zabin, L. S., Kantner, J. F., & Zelnik, M. (1979). The risk of adolescent pregnancy in the first months of intercourse. *Family Planning Perspectives, 11,* 215–222.

Zelnik, M., & Kantner, J. F. (1980). Sexual activity, contraceptive use and pregnancy among metropolitan area teenagers: 1971–1979. *Family Planning Perspectives, 12,* 230–237.

11

The Meaning of Family Policy in Western Europe and the United States

WILFRIED DUMON
*Sociological Research Institute, Katholieke Universiteit
Leuven, Belgium*

INTRODUCTION

In 1965 I had the opportunity to discuss family policy with Reuben Hill. He then, not without some sense of humor, suggested that the real meaning of family policy was the process of decision making within the family. He did not refer to the division of power but to the family as a unit, saying that it reaches decisions on group-relevant issues through coping behavior. Not "who is making decisions" but "what decisions are being made" was the Hillian version of family policy. This "mock" definition of family policy was a challenge to a then young European student.

In 1961–1962 Hill had spent the academic year in Leuven with Pierre de Bie, one of the authorities on family policy in Europe. He was very familiar with the typical European approach to family policy, which in de Bie's formulation at that time read:

> The aim of family policy is the well-being of families. It is guided by an attachment to the family, by a desire for protecting and helping it, not by substituting for it but by enabling it to fulfill its functions more properly and to set conditions for its development. (English translation of de Bie, 1963, p. 6).[1]

The translation of this statement might be almost without sense or very misleading for a United States or non-European audience. The word "government" does not occur explicitly in this definition although it is implicitly present. For any European, it is self-evident that family policy is not action taken by the family, but action taken by the government, by a public authority, local, regional, or national.

Hill became acquainted with the family organizations in Belgium or, as he would prefer calling them, "family unions." In 1965 he told me that, in his opinion, these organizations were "too militant." Hill represented the at that time still unquestioned value-free stance of the scholar versus the advocacy position of the family unions. The European

scholars of that time might seem somewhat familistic in their orientation. Thus, it was the Norwegian scholar, Eric Grønseth, who in 1967
for the first time defined family policy as "a more or less coherent and
explicit theory and practice with the aim of influencing the structure
and function of nuclear and of extended family units" (p. 9). This
definition also implicitly refers to the government. New, however, is the
statement that the government is aiming at change, the direction of the
change not explicitly being stated as in favor of the family. Without
questioning Hill's scientific nonpartisan stance, there is no evidence
available that his European colleagues would have been more (or less)
familistic.

The difference could, to some extent, be due to differences in
scientific approach. European family sociologists in the 1960s were far
more oriented toward an institutional conceptual approach. Hill was
very instrumental in spreading "the good word" (a skill he developed in
his youth in Belgium) of the interactional approach. Due to his efforts,
Leuven became a center where Andrée Michel of France and others
from other countries became aware of the interactional approach. They
replicated the Blood and Wolfe Detroit survey (1960) with great eagerness, which resulted in many articles and book-length publications.[2]

It is my impression that the exchange was somewhat unbalanced, so
that we gained more from this relatively new interactional approach
than Hill learned of the typical European institutional approach. This
was not due to a language barrier. Hill felt confident in French and was
not unfamiliar with German. Moreover, René König, the great European family institutionalist, although publishing in German, speaks
French literally as his mother tongue. Hill and König had already in the
mid-1950s met, and they coedited a book on comparative family sociology (Hill & König, 1970). But Hill had never been very much attracted
to the institutional approach. I can recall several instances in which he
claimed that the micro analysis of families would be the most strategic
way of explaining family life.

Family policy in the European sense hardly can be understood from
a micro approach; it can only be studied from a macro perspective. Hill,
despite his many contacts, long periods of residence in Europe, and field
research there has bypassed the developments in family policy. Although
he has studied world trends in applied family sociology (Hill, 1959),
governmental action with respect to families on a worldwide scale has
not been his central concern.

This does not imply that Hill has not studied family policy. He co-
authored an article with Joan Aldous on "Breaking the Poverty Cycle"
(1969) that directly relates to governmental action. However, the title
runs in full: "Breaking the Poverty Cycle: Strategic Points for Intervention." This means that the scope of the article is more directed to an

analysis of the changing balance of needs and resources over the family life span (an interactional approach) than to what governments actually do (an institutional approach). Aldous and Hill here identify two periods in which poverty-prone families would benefit most from an income maintenance program. First is the childbearing stage, which they claim to be most vulnerable owing to insufficiencies of instrumental resources. A second period is the phase of adolescence, when families face most acutely the problem of the social placement of their offspring. This approach contrasts with an institutional approach in which the government would be the focus of attention, not the family. A typical question would concern when European governments cut down on family allowances. The answer to this particular question would be that they do so at times of recession (eg., the early 1980s), when families are most in need of them.

FAMILY IMPACT VERSUS FAMILY POLICY

In 1976, Hill proudly announced in Leuven that the Minnesota Family Study Center would introduce a program for training family impact analysts, a program that paralleled an already existing seminar at George Washington University. That program was conceived as "a recognition of the need for family impact assessments to parallel environmental impact statements as public policy changes and legislative enactments are opened for public debate" (Minnesota Family Study Center, 1975, p. 1). This statement clearly overlaps to some extent with the definition of family policy. However, it is at the same time far broader in some respects and more restricted in other aspects. It is far broader and in my opinion less well defined as a concept than family policy on two accounts. First, it lumps together all implications for families of every governmental action, referring to "the consequences for the family of changes of such diverse spheres of the family's environment as the economy, the educational system, technology, the ecological structure or any other sphere of the total society which may impinge upon the family" (Minnesota Family Study Center, 1975, p. 1). Second, it states in even broader and certainly less well-defined terms the other feature of family impact:

> Not only will planned (eg., policy based) change be relevant to family impact analysis, but also those factors which create differential response to unplanned change such as natural disasters, unemployment, inflation or recession or widespread public disorder. (Minnesota Family Study Center, 1975, p. 1)

The authors (Hill and others) were, however, aware of the vagueness of the term "family impact." In the very last paragraph of their brochure they recognized the concept of family impact analysis to be "formative rather than definitive" (Minnesota Family Study Center, 1975, p. 8). They added, not without some naiveté or conceptual misjudgment, "Experience with the program and especially the accumulation of case records of impact analysis will enable clearer conceptualization" (Minnesota Family Study Center, 1975, p. 1).

The European notion of family policy, by comparison, is far more restricted in scope. It does not encompass all government measures that have implications for the family. If this were to be done, the entire policy of the nation would in fact be aimed at the family, and the prime minister would have to be called a "Minister of the Family" (Van Mechelen, 1981, p. 58). Therefore, as Dumon and Aldous (1979, p. 43) have argued, family policy refers to governmental goals concerned with family well-being and resultant activities directed toward families having children. The latter definition enables an approach in which the goals versus the effects of governmental action can be distinguished. The notion of family impact analysis leads to a blurred vision of governmental action. For any governmental action, two differentiated elements can be distinguished: (1) the symbolic meaning of the action, which in many instances outweighs (2) the instrumental effect. The American expression "lip service" is a form of symbolic action.

There is, however, a second distinction that is even more important. It is between the goals set by the government and the results attained. The family allowances program provides a good example. Although there should be a very clear distinction between demographic policy and family policy, the family allowance program in Europe once had natalistic overtones. Several governments advocated new family allowance measures with natality-oriented arguments. This was especially the case in the 1930s and still is not totally absent in the 1980s. However, family allowances have not automatically led to larger families. The evidence available is not conclusive, but if any evidence is to be found, it lies in the opposite direction. Economic support of the family has contributed to smaller family units and has been instrumental in developing what Kooy (1967) has labeled the "individualized family."

Two conclusions can be drawn. The first is that since family policy has been more clearly defined than family impact, it is a more powerful concept for one analysis of relationships between family and government or family and society. Secondly, the vagueness of the concept, although not necessarily the key factor, may have played some yet unrecognized part in the limited success of the family impact analysis training program. This program eventually was discontinued at the Minnesota Family Study Center, allegedly due to the lack of governmental financial support.

In a personal communication, Hill (1981) stated that he had never really cherished the idea of family impact analysis. In his own work, the main emphasis has been on internal and intrinsic family development in the broad sense of this term. Family impact, to the contrary, leads to the conception of the family as being the result of external societal developments. It implies the conceptualization of the family as the product of a given socioeconomic structure, rather than as an autonomous group with its own interaction and organization.

The interactional studies by Hill remain of great value for policy makers, and some results can be turned into policy measures. The classic study of fertility control in Puerto Rico (Hill, Stycos, & Back, 1959) is an example. The point I wish to make, however, is that it is unfortunate that the studies on family policy in the United States are heavily oriented toward social work. Although it is difficult to distinguish cause from effect in regards to this orientation, it is nevertheless important to recognize that there might be a link between the typical American approach of family policy analysis and a social work orientation, along with the relative absence of a sociological approach.[3] The greatest interest has been raised by social workers such as Catherine Chilman, Shirley Zimmerman, and members of the Columbia School of Social Work. For example, the outstanding book by A. J. Kahn and S. B. Kamerman (1975) is entitled *Not for the Poor Alone.* This title refers to their view that family policy is linked to help (self help) and other typical social work activities. Even Leik and Hill (1979) borrowed more from social work concepts than from a sociological frame of reference in assessing "What Price National Policy for Families?"

Leik and Hill recognize that there are obvious reasons for advocating an explicit "family policy." However, their notion of family policy coincides to a large extent with "family impact." In the first page of their article, the term "impinge" appears twice, as it does in their brochure on the training seminar mentioned above. One of their statements reads: "Government at all levels, and private business as well, operates according to laws and practices which impinge on families" (Leik & Hill, 1979, p. 457). Further, they refer to "favorable consequences" as well as to "serious negative effects" on families. I am not pointing to the value judgments implied here, but to the lack of sociological analysis. This is the more striking, since the work of Leik and Hill is known to be outstanding, conceptually as well as methodologically. It is seemingly only when dealing with family policy do they replace sociological rigor and analytical concepts with everyday notions, the self-evidence of which is either taken for granted or at least left unquestioned.

Although Leik and Hill are rather cautious in putting the need for a family policy into the mouths of the alleged "advocates," they are somewhat less prudent in setting out the goals of a family policy. For them, family policy is developed explicitly "to increase family stability and strength" (Leik & Hill, 1979, p. 457). These are interactional categories. In a European sense, family policy is not aimed at family stability, although it might be aimed at family strength. In order to make this clear I will describe very briefly the three main characteristics of family policy in Europe and contrast these with the Leik and Hill version, before concluding with some final remarks.

CHARACTERISTICS OF FAMILY POLICY IN EUROPE

Family policy in Europe, from its very origin after World War I, has been based on the idea or ideology of social justice, more than on any type of charity, help, or welfare. The French term "prestations famili-ales" (family payments) refers to a positive reward for a societal achievement rather than to an alleged deficiency in income. Therefore, family policy was not directed to deficient families, and as Kahn and Kamerman (1973) put it very well, "not for the poor alone." Since many family policy measures, particularly family allowances, were part of wages, any wage earner with dependent children—even the Prime Minister—received and is still receiving them. It was only in the 1960s that some categories of families not in the labor force such as unemployed, unmarried mothers, began receiving family allowances. Thus, family policy, in some parts of the world, does belong to a social security system, a system of social insurance. Such a system might be directed toward persons seen as needing help who can be described in terms of "poverty," "deprivation," or "exploitation," depending on ideological stands. Thus the Leik and Hill approach, confining itself within the American descriptive frame of reference, could be broadened by a comparative perspective in which a more analytical sociological frame of reference concerning the politics of scarce resource allocation would be introduced.

Leik and Hill (1979) do point to the need to decide whether policy should be focused on conditions *affecting* families or conditions *of* families. They implicitly recognize here a distinction between family impact and family policy. The conditions of families to which European family policy confines itself is covered by "financial adequacy, mutual supportiveness, ability to care for and nurture children" (p. 457). These three types of family policy measures actually correspond very well to the Dumon and Aldous (1979) differentiation among three types of family policy: (1) policies aimed at strengthening families economically, (2) remedial policies, and (3) substitutional policies (p. 43).

The first type can be viewed as economic enabling policies. Two main policies can be identified: family allowances and tax reductions. It should be noted that family allowances are not income related, and that tax reductions are also applicable to high income groups. Both measures constitute the bulk of the original family policy and are supplemented by other non-income-related measures such as reduced rates for public transportation. Therefore, they aim at a horizontal redistribution of income from small to large families. They are not aimed at a transfer of money from the rich to the poor.

From an evaluative point of view, this type of policy can be characterized as social-stratification blind. It favors social equality or inequality according to the distribution of children over the different social classes. This policy, therefore, is child and family centered. It is child centered because the allowance goes to the one who takes care of the child, regardless of the marital status of the caretaker. It is family centered because the family is the residential unit. Family allowances go up according to the age and birth order of the child. Many of the same criteria apply to tax rebates and other financial measures. There is no "qualifying" for family assistance; the very fact of having a child or taking care of a child gives a right to the child allowance.

A second type of policy introduced after World War II in many European countries consisted of family life education and information on family matters. Leik and Hill (1979) point to the fact that it must be decided whether such action should be undertaken by public agencies or the private sector. In many European countries the question cannot be answered by simply indicating the former or the latter.

After World War II, "ministries for the family" were established in many European countries. They developed the so-called "nonmaterial" family policy, in contrast to the monetary family policy. This new policy did not substitute for but rather supplemented the older one. Tax rebates usually fell under the jurisdiction of the Minister of Finance, and family allowances under that of the social security system. The new policy, however, was in the realm of the newly established Ministries of the Family.

The solution to the problem of the state interfering in family life in such matters as family planning and education for family life was solved in most countries by subcontracting these matters to private institutions. This was usually effected by subsidizing the activities of such organizations, sometimes with up to 100% support. The distribution of government money for this purpose was ordinarily allocated according to the ideological, church oriented, regional, ethnic, or other divisions that were characteristic of the countries involved. This procedure is one of the expressions of the so-called "quota democracy."

The well-developed American services for counseling and therapy should be mentioned here. They illustrate a characteristic of this second type of family policy: Far more emphasis is given in these policies to individual well-being than to the well-being of the family as a group. The focus of attention usually is on individual or interpersonal aspects rather than on situational elements, which are far more prominent in the older type of policy.

A third form of family policy developed in the early 1970s, when a substitutional approach became prominent. It somewhat lagged behind the economic development of the late 1960s. Then, not only more women but women from a broader range of social classes, along with young married mothers, increasingly stayed in the labor force. Church organizations and day-care centers for children were fast spreading, with government financing. A new policy was the provision of household substitutes for mothers, and later on for either parent falling ill or being disabled on a temporary basis.

As was the case with the second type of family policy, this policy is also indirect and subcontracted, and it calls for the development of a new group of professionals. With this policy, the professionals and their claims sometimes tend to take priority over the needs of the families they serve. A remarkable new aspect of these services is that they are paid for under the style of "fee for service." The amount of the fee is income related, from being almost free for lower income groups up to amounts competing with the free market system for higher income groups. However, low income groups receive priority for service.

This summing up of different types of family policy, which now exist in many European countries, shows how European governments have dealt with the questions put forward by Leik and Hill (1979) on the scope of family policy. The authors felt that a distinction must be made as to whether family policy should pertain to the following: (1) the *monitoring* of current circumstances, (2) the *preventing* of undesirable consequences for families, (3) the *treating* of existing problems, or (4) the *developing* of family capabilities for self-help (Leik & Hill, 1979, p. 458).

Another issue relates to the politics of family policy. At the organizational level, Leik and Hill claim that there are appropriate roles for national government, state or regional government, local government, and private sector participation. European experience has shown that family policy measures are provided by national and regional as well as local authorities. The services are mostly complementary, but sometimes they overlap. In general, the old family policy measures (the financial and social security measures) are being debated, legislated, and implemented on the national level. International agreements increasingly structure this type of family policy. The more person-centered measures such as the nonmaterial family policy tend to be more regionally diversified.

In a European setting, the politics of family policy tend to be related conceptually to programs of political parties, and in their realization are the result of bargaining in coalition governments. Family unions and other social organizations such as trade unions, employers' organizations (the so-called "social partners"), and civil organizations play an important role in developing ideas. These organizations are only powerful insofar as their ideas are taken over by politicians either at the legislative or the executive level. The important point, however, is that family policy is linked with ideology and is based on political power.

One way in which governments tend to cope with partisan positions and yet try to develop a family policy that appeals to a nonpartisan, general interest is by setting up consultative bodies in which the representative organizations take part. These advisory bodies have a double function of evaluating measures the government is about to take and initiating and stimulating government action. Given the pluralistic composition of such high councils for the family, the former function outweighs the latter.

This form of organization is an alternative to the Leik and Hill (1979) proposal to make policies maximally adaptive to the special needs of what they identify as "differentiated cultures." Their alternative solution, to formulate family policy at as local a level as possible, might constitute a valuable alternative for policy making in an American setting. Still, a more thorough knowledge of the European situation might help in two ways. First, it indicates how the organization of family policy is differentiated according to the political systems of different nations. Second, such knowledge can also include evaluative research assessing the effectiveness of a policy according to the political organization.

This calls for sociological research rather than for a social-work orientation. As long as family policy is put in terms of help or self-help to overcome inadequacies, it will tend to be more social-work related. The more it is defined as a way to distribute scarce goods (material and nonmaterial), based on criteria society puts forth, the more sociologists are likely to be involved.

The politics of family policy have changed over time. Since the 1960s, a growing vagueness in the concept as well as in the concrete measures encompassing family policy occurred. Two elements in the change can be identified. In the late 1950s and early 1960s, there were new types of policies. They expanded and implemented, in the Leik and Hill terminology, policies with respect to collectivities rather than families. Social categories such as "the aged," "youth," and "the disabled" gained far more political attention than in any previous period. These policies, geared toward unidimensional categories rather than toward multigenerational groups such as families, have led to confusion, particularly since the target groups usually are family related. Increasingly, family policy is being integrated into a policy of "social well-being," quite different from a social welfare policy. One of the ideological and political debates going on is whether the individual or the family should be the focus of policy measures.

A second development since the 1960s has been the growing bifurcation between family policy and "emancipation" policy. One indicator in the political and also the scientific world is the recognition of women's studies and gender roles. The increased political attention to feminist demands led to policy measures, sometimes taken under the heading of family policy, but mostly in clear opposition to traditional family policy. The conflicts have been almost exclusively situated in the domain of economic family policy. The bifurcation has had a symbolic expression, since both types of policies are usually located in different ministries represented by different secretaries of state (often both female).

The above two developments point to people no longer seeing family policy as unquestionably beneficial for the whole community. Family policy has been criticized by some as being oppressive to some.

CONCLUSIONS

The history of family policy in Western Europe can lead to many conclusions, of which two are most relevant here.

One conclusion is that family policy in Europe was never based explicitly on a monolithic family model. However, the old type family policy was clearly based on a type of household structure with an employed husband/father and a nurturant and housekeeping wife/mother.[4] The focus of attention was directed to the children, based on family size. The whole policy assumed that the family should not be relatively deprived by having children, that the community, via the state, should compensate for the cost of children. This ideology is now being questioned on two grounds. First, horizontal redistribution is being replaced by vertical redistribution. The latter is not completely realized, and compromises increasingly are being made. Second, the family or household as the unit of attention is being replaced by such categories as women, the aged, the disabled, youth, and so on. In this realm there is no ultimate winner or loser. Compromises are being made here also. Family policy, consequently, is becoming a far looser concept, since the target group is ambiguously defined.

A second conclusion to be drawn is that, like any other topic, family policy can be analyzed from the conceptual frameworks used in disciplines such as social work, political science, and sociology. In the United States as well as in Europe, most advances in this respect have taken place in the fields of social work and social administration, with sociologists lagging behind. The relative absence of sociologists in this area, as well as the recent growing interest in it, indicates that social change is taking place and scientific approaches are shifting. The two phenomena might be interrelated.

Social change does not necessarily point to weaker or more deficient families. It has to be understood, paradoxically enough, in the light of growing deinstitutionalization of the family. This can be put either in terms of a loosening of state/church control or in terms of the growing autonomy of individuals or individuation, thanks to increased economic prosperity.

The prospect of growing interest and higher value in an approach showing how families affect society as well as the reverse could increase interest in family policy. This has been defined by Stolte-Heiskanen (1972) as the point of intersection of family and society. Thus, family policy analysis has the potential of becoming a field in which a transactional approach is stimulated and advanced.

NOTES

1. The aim of family policy is the well-being of families. It is guided by an attachment to the family, by a desire for protecting and helping it, not by substituting for it but by enabling it to fulfill its functions more properly and to set conditions for its development.

2. The typical Louvain/Leuven versions were "La dyade conjugale" and "Het echtpaar," a French/Dutch publication by de Bie, Dobbelaere, Leplae, and Piel (1968), with an introduction by Hill.

3. This is only typical for the post-World-War-II American approach. Before the war, far more emphasis was given to macro views of family policy, as is indicated in the excellent overview by Paul Howard Douglas (1925).

4. His wages should be sufficient to provide for "wife and children," the so-called "family wages" (Kaufmann & Messu, 1982).

REFERENCES

Aldous, J., & Hill, R. (1969). Breaking the poverty cycle: Strategic points for intervention. *Social Work, 12*(3), 3–12.

Blood, R. O., & Wolfe, D. M. (1960). *Husbands and wives: The dynamics of married living*. Chicago: The Free Press.

de Bie, P. (1963). Politique familiale et politique demographique. *Population et Famille, 1*(1), 6–17.

de Bie, P., Dobbelaere, K., Leplae, C., & Piel, J. (1968). *La dyade conjugale: Étude sociologique*. Brussels, Belgium: Vie Ouvriere.

de Bie, P., Dobbelaere, K., Leplae, C., & Piel, J. (1968). *Het echtpaar: Een sociologische studie*. Antwerp, Belgium: De Standaard.

Douglas, P. H. (1925). *Wages and the family*. Chicago: University of Chicago Press.

Dumon, W. (1987). La politique familiale en Europe occidentale. *L'Année Sociologique, 37*, 291–308.

Dumon, W., & Aldous, J. (1979). European and United States political contexts for family policy research. *Journal of Marriage and the Family, 41*(3), 497–505.

Grønseth, E. (1967). Economic family policy and its guiding images in Norway: Inconsistencies and consequences. In P. de Bie, & C. Presvelou (Eds.), *National family guiding images and policy* (pp. 9–64). Leuven, Belgium: International Commission on the Family.

Hill, R. (1959). Recent world developments in applied family sociology. In *Transactions of the 4th World Congress of Sociology* (Vol. 2, pp. 81–126). London: International Sociological Association.

Hill, R., & König, R. (1970). *Families in east and west*. Paris: Mouton.

Hill, R., Stycos, J. M., & Back, K. W. (1959). *The family and population control: A Puerto Rican experiment in social change*. Chapel Hill, NC: University of North Carolina Press.

Kahn, A. J., & Kamerman, S. B. (1975). *Not for the poor alone*. Philadelphia, PA: Temple University Press.

Kaufman, J. C., & Messu, M. (1982, August). *Working class families, the diffuse social movement and the labour movement: Outline of a political-historical interpretation*. Paper presented at the 10th International Sociological Association World Congress, Mexico City, Mexico.

Kooy, G. A. (1967). *Het modern-Westers gezin*. Hilversum, The Netherlands: Paul Brand.

Leik, R., & Hill, R. (1979). What price national policy of families? *Journal of Marriage and the Family, 41*(3), 457–459.

Minnesota Family Study Center. (1975). *A program for training family impact analysts*. Minneapolis, MN: Author.

Stolte-Heiskanen, V. (1972). *Holistic versus particularistic approach to family policy: Social policy or societal planning?* Paper presented at the 3rd International Commission on the Family/International Union of Family Organisations, Dubrovnik, Yugoslavia.

Van Mechelen, F. (1981). Non-governmental activities: Participation in family policy. In *Family Policy in Europe/La Politique Familiale en Europe* (pp. 57–65). Milan, Italy: CISF.

12

Internal Family Policy Making and Family Problem Solving: Toward a Structural Exchange Model of Family Goal Achievement

GERALD W. McDONALD
THOMAS A. CORNILLE
Florida State University

Renewed attention has been given recently to the internal dynamics of "normal" families. Attention has been drawn to those characteristics and patterns that seem to assist families to contend effectively with routine and extraordinary problems of daily living. The efforts of Reiss and Oliveri to examine the interaction patterns that families develop for problem solving exemplifies this attention (Reiss & Oliveri, 1980). However, this recognition of the importance of various family dynamics is not a recent discovery.

This chapter focuses on one of the concepts developed by Reuben Hill and his colleagues in several landmark works and presents an explanation of the potential utility of an underlying model for further family research. Hill and others have suggested that families develop policies to help them contend with repetitive issues in their daily living. These policies are rooted in the values and goals to which a family subscribes and result in rules for daily living in each family. In order to place the framework of internal family policies in a historical context, several works of Hill and his collaborators will be reviewed briefly. Attention will be paid primarily to the role of family "policies" in planning and executing a life course. A hierarchical model of policies in families is presented along with an examination of how this model fits into a structural exchange theory. This model proposes that families develop a style of contending with day-to-day issues by basing decisions on shared

Gerald W. McDonald died suddenly, shortly after the completion of the first draft of this chapter. The revision of the chapter could not have been accomplished without the support, advice, and encouragement of the editors of this book, Joan Aldous and David Klein. Feedback to the first draft provided by Reuben Hill and David Klein was especially appreciated.

values given priority by the family, resulting in a "standard operating procedure." Some of the implications of this model for both family researchers and practitioners are suggested in the discussion of the potential utility of the framework for understanding and strengthening families.

REUBEN HILL'S DEVELOPMENT OF THE "FAMILY POLICY FORMATION" CONCEPT

Hill's substantive interests have focused on various aspects of family functioning. These have included but are not limited to an examination of the following issues: families' capabilities to cope successfully with crises (Hill, 1949); the process that families undergo to deal with family planning (Hill, Stycos, & Back, 1959); the stability and change of internal "family policies" across generations as families strive to achieve their long-term economic and especially consumption goals (Hill, Foote, Aldous, Carlson, & MacDonald, 1970); and the family problem-solving process as families seek to overcome barriers to goal achievement (Klein & Hill, 1979). One of the most consistent themes that pervades Hill's contributions to theory construction and empirical research about family relationships and interaction is that the family (1) has both a history and a future, (2) is a decision-making unit, (3) has the capability of utilizing its resources, and (4) structures its future as it moves through different stages of family development in attempting to achieve its long-term goals. Whether the central issue concerns the resources that families have at their disposal in coping with a crisis, decision making about fertility or consumption, or the determinants of family problem-solving effectiveness, this theme has been carried throughout.

The theme of policies developed by the family emerges as one salient concept in understanding the capacity of a family to confront a crisis successfully. Hansen and Hill (1964) cite the contributions of Parad and Caplan (1960) in their use of the central concept of family life style and Angell's (1936) emphasis on family integration as relevant to the examination of existing family styles that aid in coping with a crisis. Hansen and Hill (1964) summarized the findings of those studies as suggesting that a well-organized family is resistant to the effects of crisis. They describe an organized family as one having the following characteristics: an agreement on role structure, subordination of personal ambitions to family goals, satisfaction with the family because it meets the physical and emotional needs of its members, and shared goals toward which the family is moving collectively (p. 811). Central to this discussion is a recognition of the importance of organization and yet flexibility in supporting the family's changing needs and goals. Each of these components contributes to the family's capacity to contend with unexpected stress.

A consistent undercurrent of Hill's research is that the family is a miniature social system (Hill, 1971; Hill & Hansen, 1960), a group or organization with a distinct set of emergent and changing characteristics. One of the major systemic characteristics is that the family has an image of itself as a coherent entity with a purpose or guiding theme congruent with "family policy formation." In research in the area of consumership, Hill (1963) emphasized several levels of the process by which families attempt to achieve these shared objectives. He described four distinct stages: planning, decision making, acting taking, and evaluation of outcomes. The results of that research also emphasized the importance of shared values about the malleability of the world, as well as such organizational qualities as found in "crisis-proof" families.

These several levels of family value orientation were subsumed in his "three generation family study" under the heading of family policies: "[the family] builds a history of problem solutions, a pattern of decision-making and a set of rudimentary family policies by which actions can be judged" (Hill *et al.*, 1970, p. 9). A range of decision areas and processes were discussed, mostly related to family consumption behavior, "which not only help in making choices in the present but give direction and structure to the future" (p. 9). As a result, the three-generation research project addressed changing patterns of policy formation within families and across family generations as a central research objective. A major aim of the project was "to describe the process of structuring the future through family policy formation" (p. v). Although this research focused primarily on financial planning and consumption, an explicit component was the investigation of family problem solving, and one of the underlying questions was "What are the predominant styles of problem-solving behavior for the three generations?" (p. iv).

Thus, Hill has provided both theoretical and substantive evidence for expanding our knowledge about family policy formation, family decision making, and family problem solving. First, he has demonstrated that policies internal to families include levels of shared value systems, specific beliefs, plans for action, and assessment of outcomes. Second, he has emphasized the importance of open, shared communication, especially in the context of family decision making. Third, he has provided extensive theorizing and research findings on the determinants of problem-solving effectiveness. And last, he has demonstrated the effect of different developmental life stages on these shared value systems.

The next section provides further development of the "family policy making" concept and attempts to demonstrate that Hill's work on family policy formation, family decision making, and family problem solving are interrelated in that they all focus on family goal achievement. The development of family policies is intended to maximize family goal achievement and minimize family problem solving by providing consistent lines of action in order to avoid most "barriers" to goal achievement. Family interaction regarding varying levels of family policy formation may involve decision making but not problem solving through "program development" and "impact assessment," the purpose of which is to circumvent recognized barriers to goal achievement. Family problem solving occurs when those barriers are encountered, that is, when program development does not appear to be moving the family toward goal achievement. Thus, family problem solving is that sector of family policy-making activities that deals with the explicit interaction that occurs to overcome such barriers when a specific family policy ceases to be effective.

INTERNAL FAMILY POLICY MAKING: CONCEPTUAL DEVELOPMENT

Hill was perhaps the first to identify as "family policy formation" the internal dynamics by which families make decisions and plans with respect to long-term goals, but such terminology did not become used widely in family literature. It did, however, surface in the home management literature (Liston, 1971; Pershing, 1979). In fact, according to Pershing, development of the home management framework was sparked by Hill's (1961) challenge that although different concepts in home management had been developed and studied, little had been done to tie the concepts together. Pershing defined the home management framework as involving "purposive behavior utilizing the management processes to guide resource use toward the achievement of family goals and satisfying relationships" (p. 573). Family policy problems were seen as involving decisions about important values, goals, resources, and general living conditions.

Of particular interest was Hill *et al.*'s (1970) finding that families having consistent policies about the use of family resources adjusted more successfully to change and had a greater chance of implementing their plans than did families without such policies. In congruence with Hill's definition of family policy, Pershing (1979) defined a "family policy" as "a general course of action, made and adopted by the family or some of its members, which is designed to guide and influence their subsequent decisions and action" (p. 574).

One framework generated out of the University of Minnesota Family Policy Research Project by Hill and his associates provided a method of identifying several facets of the relationship between families and their larger environment.[1] Four levels of the family policy-making process were identified: meta-policy, policy, programs, and outcomes or impacts. *Meta-policy* refers to that set of general goals and values that are held by society and by those formulating public policy for families, and are identified as desired ends in themselves for families. The effort of putting these values into action requires some assignment of priorities from most to least important. The next level of policy making, *policy formation*, incorporates this process of ranking.

A simple statement of policy is inadequate in providing direction toward achieving any identified desired goal unless some specific plans are promulgated regulating the day-to-day responsibilities of the people concerned. *Program development*, then, is the implementation of policy through the development of laws, regulations, social programs, and so on, which provide specific guidelines for action to achieve specific goals derived from the policy and certain rules of procedure.

The final level of this framework, *impact assessment*, is the examination of the impact or consequences of programs in light of the identified goals and values that are presented. Evaluation research in social service agencies addresses this level of the framework. Much of the research generated within the Family Impact Analysis research project at the University of Minnesota, developed by Hill and associates, focused on the intended and unintended consequences of social policies and programs. Thus, there is some kind of prioritizing of general values and goals, or meta-policy that is implemented at the program development level, which has subsequent impact on the population affected by the policy and resultant programs, and is evaluated in order to determine the degree to which goals are being achieved.

The basic contention of this chapter is that the above-mentioned framework for the study of family policy at the macro level (societal) can be utilized also at the micro level (intrafamilial). Such a micro level approach should help us understand and investigate how families attempt to develop and implement policies themselves (Cornille & McDonald, 1982).

Internal family policy making is defined here as the establishment of a consistent line of action for family members, first through the ranking of family values, whether implicitly or explicitly stated (policy formation). The ranking is based on a general family value system (meta-policy), initially designed to avoid or resolve conflicting interests within the family (program development), while also guiding and influencing their subsequent decisions and actions (impact). The ultimate outcome ideally is achievement of a variety of family goals, the most general of which are effective family functioning and overall family well-being (meta-policy).

This definition is comprehensive in that it includes the differing elements of family policy making that need to be considered in having a general perspective on family functioning at the micro level. Meta-policy, policy formation, program development, and impact assessment parallel Hill's (1970) model of the differing phases of the family consumption process, including (1) identifying unmet needs, (2) choosing a course of action or process of decision making, (3) taking action, and (4) evaluating the adequacy of actions taken. This conceptualization of internal family policy making, given its differing dimensions, could be argued to constitute a miniconceptual framework, and, though generated out of macro family policy concerns, can be utilized to systematize Hill's work as it relates to family policy formation. In order to do so, it is necessary to develop further the conceptual dimensions in the conceptualization internal family policy making.

Meta-Policy

Meta-policy can generally be considered "policy-on-policy." In other words, the meta-policy of a family is the general family value system or those family value statements that help to determine basic directions and aspirations of the family. Such family values may be imbedded in the family through the societal expectations and cultural norms for families, passed through kinship systems from one generation to another, or they may arise from the unique characteristics of the family and the orientations of individual family members. Such values imply a variety of family goals and are generally assumed by the family rather than being explicitly stated or developed. For example, children are highly valued in most families, and this value is usually at or near the top of the value priority list. In a sense, then, family values specify the major long-term goals of the family.

Policy Formation

The policies of the family spring out of the family meta-policy or primal family values, and they specify consistent lines of action for family members. Ideally, each family member has a psychological commitment to the goals inherent in the meta-policy and acts in accordance with that commitment. If children are highly valued by the family, the parents generally develop certain lines of action, or commitments. These ensure that children are protected, loved, cared for, and socialized for later success in functioning as healthy, productive members of the larger society—an implied goal of the meta-policy valuing children.

Further, family policies serve to rank those family values both cognitively and behaviorally for family members, so that family members are functioning in accordance with each other rather than working against each other. The process of policy making is dynamic in the sense that family value priorities are generally stable but not static. Value priorities of families change over the life cycle of the family and, with each new stage, family value priorities must be reassessed. For instance, priorities generally shift considerably in families with the birth of the first child or when the last child leaves home. Commitments are altered and new policies must be developed that realize the changed priorities of family members.

Family policies may be systematic or inadvertent and explicit or implicit. Systematic policies tend to be explicated more, while inadvertent policies are usually implicit. Systematic, explicit family policies would be expected in families with open communication, policies that are far-sighted, and that carefully consider and plan for the achievement of family goals (Hill *et al.*, 1959). Inadvertent, implied family policies tend to be found in those families that function on a day-to-day basis. They confront problems as they arise and deal with them in an isolated manner, using readily available "intervention strategies" rather than planning for their prevention or resolution. The degree of problem solving in which families engage may then be inversely related to the degree to which families have systematic, explicated internal family policies and the degree to which their prioritization is shared by the family members. Many families have only inadvertent, implied family policies, as suggested by Weick's (1971) "organized confusion" theory. With respect to family problem solving, Klein and Hill (1979) characterize this perspective as follows:

> On the one hand, the principles governing family problem-solving are ultimately knowable and upon occasion may be articulated by family members, even if only after the fact and in a rationalized manner. In this sense, family problem-solving is organized. On the other hand, the surface manifestation of family problem-solving in operation is highly disorganized and difficult to grasp and conceptualize. In this sense, family problem-solving is confusing. (p. 511)

In this regard, Hill *et al.*, (1970) found that families had policies to facilitate change in consumption behaviors only about one third of the time.

Program Development

While macro level public policies are implemented by the development of social programs that may be considered the "means" to the desired "end," families implement policies in the form of family rules and rule enforcement. While family policies may be more often implicit, family rules are generally more formally stated. For instance, families may have a rule that all family members eat dinner together every night, and this might be formally stated. However, the basic family value underlying such a rule may be less clearly formalized for the family members. It may reflect a value of togetherness (meta-policy) and a highly prioritized desire for family interaction on a regular basis (family policy). Alternatively, it may be generated by a highly prioritized value of process, whether intentional or inadvertent. This serves to restrict the range of behaviors and determines what decisions are relevant and, probably, who makes what decisions for the family and which ones are negotiated among family members. Additionally, this level might provide rules or strategies for problem solving when barriers to goal achievement are confronted by families.

Impact Assessment

This final level of internal family policy making entails evaluation of the outcomes of the policy-making process. It is the assessment of the intended and unintended consequences of policy making, providing feedback to family members about the degree to which the desired outcome has been achieved. The assessment of impact can probably be undertaken most easily with regard to program development, since this includes the implementation of procedures to achieve family policy goals through the development of rules and rule enforcement. Consideration can be given quite specifically to whether such rules have been maintained and enforced and how successful families are at renegotiating and changing family rules as is necessary to resolve conflicting interests or to increase problem-solving effectiveness.

In family policy research, evaluation studies and family impact analyses are increasingly popular for determining how well social programs have achieved their specific goals (Cox & Cox, 1984; Stuart, 1984; Voydanoff, 1984). Similarly, the internal family policy model encourages the assessment of impact with respect to family goal achievement, problem-solving effectiveness, and the successful completion of "developmental tasks" through each stage of the family life cycle. Theoretically, impact assessment examines the success (or failure) of the internal family policy-making process and provides an indicator of the degree to which family meta-policy and policy goals are being or have been achieved. This assumes that there is a "consistency of flow" as families move from meta-policy to specific policies to program development and rules and, finally, to impact assessment. The degree to which this in fact occurs is an empirical question.[2] The advantage of this framework for internal family policies lies in its potential for guiding the examination of these and related questions while also providing practitioners with a conceptual model for facilitating families to achieve their goals successfully.

INTERNAL FAMILY POLICY MAKING
AND STRUCTURAL EXCHANGE

Social exchange theory addresses interaction patterns between and among individuals and has been widely utilized in explanations and investigations of marital and family interaction (Broderick, 1971; Edwards, 1969; Ihinger, 1975; Nye, 1978; Richer, 1968; Scanzoni, 1972). The basic premise of social exchange theory is that individuals in social interaction attempt to maximize rewards and minimize costs to obtain the most profitable outcomes. As social interaction becomes stabilized, the assessments of outcome (reward minus cost) in enduring interpersonal relationships become governed by considerations of equity, distributive justice, and available alternatives (Homans, 1974).

McDonald (1981) has argued that social exchange theory has largely focused upon interpersonal transactions as though they were occurring in a social vacuum, with all social interaction being governed by the assumption of human as accountant or bookkeeper. As such, it has had limited utility for the study of stable marital and family interaction. The problematic application of social exchange principles to the study of marriage and family relationships relates to the unique characteristics of the marriage and family institutions.

Marital and family relationships generally have a lengthy duration, moving through a progression of life cycle stages, and are subject to structural and normative constraints (Aldous, 1978). These result in differential role expectations and obligations of family members, and an unequal distribution of resources often contributing to relationship imbalance and thus to an asymmetrical exchange context. The temporal and structural dimensions of such social relationships have been deemphasized in most social exchange formulations. Additionally, much family interaction tends to be cooperative rather than competitive in nature (Nye, 1976), and thus necessitates a consideration of more cooperative exchange dynamics.

McDonald (1981) has attempted to reformulate social exchange theory in order to remedy these theoretical deficits. A structural exchange theory is presented here that recognizes the importance of social time and social structure on the cognitive orientations of family members and on the subsequent exchange relationship.

The basic dimensions of a structural exchange approach include the following:

1. *Normative orientations:* the culturally internalized expectations of marriage and family relationships generally, and of the roles of marital partners and family members in particular. These expectations are based on common patterns of socialization among members and on the

similarities in the motivations and values they have acquired (Abramson, Cutler, Kautz, & Mendelson, 1958).

2. *Cognitive orientations:* the beliefs, values, and general relationship orientation of the individuals in the family. This includes their personality and attitudinal structures. General socialization experiences, particularly the existing "normative orientation," as well as the individual's unique socialization experience, internalized gender roles, and the past bargaining or exchange experiences of the individual largely determine an individual's cognitive orientation.

3. *The exchange relationship:* the general patterning of social transactions, involving the availability and/or exchange of valued resources between spouses and among other family members, the costs and rewards associated with these transactions, and the expectations that result in each partner's appraisal of the benefits and costs of the relationship.

The exchange relationship is dynamic and ongoing in nature and tends to change as the family moves from one stage of the family life cycle to another. Also of major concern is the cooperative or competitive nature of family interaction. Cooperative relationships are those in which the family members work together to increase their joint profits, while competitive relationships are those in which each family member is trying to maximize his or her individual profits. Cooperative exchange relationships tend to be characterized by commitment and trust in the family as a group, whereas competitive relationships often involve mistrust, a lack of commitment to the relationship, and an overriding concern with individual gain.

This theoretical framework has considerable utility for the study of the interactional dynamics occurring in the internal family policy-making process as families strive toward and attempt to overcome barriers to family goal achievement. In particular, it expands our focus beyond traditional social exchange theory considerations by including a direct concern for the internalization of culturally prescribed norms that affect the development and stabilization of family interaction and decision-making patterns and the establishment of rules of exchange.

From a structural exchange perspective, then, the internal family policy-making process can be viewed as an ongoing group attempt to: (1) maximize rewards through the optional achievement of family goals, (2) minimize costs through the avoidance of barriers to goal achievement, and thus (3) achieve "maximum joint profit" (Scanzoni, 1979) for the family in its goal-achieving efforts. Congruent with Klein and Hill's (1979) assumptions about the nature of families and family members, this model assumes that (1) social structural factors affect family life; (2) families are active agents in their efforts toward goal achievement; (3)

human behavior is active, coping, and achievement oriented rather than passive or fatalistic; (4) families can learn from their goal-seeking experiences; (5) rationality is a major component in families; and (6) families have a strong temporal element in that they have both a past and future.

This approach also assumes a degree of coordinated family behavior with the success of the policy-making process being largely determined by orientations of group interest rather than individual gain. The degree to which this is the case influences the extent to which a family has explicit and systematic policies and programs, thus successfully avoiding many problems and facilitating coping with crises. The explication of such assumptions lays the groundwork for a more systematic discussion of the dimensions of the internal family policy-making model from a structural exchange perspective.

Family meta-policy, or the general family value system, largely results from normative orientations regarding the role and function of families in society. Such culturally prescribed values imply a variety of family goals that are generally inferred or assumed by the family rather than explicitly stated or developed. The elaboration and specification of family values and goals, whether implicit or explicit, are further shaped by the cognitive orientations of the family members, particularly the spouses or parents. These cognitive orientations tend to be rewarded if displayed by children, and thus are shaped through the socialization process, so that the individual orientations of family members toward family values and goals are likely to be reciprocated and congruent at any point in the family life cycle. Such family goals may include, for instance, the value of children and their effective socialization toward healthy functioning in society, emotional closeness, economic well-being, and effective family functioning.

Family policy is the result of translating meta-policies into consistent lines of action for family members. The cognitive orientations of family members, particularly the adult members, primarily determine the process and outcome of policy formation. At this level, basic family values, or meta-policies, become prioritized both cognitively and behaviorally for family members. The individual's value priorities and belief systems, both personal and familial, go through a process of dynamic alignment via ongoing interaction. The matching of cognitive orientations occurs through the process of generalized reciprocity. However, this process may not be explicit in nature; husbands and wives or other family members may not—and probably do not in most cases—make a formal listing of family policies or rank their family goals. Rather an emergent consensus tends to arise in family interaction and exchange as family members come to determine over time what are the expectations and obligations of family members.

Program development includes not only the development of rules governing day-to-day family life, but also some formulation about the consequences of either complying with or violating norms. These rules and consequences are determined in large part by the reciprocated cognitive orientations of the family members, particularly the spouses/ parents.

The nature of rule formation and regulations is similar to Meeker's (1971) "exchange rule" and Cook's (1975) "distribution rules." They specify the nature of the exchange relationship and how the dimensions of evaluation in a social system are related to the allocation of valued outcomes in that system, and under what conditions felt inequity occurs. Such exchange or distribution rules are generated principally from spouses' normative orientations regarding how exchanges are to take place, how decisions are to be made, how problems are to be solved, and how goals are to be achieved in families.

Reciprocated cognitive orientations further take into account the "exchange-orientations" (Murstein, Cerreto, & MacDonald, 1977) of the family members. For instance, social class variations in normative orientations and the resulting bargaining or exchange experiences in the spouses' families of orientations relate directly to the implicit norms monitoring the exchange relationship and affect the style of family decision making and/or problem solving.

Broderick (1975) refers to this process as "family governance," or the process of managing or resolving conflicting interests in the family. In this regard, Broderick outlines three different types of rules. *Rules of direct distribution* allocate family resources directly and function to preclude power confrontations through the heading off of potential problems. *Rules allocating authority* appropriate the role domains of family members by indicating who gets to make decisions in certain content areas of the family and by specifying who may participate or "vote" in those family decision-making or problem-solving areas. This reduces conflict by allocating a legitimate right or authority to make certain categories of decisions. *Rule-bound negotiation* specifies how contested decisions may be *fairly* negotiated, with such questions addressed as who enforces the rules and who is free to challenge or change the rules.

These differing family governance norms provide the parameters for the exchange relationship with respect to family decision making and family problem solving, and they dictate the distribution rules of exchange. The interactional dynamics in the family provide for the stability or modification of rules. They can be seen to be influenced by the "cooperative" nature of family interaction and by the relative degrees of symmetry/asymmetry and equity/inequity in the family unit. Movement toward relationship symmetry and equity-based exchanges is determined, in large part, by the relative levels of trust and commitment on the part of the family members. Thus, as families shift from asymmetrical, power/dependency relationships toward cooperative, commitment-based relationships, we might expect to see families shift in governance norms from the authoritarian structure toward "rule-bound negotiations." Such shifts might also occur as a result of changes in the family life cycle, as a result of increased maturity of family members or a history of shared beliefs and expectations.

In this sense, the establishment of internal family policies may function to avoid direct power use by individuals in family interaction. These policies provide a cooperative exchange base rather than a more competitive power-oriented exchange orientation and thus provide policy and programmatic agreements among family members with respect to family and individual goals. The manifestation of competitive exchange behaviors, or the shift from cooperative to competitive exchange, disrupts equilibrium in the family with the subsequent lessening of interpersonal commitment and trust among family members. Meta-problem-solving toward family goal achievement in this instance would be focused on restoring family equilibrium and establishing or reestablishing group goal consensus.

The program development level, then, serves to guide and influence the decisions and actions of the family subsequent to the policy-making process. It may be particularly significant in giving recognition to the existence of a "problem," shaping the style of problem-solving activity, and determining the relevant criteria by which to assess problem-solving effectiveness. This serves to restrict the range of behaviors, determines what decisions are relevant, and influences who makes what decisions for the family and which are negotiated among family members. Family regulations grow out of the exchange relationship and are the rules and regulations regarding the explicit role expectations of all family members and the extent of equity in the group.

The final element of internal family policy making, *impact assessment,* entails the evaluation of the outcomes of the policy-making process. From a structural exchange perspective, this evaluation of impact is a dynamic ongoing process. It occurs at any point in the exchange relationship among the family members, but feeds back to influence cognitive orientations and, thus, feelings of trust, commitment, and possibly a reassessment of one's comparison level of alternatives. This reassessment, in turn, may change the patterning of the exchange relationship as family members or the family as a unit attempt to develop more efficient and effective interactions, exchange strategies, or policies.

This exchange approach to the internal family policy-making process allows for the assessment of impact with respect to problem-solving effectiveness and the successful completion of developmental tasks. It is this evaluation of the outcome (rewards minus costs), with a consideration of available alternatives, by which family members can increase rewards and decrease costs in order to achieve "maximum joint-profit" (Scanzoni, 1979) in decision-making and problem-solving processes. The systematic application of the structural exchange perspective will require further explication in order to generate theoretical propositions and testable hypotheses regarding family policy making and problem-solving processes.

RESEARCH, EDUCATIONAL, AND CLINICAL ISSUES

Structural exchange theory provides some plausible relationships between internal family policies and successful family functioning. For example, one might expect that families with shared goals and expectations would be more effective problem solvers than those families with goals that openly compete with one another. However, these relationships have not been tested empirically. One of the first issues that needs to be addressed before any research can be attempted is the operational independence of the levels of policy formation. Until that independence is verified, it will not be possible to assess their impact on successful goal attainment.

Nevertheless, some of the issues commonly addressed by family researchers involve the relationship between components of family policy making and factors known to affect family life. For example, the positive relationship between strong commitment to a religious community and a sense of family well-being has been documented (Stinnett & DeFrain, 1985). Research on the degree of interdependence between the commitment to a religious community and the family's need for consistency between meta-policy, policies, and programs would provide greater understanding of the importance of shared values and goals in family functioning.

The examination of development of policies within families is certainly an area that could provide a wealth of information about the dynamics of communication and decision making. As was noted earlier, it would appear from casual observation that families do not openly address the policies that influence their lifestyles. However, it has been shown that families who demonstrate greater openness in communication also experience greater success in problem solving (Klein & Hill, 1979) and crisis management (Hill, 1949).

Whether families with more open styles of communication also are more likely to share in the development of family policies or not is a research question worth pursuing. Research findings also would be important for family life educators and therapists. Drawing attention to the consistency within and between internal family policies could assist educators in developing curricula to help families develop greater sensitivity to the ways families structure their daily lives.

Family therapists have focused for some time on the importance of the structure and dynamics of families in trouble. In particular, many have drawn attention to elements in family living that bear strong resemblance to the component of internal family policy making. For example, Jackson (1965) and Riskin (1963) stressed the importance of family laws, family rules, and dynamic issues in problem families. Laing (1971) addressed the role of values, meta-rules, and rules in families, but with little attention to the relationship between these concepts. The idea that family members share a view of the world that may not be rooted in the outside world has been the subject of researchers and theorists alike (Reiss & Oliveri, 1980; Watzlawick, Weakland, & Fisch, 1974). Within each of their frameworks, one or two of the components of the internal family policy framework are usually included. Research that gives greater attention to the fit between family policies and family functioning could prove to be of substantial benefit to therapists dealing directly with conflicts in families.

Our knowledge of conflict management and decision making in families might be enhanced by exploration of the capacity of families not only to develop family policies, but also to change them as the developmental needs of the family members change. One might expect that some families have not developed policies for day-to-day issues or have developed rules that overcontrol the activities of family members. Such extremes would be similar to those families described by Olson, Sprenkle, and Russell (1979) as chaotic or rigid, respectively. The significance of internal family policy in affecting family structure or vice versa is not yet clear.

The purpose of this chapter has been to present a conceptual framework of internal family policy making for the consideration of family scholars. The historical development of this framework from early family crisis research to more recent studies of family problem solving has been outlined to root the model in the broader area of successful family functioning. The central tenets of structural exchange theory have been shown to accommodate easily the concepts of the model.

The possible utility of the internal family policy model in expanding our knowledge of several substantive areas of family studies and applications has been addressed. However, the next step toward examining the merits of the model must be an examination of the relationship between its elements and other key concepts that have been utilized in family research and intervention.

NOTES

1. During the years of 1977–1978, a Family Impact Analysis Training Program was developed by Hill and others at the Family Study Center, University of

Minnesota. Although the authors were unable to identify a specific written source for the family policy framework, an oral tradition exists. Based on the recollections of the first author, who participated in that program and interviews with several other individuals who shared that experience, the framework was developed and utilized at the Center, under Hill's guidance.

2. It would appear that families infrequently review or reflect on the extent to which their day-to-day activities are in compliance with their goals. Periods of reflection may be triggered by conflict over policies, such as curfew for adolescents. They may also be linked to celebrations, such as birthdays or wedding anniversaries. These events may stimulate questions such as "Is this where we are going?" The tasks facing all family members at each developmental stage bring into focus the degree of conformity between family goals and individual needs.

REFERENCES

Abramson, E., Cutler, H., Kautz, R., & Mendelson, M. (1958). Social power and commitment: A theoretical statement. *American Sociological Review, 23*(1), 15–22.

Aldous, J. (1978). *Family careers: Developmental change in families.* New York: Wiley.

Angell, R. C. (1936). *The family encounters the Depression.* New York: Scribner.

Broderick, C. (1971). Beyond the five conceptual frameworks: A decade of development in family theory. *Journal of Marriage and the Family, 33*(1), 139–159.

Broderick, C. (1975). Power in the governance of families. In R. Cromwell & D. Olson (Eds.), *Power in families* (pp. 117–128). New York: Wiley.

Cook, K. (1975). Expectations, evaluations and equity. *American Sociological Review, 40*(3), 372–388.

Cornille, T., & McDonald, G. (1982). Internal family policymaking: A framework for the assessment of family functioning. In N. Stinnett, J. DeFrain, K. King, H. Lingren, G. Rowe, S. Van Zandt, & R. Williams (Eds.), *Family strengths: Positive support systems* (pp. 185–201). Lincoln, Nebraska: University of Nebraska Press.

Cox, M. J., & Cox, R. D. (1984). Foster care and public policy. *Journal of Family Issues, 5*(2), 182–199.

Edwards, J. (1969). Familial behavior as social exchange. *Journal of Marriage and the Family, 31*(3), 518–526.

Hansen, D., & Hill, R. (1964). Families under stress. In H. Christensen (Ed.), *Handbook of marriage and the family* (pp. 782–819). Chicago: Rand McNally.

Hill, R. (1949). *Families under stress.* New York: Harper.

Hill, R. (1961). Patterns of decision making and the accumulation of family assets. In N. Foote (Ed.), *Consumer behavior (Vol. 4): Household decision-making* (pp. 57–80). New York: New York University Press.

Hill, R. (1963). Judgement and consumership in the management of family resources. *Sociology and Social Research, 47*(4), 446–460.

Hill, R. (1971). Modern systems theory and the family. *Social Science Information, 10*(3), 7–26.

Hill, R., Foote, N., Aldous, J., Carlson, R., & MacDonald, R. (1970). *Family development in three generations: A longitudinal study of changing family patterns and achievement.* Cambridge, MA: Schenkman.

Hill, R., & Hansen, D. (1960). The identification of conceptual frameworks utilized in family study. *Marriage and Family Living, 22*(4), 299–311.

Hill, R., Stycos, J., & Back, K. (1959). *The family and population control: A Puerto Rican experiment in social change.* Chapel Hill: University of North Carolina Press.

Homans, G. C. (1974). *Social behavior: Its elementary forms* (rev. ed.). New York: Harcourt Brace Joranovich.

Ihinger, M. (1975). The referring role and norms of equity: A contribution toward a theory of sibling conflict. *Journal of Marriage and the Family, 37*(3), 515–523.

Jackson, D. (1965). Family rules: Marital quid pro quo. *Archives of General Psychiatry, 12*(6), 589–594.

Klein, D., & Hill, R. (1979). Determinants of family problem-solving effectiveness. In W. R. Burr, R. Hill, R. I. Nye, & I. L. Reiss (Eds.), *Contemporary theories about the family* (Vol. 1, pp. 493–548). New York: The Free Press.

Laing, R. D. (1971). *The politics of the family and other essays.* New York: Pantheon Books.

Liston, M. (1971). Home management and family economics. In L. Deighton (Ed.), *The encyclopedia of education* (Vol. 4, pp. 451–454). New York: MacMillan.

McDonald, G. (1981). Structural exchange and marital interaction. *Journal of Marriage and the Family, 43*(4), 825–839.

Meeker, B. (1971). Decisions and exchange. *American Sociological Review, 36*(3), 485–495.

Murstein, B., Cerreto, M., & MacDonald, M. (1977). A theory and investigation of the effect of exchange-orientation on marriage and friendship. *Journal of Marriage and the Family, 39*(3), 543–548.

Nye, F. (1976). Ambivalence in the family: Rewards and costs in group membership. *The Family Coordinator, 25*(1), 21–31.

Nye, F. (1978). Is choice and exchange theory the key? *Journal of Marriage and the Family, 49*(2), 219–233.

Olson, D. H., Sprenkle, D. H., & Russell, C. S. (1979). Circumplex model of marital and family systems: I. Cohesion and adaptability dimensions, family types and clinical applications. *Family Process, 18*(1), 3–28.

Parad, H., & Caplan, G. (1960). A framework for studying families in crisis. *Social Work, 49*(3), 3–15.

Pershing, B. (1979). Family policies: A component of management in the home and family setting. In G. McDonald & F. Hye (Eds.), *Family policy* (pp. 114–122). Minneapolis, MN: National Council on Family Relations.

Reiss, D., & Oliveri, M. E. (1980). Family paradigm and family coping: A proposal for linking the family's intrinsic adaptive capacities to its responses to stress. *Family Relationships, 29*(4), 431–444.

Richer, S. (1968). The economics of childrearing. *Journal of Marriage and the Family, 30*(3), 462–466.

Riskin, J. (1963). Methodology for studying family interaction. *Archives of General Psychiatry, 8*(4), 343–348.

Scanzoni, J. (1972). *Sexual bargaining: Power politics in the American marriage.* Englewood Cliffs, NJ: Prentice-Hall.

Scanzoni, J. (1979). Social processes and power in families. In W. Burr, R. Hill, F. Nye, & I. Riess (Eds.), *Contemporary theories about the family* (Vol. 1, pp. 295–316). New York: Free Press.

Stinnett, N., & DeFrain, J. (1985). *Secrets of strong families.* Boston: Little Brown.

Stuart, A. (1984). Family impact statements in South Australia. *Journal of Family Issues, 5*(3), 383–399.

Voydanoff, P. (1984). Economic distress and families: Policy issues. *Journal of Family Issues, 5*(2), 273–288.

Watzlawick, P., Weakland, L., & Fisch, R. (1974). *Change: Principles of problem formation and problem resolution.* New York: Norton.

Weick, K. (1971). Group processes, family processes, and problem solving. In J. Aldous, T. Condon, R. Hill, M. Straus, & I. Tallman (Eds.), *Family problem solving* (pp. 3–32). Hinsdale, IL: The Dryden Press.

Index

Italicized numbers indicate material in tables and figures.

265